Hans-Georg Behr was born in Vienna in 1937. He studied medicine, clinical psychology and linguistics, and has written for *Die Zeit* and *Der Stern* among other publications. He divides his time between Hamburg and Vienna.

Anthea Bell has translated a wide variety of fiction and non-fiction from German and French. She has received a number of translation prizes, including the Schlegel-Tieck award and the Independent Foreign Fiction Prize.

'*Almost a Childhood* is a daring literary achievement, telling the story of the Hitler years through the blurred and shocking reality of Nazi childhood. Honest, ironic and very moving, Hans-Georg Behr goes to the heart of moral chaos with a great eye for the truth' Hugo Hamilton

'Behr achieves the near impossible: he recreates the many discordant voices of a lost aristocratic childhood, recapturing the bewildered curiosity of a boy surrounded by the increasingly fantastical world of the Nazi elite at war and in defeat. A compelling read' Nicholas Stargardt, author of *Witnesses of War: Children's Lives Under the Nazis*

'The real fascination of this book is its ability to recall everything as seen by the youngster at the time, all in a spare, laconic, third-person style . . . As the reader, we slowly begin to comprehend matters that the boy himself barely comprehends . . . a tale told by an infant, full of sound and fury and a great deal of sly humour . . . a sad, compelling read' *Jerusalem Post*

ALMOST A CHILDHOOD

HANS-GEORG BEHR

Translated from the German
by Anthea Bell

Granta Books
London

Granta Publications, 2/3 Hanover Yard, Noel Road, London N1 8BE

First published in Great Britain by Granta Books 2005
This edition published by Granta Books 2006
First published by Eichborn AG, Frankfurt am Main 2002, under the title
Fast eine Kindheit by Hans-Georg Behr

This book is supported by the Federal Chancellory of Austria –
Department for the Arts

Copyright © Eichborn AG, Frankfurt am Main, 2002
Translation copyright © Anthea Bell, 2005

A CIP catalogue record for this book
is available from the British Library.

1 3 5 7 9 10 8 6 4 2

ISBN 13: 978-1-86207-866-6
ISBN 10: 1-86207-866-1

Typeset by M Rules
Printed and bound in Great Britain
by Bookmarque Limited, Croydon, Surrey

CONTENTS

'. . . I have resolved to strive for the truth in every particular, and to record every action exactly as it happened' *Zahiruddin Mohammed Babur Padishah, 1529*

'A heap of things thrown together at random is the best kind of world order' *Albert Paris Gütersloh, ascribed to Heraclitus*

Christmas 1939

THERE'S A WAR ON

The child had been cured early of any notion that he was the centre of the world, and had learned that it is less painful to be inconspicuous. He was not entirely happy with that state of affairs in the endless sequence of 'Now you must do this' and 'That's not done', and withdrew as often as possible from the verbal world back into a shady or partly shady green one, half visible, half-imagined, where human beings could be heard only from a distance, far away beyond the croaking, chirping, cheeping sounds, lingering in it until he was summoned back to the house. Or the houses, because he couldn't really tell one from the other too well yet. A house was big, so big that everything in it must have its proper place if it was to be found again. That was called tidiness, and anyway there was a war on. For the moment both these ideas were foreign to the child, but he learned quickly, for he was trying to avoid the ever-reproachful tone in which the necessity for tidiness was drummed into him, and if he didn't instantly recognize the warning in that tone there was usually a spanking. Spanking hurt the bottom, slapping hurt the face, and the two together were known as a good hiding. There wasn't quite so much of that at Grandmother's, although she lived in an even bigger house. 'You must be neat and tidy,' the child was always told, but he neither knew nor understood the fundamental principle of the making of a human being whereby all imagination, desire and dreams must be pruned away, or else tied tightly until they dropped off like lamb's tails, and what was left would pass as a useful member of society. 'A jewel must be cut and polished,' they said. Such had always been the case, and anyway there was a war on. The child didn't understand what that meant until he was forbidden to bring a little hedgehog into the house because it had fleas. Which house was it where you couldn't have a hedgehog because there was a war on? Mother's, maybe?

The reason for the similarity between the houses that so confused the child lay in the similarity of their setting and history. Four or five generations ago they had been gentlemen's residences not far from riverbanks, and they had been destroyed and rebuilt in the passage of the centuries, through wars and changes of ownership, until they acquired something like their final form. The land provided a living, and mills and industries stood along the riverbanks. A hundred years or more before the child's time, railway lines were built beside the rivers too, land was sold to the railway companies in return for a share in the profits, and now an almost obsessive development began: Vienna was bursting at the seams and needed the forests of the great estates to supply more and more timber for construction work. The mills became sawmills. There would be a pulping works too, to exploit the wood waste, and a small paper-making factory. The advantage of all this was that it provided a livelihood for those of the growing throng of labourers' children who could not be employed in forestry. And a great many people arrived from the east of the monarchy,[1] walking barefoot, as their grandchildren were still told, to find a new home here. Since the economy must expand, timber was soon being bought in from landed proprietors who were not blessed with a river and a railway line on their own estates, and thus – gradually, but quite rapidly as it affected the local population – the feudal agrarian idyll turned into a timber and woodworking industry with a little castle and a home farm attached. In these houses, so buffeted by progress, everything must have its own place for the sake of peace, and must stay in that place or return to it, for the people of the house hardly knew what period they really belonged to, and were therefore anxious both to preserve the grandeur of the past, inflated as it was by many anecdotes, and to offer profitable defiance to the present.

The child was often – constantly, it seemed to him – taken into a large yellow room where all kinds of people were hung up in effigy as oil paintings, and then he was told who had been what and when, who had married whom and why, how many children they had had and what became of them. Many of the men wore the stuffing of horsehair mattresses on their heads and had metal items buckled over their bellies, like the things that hung over the stairs but you mustn't play with them. There were few tales to be told about these men, or the women in their stiff dresses, so mercilessly tight-laced that their breasts swelled out up near the neckline. The closer the pictures came to the present day, with uniforms and dark suits and silk cravats which the child recognized in shrunken form as neckties, the more bald heads and the more stories there were. The child listened to the stories as if they were fairy tales, and he had known that fairy tales weren't true ever since he chased a rainbow to find the pot of gold at its foot and was spanked for getting dirty. Armed with the scepticism thus acquired, he let the family stories wash over him and even learned some of them off by heart. If he recited one successfully he got a pickled gherkin as a reward. He always liked sharp flavours better than sweet.

That must have been in Mother's house, because while Grandmother too had ancestors, indeed even more of them, her relationship with them was not the same. She didn't want to be constantly under the eye of important forebears who weren't even her own real family, and consequently had banished them to a large unused room where they hung in triple rows, looking down on the dust that collected on the huge, worn, plush-upholstered furniture. And Grandmother knew stories too, she knew even more stories, because Mother herself had not always paid attention to them. Furthermore, as there was a war on, Grandmother didn't always care so much about what was and what was not fit for childish ears, so the child thought her a better storyteller. There had been her father-in-law, whom Grandmother herself never knew, since he was so busy in his prime with the industrial conversion and expansion of his inheritance that he died of a stroke as a result of mucoid impaction. His son, who was her husband and the child's grandfather – he discovered only later that these three were one and the same man – took that as a warning, spurned industry and sold the paper factories, or what was left of them after the First World War, to an industrialist from the German Reich. 'And he's your father. So there we are.' It all sounded rather odd, and the child was interested, but only many years later did he find out how it had really been. Father had bought the factories and Mother along with them, and she became his wife, but his grandparents did not approve because Mother had not asked their permission. She had been married once already, when she was still a lyric soprano, but then her husband had turned his attentions to the dramatic soprano, and Mother came home with the child's brother and sister. The brother was at boarding school now, and so was the sister, but the child didn't understand what that meant. All Grandmother did was sigh and say, 'Green shutters don't always do what you expect of them.'

For some time these 'green shutters' conveyed nothing to the child, unlike 'Swedish curtains'. It was easy enough at the time to discover what Swedish curtains were. The child first came across this colloquial expression when the ancient gardener who was always saying bad things about the Führer suddenly disappeared. The child had hardly noticed his departure in the morning. There had been rather more noise than usual in the house below, but since the child knew that noise like that boded no good, he pulled the covers up over his head, pretended to be asleep, and had soon forgotten all about it. After all, the noise was nothing to do with him. That afternoon, however, he missed the gardener, who would always give the child a few raspberries from the canes that he couldn't reach. The child asked two women working in the garden about him, but they acted in an oddly mysterious way. So he went indoors and asked Grandmother.

'They've taken him away,' sighed the old lady. 'He's behind Swedish curtains now.' The child had an aunt in Sweden, but he couldn't visit her because there was a war on.

'Has he gone to see Auntie Grete, then?'

The old lady, rather put out, looked at the child. 'He's in prison.'

Then she explained that Swedish curtains were thick iron bars, much thicker than the gratings over the ground-floor windows, and the bars were in a building where you got spanked, and which you couldn't leave.

The child had often come upon the expression 'green shutters' when people working in the garden or on the farm talked about 'them behind the green shutters there', but as they were obviously not referring to him, he didn't mind not understanding. A few days after the incident of the Swedish curtains, however, he did ask Grandmother.

'Are Swedish curtains shutters?'

'No, those are shutters.' And she pointed to the window.

'But that's a window!' Knowledge is power.

'And there are shutters on the other side of it.'

Aha – and furthermore, they were green. The child was surprised, because he had always lived behind green shutters.

His mother's house had them too. Green shutters were sturdy items made of wood and rusting iron, constructed on the Venetian blind principle. They were outside the double windows and consisted of two large wooden frames, one that you opened and another inside it that you could push up. Inside the frames were thinner slats of wood that could have been adjusted to various positions with yet another mechanism, if rust and many layers of oil-based paint had not clogged them up long ago. Opening the shutters or adjusting them to their 'summer position' was impossible not just for the child but for Grandmother too. The maid did it. She also, said Grandmother, opened the shutters up every other year, and then men brought ladders, took them off their hinges and carried them out to the farmyard, where the splintering and now dull wood was given a new coat of green paint. The child heard the painters say that it was called 'enamel varnish', and the stuff that had such a fascinating smell was turpentine.

Because the green shutters didn't work any more there was always twilight in all the rooms on the first floor, which the child had discovered was called the 'peeyanobilay'. You couldn't see straight out through the gaps between the slats, you had to squint down through them, which could be done only if you fetched a stool, clambered up on it and got on the window sill. Opening them must have been quite an adventurous business too. Once the child heard a frightful scream and a loud crash, and when he managed to peer through the slats of the shutters he saw that the maid had fallen out of the window of the 'boodwaah' two rooms away, shutter and all, landing among the runner beans that grew between the flower-beds and the wall of the house. She limped for several days, the shutter was smashed to bits, and since there was a war on it couldn't be either repaired or replaced. Grandfather gave orders for all the shutters in that room to be taken down and stored in the stable. Grandmother complained of the unaccustomed brightness and got green roller blinds – 'because of the blackout, too' – but for a long time the house still looked very odd, as if it had opened three eyes by mistake.

Long after the child was no longer a child, he heard it said now and then that someone had 'grown up behind green shutters', an expression meaning that such a person's behaviour was unusual and rather peculiar. Everything was normal to the child, in so far as anything seems normal to children. It began, once you had learned to sit still, with learning which 'you' pronoun to use when speaking to whom. The polite *Sie* was to be used in addressing your mother, your father if he happened to turn up, your grandparents and your other granny, all those uncles and aunties, and indeed the world in general with the possible exception of other children. But those were 'the servants' children', and you could play with them only if Grandmother gave special permission. There was much more to learn too, for instance that, as Grandmother put it, 'One is not "I".' She, Grandfather, Mother and the close family, even those related only by marriage, were 'one', while other folk were 'them'. It was all right for 'them' to say 'I', but such a faux pas on the family's own part could be avoided by refraining from the pronoun, even when they really did mean 'I', and saying only, 'One might just ask whether . . .', or, 'One would be glad if . . .'. Then there were a number of nice words that couldn't be used, because there were other words for the same thing that didn't sound so good but were apparently the right thing to say. For instance, you didn't have the trots but diarrhoea, nor did you have the collywobbles, you had stomach-ache instead. As for crapping and puking, that was to be described as diarrhoea with vomiting, not that anyone would want to have it. Such common words, you were taught, were suitable at most for the servants, although even the child's grandparents could sometimes be caught using them. Now and then even Grandfather spoke of 'farting' instead of 'breaking wind', and come to think of it, was wind breakable anyway? But the child himself must use only the right kind of words, and if he didn't he often got a smack on the head to teach him not to use the wrong ones. So he remembered the others, but he mustn't say them. He was taught quite early to 'make a nice bow' and kiss the hands of married ladies, placing the kiss in the air just above the right hand, since the left belonged to the lady's husband. And he learned not to enter a room without knocking twice, and then only if he heard a quiet little bell ringing inside. Of course mistakes were sometimes made. Once, for instance, the child was sitting with the old maidservant outside his grandparents' dining-room. The bell inside rang, and the maid went over to the dumb waiter and rang another bell herself. Meanwhile, however, the child entered the room where his grandparents were sitting at table. Grandfather looked at him in surprise. 'But I didn't call for you!' Luckily the maid came in with the tray at that moment, and the child managed to make his escape.

Other kinds of normal behaviour were worse. If you came in from out of doors you had to wash your hands. If you had touched something you had to wash your hands. If you had been playing you were washed, and there wasn't any hot water except at midday. And when you had your 'best clothes' on, you had to keep perfectly still, because the tiniest little dirty mark on them meant trouble. Once the child was wearing his best knitted trousers with the shoulder straps and his white shirt because an auntie was coming to visit. But the auntie didn't turn up and, feeling bored, the child slipped out into the little garden where he had seen a bird's nest in a tree a few days ago. As he looked up, something splashed down on his hair and his shirt, and then he heard a car coming and ran back to the house with his bunch of flowers. Mother was already standing on the steps outside the door. She was horrified: 'What on earth have you been doing now?' He never saw the auntie, because he was locked in his room for going into the garden in his best clothes, and they didn't let him out until she had gone away again.

He hadn't even seen the car, which would have been interesting. Cars were a rarity, having been 'requisitioned' because there was a war on. But his grandparents had their big Maybach, and Mother had her 1930s Steyrer, and all the uncles and aunties had cars too, the only ones who didn't were 'the common people', who said bad things about 'them behind the shutters there' as a result.

The common people were a problem anyway. Leaving aside the uncles and aunties, they were everyone else but also, on occasion, they were individuals. The child had to learn their names, as well as the fact that some were people who lived in and around the house, but there were others whose names he was free to forget at once. And the closer the common people were, the more carefully a proper distance had to be preserved. They were addressed not directly but in the third person, and with a shift in the sequence of tenses too. The child didn't understand, but was impressed, when Grandmother announced that 'Anna is bringing in the washing.' Whereupon Anna ran out to the drying ground, took the washing off the line, damped it down in the ironing room – the child watched with interest – let it 'rest' for three hours – the child waited for the washing to perk up and show some sign of life – then ironed and stacked it and finally, in the evening, took it in to Grandmother in the present tense. He was also impressed when Grandfather went to the window after telling off a drunken manservant and stated: 'He's gone.' The swaying figure turned, perhaps to make some rejoinder, but then he did go, and the child never saw him again.

Herr Wittmann had some difficulty in teaching the child the sequence of tenses, which worked differently in real life, saying many times a day what a trial he found 'it', and there was another 'it' that was a trial too. One of these 'its' was the child, whom Grandfather also called 'it' when he was angry.[2]

The child understood about the other 'it' that gave grounds
for complaint only when he was no longer a child: Herr
Wittmann and his wife Ellen had married over forty years
ago, to come and be tutor and governess to the little girl who
grew up to be Mother, and although they were now well past
retiring age, here they were again with demands being made
on their educational skills, just because of the child, and they
feared for their pension. The child was delivered up to them,
and they to him, for four hours a day. He and they cordially
loathed each other. The child was supposed to be learning the
violin. It was fun at first, but the horrible fiddle kept slipping
out of his hand when he put the bow near it, and then Frau
Wittmann scolded him until he cried. This went on for weeks,
and one day Mother came in. 'That child's holding the violin
the wrong way,' she said after a brief glance. Frau Wittmann
raised her claw-like hands, which were crippled with arthritis,
to Mother's face and said severely, 'You expect me to teach
him with these?' And when even the child could see that this
had taken effect on his mother, she added: 'I can't play the
piano any more, either.' Mother was silent for some time and
then said, 'Very well, carry on.'

The child had already discovered in Mother's house how horrible it is to be a child, and in case he forgot what he was
suffering, the point was driven home for years by adults who
were really kindly disposed to him. These adults were the size
of giants and were mean with their time, themselves and anything asked of them, granting at most only a fraction of
themselves and asking a horrendous price in return. Such bar-
gains were humiliating, for the adults involved in these
transactions were unaware that the value of the payment
asked was quite different for the child, though it might look
the same as their own idea of it. A nice little kiss was the tiniest of coins, yet the child often found it hard to bear. He
frequently thought those whose cheeks he had to kiss repul-

sive, sometimes even when they were people with whom he usually had no problems – but being obliged to give a kiss is no fun. When the child had made a good tower with his building-bricks, he would kiss the top brick as a matter of routine or to express his pleasure, and he did it so skilfully that the brick seldom fell off, but that was of his own free will. And even a kiss was small change compared to having to sit still, stand up straight or eat his dinner, especially when he wasn't hungry.

Being made to eat was always terrible. No sooner had the child learned how to reject nasty flavours by spluttering, and how to anticipate uncomfortably hot or cold food by watching whatever adult was present take a trial spoonful, than the magic trapdoor gave way again, and once he had seen through every terror another stood behind it, so like the first in the way it worked that it became ever more real, more puzzling, and thus a permanent fixture.

The apron spirit was the first terror. It emerged from the darkness beside the table when the child didn't want to eat any more, coming between mother and child. It assumed different colours but always looked the same: a round, faceless head crowned by a flame that never changed its colour and bobbed back and forth. The spirit gradually merged into Mother's apron, but the child seldom dared look that far, for it moved in a strange, swaying way and told the child to eat up nicely now, in a deep voice that only very slightly resembled Mother's. But the thought of eating was impossible, for the talking knot terrified the child so much that he sometimes began to scream in panic. It was the talking that was so horrible, and it didn't help when, before her child's distrustful eyes, Mother slowly knotted a corner of her apron, ostentatiously pushed her forefinger through the knot, and waggled the folds of the apron with her thumb and her middle finger – as soon as the knot began to talk, even in Mother's unmistakable voice, his horror was such that he couldn't see Mother herself any more. The apron spirit hung about for a long time, even when it stopped manifesting itself. Once Mother put her apron on, the child knew he would soon have to eat a meal, and he protested ahead of time as a precaution.

Only slightly less terrible was the crocodile. On its first appearance its function was the same as the apron spirit's, but since it only snapped its long jaws it lacked the ultimate power, and you were free to hate it. It was a pest. It would often appear unexpectedly on the child's horizon on the far side of the table, snatching away the toy that had just come to life. Then it was usually time for a meal again, but the child didn't want to eat. It was when the crocodile ate Purzel, the child's beloved dog whose ears and little tail were now nothing but stout bits of bent wire, that it became an enemy of the first magnitude – a phrase with which the child had been much struck when he heard it on the radio. Loud as the child yelled, Purzel, rigid with shock, was swept right across the table and down into the depths, and the child was inconsolable. It was no comfort to find Purzel back in his bed that evening, in reasonably good condition – war was now declared on the crocodile, and must be fought until the final victory was won.

Over the next few days Mother and the servants were surprised by the apparently aimless way the child wandered around, and the fact that he seemed to have lost interest in his toys. Of course he took care not to mention his mission, but one sunny afternoon, when there was no one in the kitchen, he found his enemy there. The crocodile had hidden in a drawer that was almost out of reach, and the child was able to get it open only because the maid had left a stool in front of it. There lay the crocodile among the cooking spoons, forks and other kitchen implements, pretending to be asleep. But the child was not deceived. He cautiously seized the enemy, who offered no resistance now, and carried it upstairs to the drawing-room and his cave under the grand piano, known as 'the instrument'.

The instrument had been the child's favourite place as soon as he could stand almost upright underneath it. He liked sitting under the black, curving roof it made, pale below and divided into little caves, particularly when Mother sat at the keyboard moving her feet about, whereupon beautiful music came raining down from above. The child didn't know when he had discovered that the music was Beethoven, but under the influence of those mighty sounds he sat quite still, enchanted and safe, watching Mother's feet move and knowing that this joy would last for ever. So this was the child's favourite cave, even when all was quiet inside it, and it was in silence that he finished off the crocodile. Its jaws shattered with a short, sharp snap, and the rest was hard work; he hurt one of his fingers badly. Exhausted but happy, he left the field victorious and was a very good boy for the rest of the afternoon, nor was his sense of triumph diminished that evening when he got a good hiding for ruining the gherkin tongs.

Luckily the child also had friends among the many things that sometimes woke to strange life. Not that he could rely unconditionally on all of them. For instance, the teddy bear who couldn't growl any more, and just had a hard thing left in his tummy to remind you that he once could, was kindly and always there when the child needed him, but left it at that, so he gradually vanished from the child's closest circle of friends. Purzel was different, although he too was of only limited value as a comrade in arms. Purzel was grey, and didn't mind having his ears or tail pulled, unlike Foxl, who was black and white and brown but always nipped, giving a sharp little yap. Also unlike Foxl, Purzel never barked and gave the child away, but hissed gently for his sake, just like Huschi, who was a grey tiger and sometimes brought the child dead mice in bed. But you couldn't play with the mice or you would get your fingers slapped, and your hands had to be well washed afterwards too.

Purzel followed the child like a real dog, and was a wonderful duck-hunting companion. The ducks suddenly appeared at Easter, all little and yellow, and mustn't be touched. Then they turned white, and there were lots of them, and they and the chickens pecked about in the meadow outside the garden, from which it was divided by a small stream with a fence on the other side. The stream was also the cause of the child's feud with the ducks. He liked to crumble his afternoon bread roll into it when no one was looking, and was glad to see bits of the bread float away. But the ducks begrudged him that pleasure, and not only ate the floating crumbs but turned aggressive, snatched the bread from his hand and pecked his fingers. The child was cross, even though they weren't as nasty as the geese, who fortunately grazed outside the child's domain most of the time, appearing in procession beyond the trees only when evening came. Then one day the little door to the garden was left open, as the ducks instantly saw, and the child enjoyed watching the gardener chase them out of paradise with curses and clods of earth. The child was pleased to see them waddling indignantly off, quacking and flapping their wings. After that Purzel came down to the stream with him, and when the ducks approached he shot into the middle of them, causing them to scatter in agitation. The child was proud of himself and of Purzel, and played this game in front of the servants too, until one day he got a good hiding from his mother for chasing the ducks.

Mother was always responsible for giving him the hiding because, as she said, Father wasn't there and she wanted the child to 'amount to something' in life. The child avoided her as best he could, but she seemed to be everywhere, and even knew things she couldn't possibly have seen. Gradually the child realized that he was surrounded by spies in the form of the servants. Whenever he had discovered some pleasure, it would always be reported to Mother, and only too often the result was a good hiding. Most malicious of all was the fat, grey, toothless kitchen maid, who kept grinning even when he got a beating. Hostilities between them had begun with the rabbit who suddenly appeared one afternoon and was a wonderful toy. At lunch next day the cook showed him a platter of roast meat. 'There's your rabbit.' The child refused to have any, finally protesting, with tears in his eyes, 'I don't eat people I know.' He soon learned to distrust the children who lived in the cottages belonging to the house too, even the gardener's daughter who had shown him that girls can do a wee as well as boys, if not so thoroughly. They were even more likely to tell tales and more malicious than the adults, although they often got a good hiding themselves, but not as often as he did because they were only the servants' children. The child had this class distinction smacked into his bottom at an early age, and he soon realized that when they played games together, for instance with the little trucks that were so easily derailed in the timber yard beyond the garden, he was the only one to get a hiding.

So apart from Purzel he had only one real friend, his oldest friend the white camel. The camel had been there ever since he could remember, looking at him from the right above his cot. And the camel was not alone. Between the bars of the cot sat a half-veiled woman, and outside the familiar circle of faces there were Arabs, Negroes, even an elephant and a lion lying there like the poodle belonging to one of the aunties, not that she was a real auntie, and one of the lion's eyes was left all smudged after the child patted him, but the camel was special, it was much more than an ordinary white camel. Whatever the child told it – and he told it a great deal every evening, in a very quiet voice – the camel always understood. You could see that from its face, which always looked different but always wore the right expression, and when the child was scared for any reason he saw that the shadowy outline of his friend was watching over him, and felt better.

The camel was his worst loss when he heard, one day, that

they were to leave here and go to join Father. The word Father certainly sounded appealing, although the child didn't really know what to understand by it, but it hurt that the camel couldn't come too. 'It stays here,' he was told curtly, and there was no chance to explain that the camel was his very best friend. Nor was it much help that Purzel was comfortably settled inside the child's travelling bag. Saying goodbye to the camel was very difficult, and he remembered it in his evening prayers for a long time to come.

Places where you do not live for long leave only sharp splinters of memory behind, splinters that are smoothed out later by the stream of time and cannot be fitted together to make a pattern, even with the putty of other people's stories. They remain somewhere in the world, with their pleasant and less pleasant aspects, but never become quite real. It was like that with Hamburg, where Father was an anti-aircraft artillery commander. They had gone to Hamburg to join him, but for some time the child doubted whether their apparently endless train journey had been worth it. Father was almost a stranger in his uniform. He picked the child up in the air and pressed him to his chest, which was prickly, being covered with jagged things called orders, and his face was scratchy too, since he needed to shave twice a day and hadn't got round to it that morning because of the train's arrival. They were living in Frau Meyen's basement in Blumenstrasse. Frau Meyen bore a vague resemblance to the camel but was not so understanding; however, there was a pretty little garden behind the house, and the child was allowed to go into it. Unfortunately there were no animals, only a few birds and a huge, smooth-coated, black dog behind the fence of the next-door garden on the left – how cramped everything was here! – a dog that was always slobbering at the mouth, and growled ferociously when the child came within ten paces of it.

But the absence of animals didn't matter too much, because

the anti-aircraft artillery post was in Hagenbeck's Zoo where, as there was a war on, a restaurant building had been requisitioned. Here, soon after his arrival, the child met Uncle Heinrich Hagenbeck, obviously the man who ran the whole show, although he wore no uniform and had to be very polite to Father. Uncle Heinrich liked the child, introduced him to his animals and their keepers, and from then on the child was allowed to go to the zoo almost daily.

There was no white camel in the zoo, but there were elephants, lots and lots of them, and their keeper was August, who didn't have to be called Uncle. The child liked him at once because he smelled like the old gardener and kept a flat bottle in his breast pocket, taking a sip from it now and then to freshen up the smell. The child thought it a pleasant aroma, and he found out that elephant dung had a pleasant aroma too; August carted off such huge quantities of it in a wheelbarrow every day that he was covered with filth. He was a wonderful old man – the child could never be with August too often or too long – and as the canteen staff usually gave him a bag of stale brown bread the elephants made friends with him as well, especially a huge old lady elephant called Roma, evidently August's assistant, for according to August she bossed all the others. One day August told the child not to be frightened, and then he said something to Roma, and the child felt something wind very gently around him, saw Roma's trunk wrapped round his waist, and was lifted right up into the air, a long way up, until he was sitting on Roma's back. It was marvellous, but Roma didn't let go of the child, she raised him in the air again and put him carefully down on the sand. The child couldn't get as much as he wanted of this, but only August knew the magic word, and he said once a week was enough. Every morning he raked the sand in the elephants' enclosure, and then you could play wonderful games there under Roma's watchful eye. Roma knew a lot of tricks. She would often raise her front leg carefully above the child's head until it looked as if he were under a roof, and that was lovely, but as soon as he caught hold of Roma's foot she withdrew it. One day the child was playing in the elephants' sand as usual when he heard a terrible lot of noise on the other side of the steep wall of the moat. A great many people were standing there, shouting like mad. The child ignored them, as August had said he was going to take a little nap on the fresh hay inside the elephant house, and then Uncle Heinrich's assistant came running up. The child knew him, but he took no notice of the child and ran straight away again. And the people went on shouting. Then Uncle Heinrich's assistant came back with Uncle Heinrich behind him, walking at his usual leisurely pace, and the shouting calmed down and then died away entirely. The child loved Uncle Heinrich, the only one of all those uncles and aunties who weren't really his relations who wanted the child to address him by the familiar *du* pronoun. 'I insist,' Uncle Heinrich had said. It wasn't easy to say *du* to such a tall old gentleman, which made Uncle Heinrich laugh and then, sighing, say something about rigid Austrian formality, but he promised the child a pony when he was bigger. Now he went over to the elephant house, and the child felt curious. He was just in time to see August wake up all of a sudden and stand to attention in front of Uncle Heinrich, who was telling him not to scare the visitors. 'Will he get a good hiding now?' asked the child. Uncle Heinrich laughed, and then explained gravely that he had twice his usual number of elephants, because the animals from his brother's circus were here too on account of the war, and elephants don't usually behave any better than human beings. At this August, still standing to attention, said something, and Uncle Heinrich laughed. 'Oh, well, if Roma's keeping an eye on him . . .' But the child wanted to go with Uncle Heinrich and see his future pony.

That was Hamburg as the child knew it. Oh, and there was something else too: his first voyage on a ship. The child was very excited the day before, looking forward to seeing Africa, but the big vessel went only as far as a café called the Alster Pavilion, where you had to sit still and be good. There were palm trees there all right, but no black people and monkeys, and you could have an anchovy open sandwich to eat, but it was covered with sliced egg and the anchovies were only very thin strips on top of the egg, so they were off the ration. Ration coupons were almost more important than money. You had to pay for everything, of course, but if you didn't have a ration card too – people snipped little corners off it for everything you bought – you could hardly get anything except on the black market.

Then one night there was a terribly loud noise, a crashing and a drumming such as the child had never heard before, and even his room vibrated. Mother had put a tiny lamp on the table, one of the kind called Hindenburg lights at the time, and she looked out of the window through a thin crack in the roller blind and muttered disjointed prayers. But the noise didn't stop, and next morning the dairy on the corner of Pölchaukamp and Dorotheenstrasse had disappeared, and so had the butcher's and the baker's and the laundry and the greengrocer's. Instead there was just a huge mound of rubble and dirt spread all over the street, and people were treading out little paths to get across it. They cursed the English, because now they'd have to get their milk from Schinkelstrasse, since there were similar heaps of rubble on the Mühlenkamp too. Mother said, 'There's a war on.' Frau Meyen said, 'Well, that's war for you,' but she seemed surprised. The child thought: is there, and is it? And then they heard that Hagenbeck's elephants were coming to clear the rubble away. Mother and child stood on the Mühlenkamp and the elephants really did come in a never-ending procession, trunk to tail, with Roma and August in the lead. The child shouted happily, 'Roma! Roma!' August said something to her, and Roma came quite close, picked the child up with her trunk, put him down on her shoulders for a moment, placed him back on the ground again and trotted on. The people watching were surprised.

Soon after that the child heard that they were going home again. It was safer there, said Father, and after all they'd been away for nearly three months, though the child could hardly believe it. Anyway, Father was being posted to Berlin, where they'd soon be able to visit him again. The child did a lovely drawing for Uncle Heinrich, lots of elephants with a pony in the middle of them, and Mother bought a bottle of rum for August. And that really was Hamburg.

But at home nothing was the way it had been before, not even the camel. The child had not forgotten his friend, although he had seen so many other houses, uncles, aunties and even real camels since they parted. But the camel was smaller than he remembered, and didn't recognize its protégé any more. Absently, with the shadow of the cot tracing its way over his body and through the neck of the half-veiled woman, he looked round the room, which now smelled strange and dusty. Noticing the child's distress, his mother told him how, two hundred years ago, a Baroque painter on his travels had painted the four continents on the walls here: Asia beside the bed, Africa behind the bed, Europe between the windows and America by the door. The child was disappointed, because he knew about pictures, but the camel had once been alive, and now it was as dead as his ancestors.

However, there was someone else here instead, Auntie Maika the U-boat.[3] She was almost a real auntie, because Uncle Richard, Grandfather's brother-in-law who was once on the Austrian imperial and royal general staff, had had a great many debts, and Auntie Maika's father had a bank. But Auntie Maika had not acted as she should, said Mother, so Uncle Richard had got a divorce and now she was here and was a U-boat. The child had never seen a U-boat except in the *Völkischer Beobachter*, but Auntie Maika wasn't made of steel, she was a rather plump lady with a long nose and an unusual red hairstyle. However, she had a little monkey on a red leash, all silky and tame. It enjoyed sitting on her shoulder, which made her look like the witch in the fairy-tale book. Sometimes the monkey made a mess on her shoulder, but Auntie Maika didn't mind, she just laughed. She was very nice, and you didn't have to sit still and be good in her company. The child loved her at second glance, and Mother was glad, because now she could go and join Father in Berlin. But after the child had spent two wonderful weeks with Auntie Maika, Mother came back to fetch him. He was going to have to go to the Führer's city now.

The Führer was a great man and had been around for ever. He was in the kitchen, not far from the crucifix and next to the radio, a colourful sight in his red, black and white frame. He was in Grandmother's kitchen too, only rather smaller, although hers was a much bigger kitchen. And he was in Father's study, where the chairs and sofa waited under white linen covers and the room was dusted once every two months. In the study he was a brownish photo standing on the desk, a very valuable photo, because he had written on it himself. So he was everywhere, and he kept watch on the child too, even from heaven on high, because the nursemaid enlivened boring bedtime prayers one day by adding an extra line, so now the child's prayers ran:

Here a little child I pray:
Jesus, guide me on my way.
As I lay me down to sleep
I hope that God my soul will keep,
And you, dear Führer, too.

The child thought this a very nice prayer, and rehearsed it industriously. And Mother, when these lines were carefully served up to her soon afterwards, looked so surprised that the child was delighted. So the Führer retained his place in the inmost chamber of the child's five-year-old heart, next to the crib. However, he stood with the shepherds near the ox and the ass, for by now the child had learned about God through one of those natural misunderstandings that so easily happened at his grandparents' house. The simple reason was that Grandfather was given no name of his own but was referred to in the house, the garden and the village merely as *der Herr*, the master – the word that was also used for the Lord God. In summer, when the child was at his grandmother's because it was her birthday, there had been so little rain that everyone was complaining of the drought, and even the priest standing before the congregation in church – the child once spoke of him as being 'on stage' there, and was teased for it long afterwards – said during Mass, 'And now let us all pray to the Lord to give us rain.' The child was proud of his grandfather and of being so closely related to him. But Grandfather had not been in church, so at lunch the child asked him to make it rain. Grandfather was baffled, but Grandmother asked a few questions and then explained to the child that the Lord in church and Grandfather as master of the estate were two different people and didn't really get on well together. As a result the Führer, like God and Grandfather, remained a human being in the child's eyes, if a very, very great and enormously important human being.

Then Christmas came, and you went to Grandfather and Grandmother's again. All the radios were broadcasting news of the heroic fighting at Stalingrad, but the child's bedtime prayer had become terribly boring, Führer and all, and was replaced by some verses from an evening hymn by Claudius.[4] The child gave them their première on Christmas Eve. The nursemaid sat beside him, holding the book, and in front of him, in a kindly semicircle, were his grandparents, his mother, and the old tutor and governess, the Wittmanns. The child had learned the lines by heart very nicely, but then he stumbled after all, making a mistake through wrongly associating ideas:

> *. . . from punishment, dear Lord, pray cease*
> *and let us sleep tonight in peace*
> *and our dear Führer too.*

Then the grown-ups stared again in a wry and helpless way which secretly pleased the child a good deal. At last Grandmother growled into the silence, 'Well, at least he's not our sick neighbour.' And Grandfather heaved a melancholy sigh with such irony that Mother sat up very straight and said sternly, 'Thank God.' Then they were all silent again in the way that the child knew meant he mustn't move a muscle. But the nursemaid heard a few days later that her services were no longer needed, since the child was big enough to dispense with them.

And now the child was almost a year older and in the Führer's city, although the Führer himself wasn't there but very far away in his headquarters, waging war. The child did not think of this as a loss because he was constantly being bombarded with new uncles and aunties. Father was living in much grander style than in Hamburg, in an army apartment not far from the Reich Aviation Ministry, and he had a new uniform too, with many more orders and stars than before and extra gold lace, but he looked positively plain beside his superior officer Uncle Hermann,[5] who was very fat and glittered even more than the embroidered garments on the skeletons of saints in the pilgrimage church the child had seen when visiting his grandparents. Uncle Hermann grinned all over his face, and there was a great deal of it, and kissed Mother's hand in a very elaborate way – Mother said later he had learned how from his wife, who was an actress. Then he approached the child, took his chin, pinched it firmly and pushed his lips up so far that the child could only say, 'Ow!'

He shouldn't have done that, because he realized it would mean a spanking, but Uncle Hermann left the child alone – he never saw him again – and afterwards, a few metres beyond the court of honour where stone soldiers with stone banners marched along the wall, all he got was a scolding.

All the Berlin uncles, as it happened, had this unpleasant urge to attack the child's cheeks and chin, and when one of them set eyes on him he instinctively took a step back. There was Uncle Albert,[6] still quite young, who wore an impressive leather coat; there was the rather smaller Uncle Josef[7] with his shoes that so interestingly didn't match; and Uncle Baldi who was almost a real uncle, being married to Mother's best friend, in his imposing naval uniform; and Uncle Ernst[8] from Linz with all those scars on his face. They were supposed to date from his student days but were really the result of a car accident. Berlin was horrible, and its zoo wasn't a patch on the zoo in Hamburg, but Mother liked having her hand kissed by all those uncles, the way no one would ever have kissed it in the Lower Danube region, and she enjoyed being asked to tea parties by lots and lots of aunties. The child hated tea parties because you had to sit still and be good, wear uncomfortable clothes and say only what was proper, or not even that, because there was often a scolding or a spanking afterwards. 'I want to be proud of you,' Mother always said.

Once the child and his mother went to tea at Auntie Magda's, and Uncle Josef's chauffeur came to fetch them. Auntie Magda was wearing a flowered brown dress with large lace flounces and had three daughters standing around. They looked very spiteful at first, but once in the playroom the children were soon getting on well together, and suddenly there was Auntie Magda shouting her head off, with the lace flounces flapping around her raised arms. Then Mother came in too and apologized profusely, but it was one of the girls who had started the doctors-and-nurses game. The child knew there was going to be a terrible hiding, but Mother couldn't get round to it yet because first they were driven home by Uncle Josef's chauffeur. All she said on the way was, 'You're never coming out to a tea party again,' and when the child innocently thanked her she was so confused that later on she forgot all about the good hiding. But she stuck to her word, and the child didn't have to go out to tea with her any more. Instead Granny came from Dresden – Father's mother whom the child had never liked, calling her 'Granny-go-away!' But still that was better than tea parties.

And then, one November afternoon, the child did see the Führer, who had come back from the war to hold a reception. After Mother had spent ages getting herself up to look elegant, and the child had been made to put on his scratchy knitted trousers, they followed a great many soldiers and other uniformed men into a huge hall, red and grey and all made of marble, with a lot of people standing around making the place echo. Down the middle of the hall there was a long red carpet that mustn't be trodden on, and people were arranged beside it: mothers with and without children at the front, then uniformed men and civilians with orders, and then, by the wall, uniformed men and civilians without orders. The child was just looking at the glass roof, which resembled his arithmetic exercise book, when a huge double door was flung open on the left, all present raised their right hands, and the Führer came in. The child didn't see him at once because of all the uniforms. The Führer wore the lightest-coloured uniform, but he looked different. However, the most impressive thing was a kind of wind that suddenly blew through the hall, more of a gentle breeze, but it smelled – and much, much later, when the child was no longer a child, he could recognize the separate aromas of that incomparable wind – it smelled of perfume, fish, leather, sweat, urine and some very feminine odours. A cloud of Chanel drifted from Mother's own afternoon dress. The crowd around the Führer came slowly closer to the child's side, and he ducked into safety behind Mother, because he feared for his chin – if all the other uncles went for him like that, what would he do? – but all the same he could see the Führer quite well. He was much smaller than the child had expected and looked, well, different. Then Mother made a curtsey and had her hand kissed by the Führer, who said something very brief, and next moment all the child could see was the uniformed backs of the escort. He saw the Führer again several times as he moved from right to left on the other side of the carpet, a back paler in colour than the others around him, and he saw him in profile too, but he was disappointed. Soon the doors on the left were flung open again, closed after the Führer and his retinue had disappeared through them, and then the doors on the right opened. There were echoing sounds once more, and a crowd of happy people made for the cloakrooms. It was like being in the theatre after Humperdinck's *Hänsel und Gretel*, when the poor witch has had such a hard time. Then the child was holding Mother's hand and standing at the top of the stairs down to the long, over-bright stone courtyard, in which people looked like little matchstick men.

'Well, what do you think of the Führer?' asked Mother when they had been walking along Wilhelmstrasse for some time. The child had kept quiet all this time, so he continued to keep quiet, priding himself on his silence. 'Wasn't he wonderful?' Mother's voice sounded hesitant, and the child noticed the way his knitted trousers scratched his thighs. 'Did you like him, anyway?' The child's silence knew no bounds. That evening Father and Mother sat side by side, staring hard at the child. 'So what was it like at the Führer's reception?' asked Father, not in uniform now. The child said nothing, because in view of those stares he was busy examining his conscience. 'He's still quite over-awed,' said Mother, and the child said truthfully, 'No, I'm not.' Father immediately inquired again, 'So what was it like?' The child froze with horror. He had broken his silence, and now, as his parents' avid glances showed, things could only get worse. After a long time he replied, 'I'm not saying.' He said this so forcefully that his parents couldn't help laughing, and with that the subject of the Führer was dismissed from the table upon which, miraculously, three oranges had appeared. In the following conversation about the oranges, and where you could get what off the ration or through connections, he found he could still preserve his silence, but it wasn't quite so good any more.

However, the Führer wasn't letting the child go so easily. The neighbour he could see across the light-well from his bedroom window, the man who couldn't fight in the war because he had lung cancer, coughed and coughed the length of a whole evening hymn and longer still before the child could finally get to sleep. In the morning he said, 'Our dear Führer was coughing all night.' Mother looked at him with a kindly but baffled expression. 'It was only a dream. You slept soundly all night.' Then the child realized that he had associated the wrong ideas again, and said: 'I mean the dear Führer and our sick neighbour too.' This so perplexed his mother that her expression stuck in the child's memory.

But Granny was a trial when she arrived a few days later. 'So you shook hands with the Führer?' 'No, I didn't.' 'What – you didn't shake hands with the Führer? Why didn't you shake hands with the Führer?' How could he explain to Granny? But the child had her to thank for a new piece of knowledge acquired during an air raid practice. He had nothing against air raid practices, and in this case nothing against Granny's company either, since he could easily get away from her and play with other children in another part of the cellar. Grown-ups were usually very cross at these times, and the children liked that, since it wasn't their fault. 'It's all Hitler's fault,' said the elderly woman keeping an eye on the children in the cellar. 'It's Hitler's fault,' crowed the child happily as Granny grumbled her way home. Granny stopped abruptly. 'Whose fault?' 'Hitler's.' 'But Hitler is the Führer!' So now the child knew that the Führer's secret name was Hitler. And older boys who played in the yards of apartment blocks a little further away told him other names for the Führer, like the Lance-Corporal, the Gröfaz (meaning the Greatest Field Marshal of All Time), or the Man from Braunau,[9] but when Mother heard about this she forbade him to play with those boys any more.

So did you say there was a war on, or just like other people that this was war? At least, here it suddenly was in the middle of Berlin, and all at once everyone was suddenly very keen not to be to blamed for it, but Grandmother had once read the child that poem,[10] and no one else knew it. News of world events kept coming over the radio, and people looked morose and irritable. Granny had finally gone back to Dresden. Before she went, she and her daughter-in-law had talked to each other very rapidly and in very loud voices – the child heard only a little of what they said. 'Oh, you and your war!' – 'It's not my war!' – 'But you wanted it!' – 'I did not!' and so on, and it all sounded just like the kind of fuss the child had learned he was not on any account to kick up – and then there was a new nursemaid, an elderly, stout woman from the Spreewald who had brought up five children of her own, her two sons were fighting in the war, and she wore the Mother's Cross as proudly as Father wore his cross that showed he was a knight. The child didn't understand the way she talked, which didn't matter, because that meant he could think his own thoughts undisturbed. He didn't like Berlin, those huge long streets, those gigantic blocks of buildings parading along them, all those uncles and aunts who were so terribly important, the snarling, sometimes jabbering tone that other people adopted, all that excruciating correctness and standing to attention, which he wasn't used to in his mother's house and most certainly not in his grandparents', but it would be Christmas in three weeks' time, and they would be celebrating Christmas with his grandparents again in the Lower Danube.

The air raid practices had been for real several times now, and you heard thudding sounds and sirens outside. Now you were back in the cellar again, sitting beside a stout pillar holding up the wall and playing with a girl. Girls in particular were fascinated by the 'caseful of junk' that you always took down to the cellar. It was a little brown cardboard suitcase with a picture inside the lid showing a happy mother and child advertising 'Dr Oetker's Pudding Powder'. Inside was a rather well-nibbled wooden rabbit, a cork for a bottle with a Tyrolean wooden head, the wooden figure of a Swedish girl in all her brightly painted glory, meant for stubbing out cigarettes, an ivory dog as a memento of August, and a number of black, white and red strings of beads. Aunt Magda had given Mother a swastika banner embroidered with little cylindrical glass beads as a cloth for a coffee table. Several beads came away the first time a coffee pot was put down on it, and then Mother removed the swastika and made the beads into a number of long necklaces, the kind of thing bound to make any girl's heart beat faster. The child couldn't remember what price he had just been asking for one of the strings of beads when there was suddenly a terrible bang, and then everything went dark and something hit him. After that, just when after that he didn't know, everything looked quite different, including the girl, who was bleeding from her ears and mouth. The child was angry and hit her because she didn't want to pay for the string of beads, but the little girl didn't defend herself, and her head flopped back and forth. Then grown-ups came along and told the child to stand up, but he couldn't because there was something heavy lying on his legs. It was taken away, but the child still couldn't stand up, and clung tight to his caseful of junk, and so he was dragged away. He was still clutching his caseful of junk when he woke up in a totally strange bed, which his mother told him was in hospital, and she said everything was all right. But he couldn't stand up because his legs were wrapped in thick, white stuff, and he had a funny buzzing in his head because, the doctor said, his left eardrum was perforated. However, the head doctor also said he'd been lucky, because the wall pillar where he had been sitting had taken the force of the blast, whereas the little girl who now visited him in all his dreams had died instantly. The nursemaid had died too, said Mother, and one of her sons had fallen at the front the week before. And then Christmas came, and they couldn't go to his grandparents. Father looked in now and then in his uniform, but there were other children and other parents in the room too, and once Father went very red in the face because the parents had been saying something with the name 'Meier' in it. Father said something in a very loud voice about 'terrorist attacks', and then he didn't come back any more. Mother said that by Meier they meant Uncle Hermann,[11] but his surname was quite different, and she said the child would understand all about it after the final victory. Then a little Christmas tree was put up in the ward, and the grown-ups were sent home. A lot of the children cried, but the child had learnt that a German boy doesn't cry, and he thought it was all horrible. So was the fact that Granny had brought him Swedish chocolate, although she ought to have known that the child didn't like sweets. The chocolate went into the caseful of junk, and was strictly guarded, because the mothers were greedy for chocolate and had stolen a bar, the one with the particularly pretty wrapping. Some days after the fuss he kicked up with the mothers over that, one of the older girls had a birthday, a girl lying next to him in even more plaster than he had, and the child generously gave her a chocolate bar. But when it was unwrapped, the chocolate bar had nothing but corrugated cardboard inside, and all the other bars were the same. Mother said Father had done it three nights ago because he knew the child didn't like chocolate. From now on he wouldn't leave the caseful of junk standing beside his bed, but took it under the covers with him where he could guard it better, because the child thought stealing was horrible ever since he had been frightened by tales of the Coal-Stealer[12] and the enemy overhearing what you said. And he was very angry with Father, particularly when he was in a friendly mood. Then he came out of hospital, and limped around for a while first on a pair of crutches, then without them, but by then he had already been to see his grandparents, where there was a Christmas tree waiting after all at the end of January 1944, the one with the real Angel Hallelujah. The story about this angel went back to several Christmases ago. The grown-ups had been singing, 'And the angel "Hallelujah" sings aloud from near and far . . .' And there on top of the Christmas tree the child saw the Angel Hallelujah, all silvery, with angel's hair and a pink wax face, and after that a Christmas tree wasn't a real Christmas tree without the Angel Hallelujah on top of it, already sooty around the hem of its dress by now. Then the child went back to Mother's house and Aunt Maika.

The child was glad to see Aunt Maika, because Purzel wasn't a good companion any more, and the camel was just silly, but even Aunt Maika had changed. The child thought she was a little stouter – Aunt Maika said that was from lack of exercise – and the red hairdo was very grey around her forehead – Aunt Maika said you couldn't get to a hairdresser these days – but above all she was more absent-minded and nervous, although she didn't tell the child why. 'She's a U-boat, that's what it is,' said Mother, but the child had seen many pictures of U-boats in Berlin, and he really didn't think she was, but Aunt Maika was wonderful and taught the child how to play chess.

Then they spent two days in Father's apartment in Vienna, which looked all deserted and grey now, like the spare rooms at the child's grandparents' house, and when they came back the little monkey had been tied to a table leg in the salon, was squealing in fear and had soiled the whole carpet. But Aunt Maika had gone. Mother spoke briefly to the servants and went straight back to Vienna.

(Her son found out the rest of the story a good fifty years later: by chance Uncle Ernst was in Vienna at the time, Ernst Kaltenbrunner, head of the Reich Security Office. It was not entirely by chance that he was in the city so often, because he had a mistress there who was an old friend of Mother's, and another who was also from an old aristocratic Austrian family and a niece of Mother's too, though not a real one. So he saw Mother at once and promised her the paper she needed. For that, and for reasons of time, Mother had to accompany him to Linz. The salon car was just reaching the city boundary when he made a pass at her. 'It was awful. He had the nastiest teeth I ever saw, and breath that smelled even worse than Hitler's. And sweaty feet too.' She got the paper and caught the next train back to Vienna, but when she had gone from the Westbahnhof to the Nordbahnhof, the train for Theresienstadt was just rolling out.)

Mother came back without Aunt Maika, and two days later the little monkey had disappeared too. 'It's been put to sleep,' said Mother, and the child wasn't to talk to the kitchen maid any more either. 'I can't fire her or she'll denounce us to the Gestapo too.' She might have guessed why the child had hated the kitchen maid so long, but she had other anxieties. She wanted to go back to Father in Berlin, so the child went to his grandparents again.

He had had a favourite room there for a long time, large, high-ceilinged and – since it had been impossible to open its blinds for quite a while – so dimly lit that you had to climb on the stool that Grandmother had put beside the door before you could switch on the light. In the middle of this room there was an ancient and rather wobbly set of chairs, with a big round thing called a globe beside it, and the walls were covered with books. Between the windows, luckily within the child's grasp, the whole world lay behind their linen and leather backs and the dust. You often had to pull hard to get at that world, now and then you fell over in the process, and sometimes you were disappointed. Once, exerting your strength to the utmost, you had pulled a particularly large book off the shelf. As it fell it landed on your hand and hurt, and then it contained only pictures in dull colours showing nothing at all, and the child was told that it was an atlas. Atlas had once carried the vault of the sky on his shoulders, but then he was tricked by Hercules, and since then he had been a mountain range in Morocco, but the child was not so keen on knowing about all that, because most of the other books were friendlier and presented him with exciting worlds in black and white, often in colour too. However, it wasn't so easy to get at the coloured worlds, because they had tissue paper sticking to them, and the tissue could be lifted off only in small pieces, if at all. 'That's the result of time,' said Grandmother, and the child hated time and the tissue paper. Once he was given a piece of cotton wool and some paraffin to get it off. The scraps of paper that had stuck to the picture below did indeed come off after a little rubbing, but then some of the picture came off too, and the desert the child longed to see, with its oasis and camels and Bedouin, ran and turned to nasty brown smears. Apart from such catastrophes, which were rare, and the annoyances, which were frequent, these pictures were a world worth living in, but Grandmother said, 'That was long before your time. It's all gone now.' The child could understand that, since he had seen the ruins of Hamburg, and yet again it was all the fault of the English, this time wreaking havoc among the Indians and many other exciting characters. With the colourful peoples of the Caucasus and the exotic uniforms of old St Petersburg it was the Russians' fault, and with everything else time was to blame, having yet more bombs in store. The child hated time, and hated himself too for not being as old as Grandmother, who said she had seen many of the pictures in real life, and he hated the world because it wasn't the same as the books.

Sometimes his hatred concentrated into a sudden rage that sent the books crashing to the floor and chased the child himself out of the library, out of the house, through the park and the nursery garden and into a barn where he had to scurry up a ladder. He came back to his right mind at last in the hay and the dim light, travelling those lost lands in his thoughts.

Usually these travels took the child south-east. He rarely visited the American Indians, the Scots, Lapps and Cossacks, and he didn't want to be an engine driver or a policeman, or even an air raid warden, an SS man or a U-boat captain, although those were the careers lauded to the skies in tones of desperation on the radio, because he didn't like the radio either. It once used to play several bars from Liszt's *Les Préludes*, and then he had had to stand very straight beside Mother, but that was a long time ago. Uncle Richard was sometimes there too, the uncle who had once been married to Aunt Maika, but Grandmother said he had been 'rehabilitated' from that marriage, and he talked an awful lot about the general staff before the First World War. He had drawn maps for them. They had had the best and the smartest army in the world, said Uncle Richard, and the only mistake had been sending them to war. The child made up his mind never to wear a uniform.

Once he was asked in front of other children what he would like to be when he grew up, and he said fervently, 'A nomad!' There was giggling, and when he was asked more questions the child explained, 'Because they have tents and camels, and they travel through deserts with them and tell each other fairy stories.' He was reminded of this for years to come. Questions of where and when were naturally of no importance in the desert, although Grandmother's linen cupboards really provided garments only for Arabs, whose skin colour could be imitated with ground-fig coffee. Once, with the aid of some red check tea towels, he spent a whole afternoon playing at Abraham and Moses, which led to a little argument that evening between Grandmother and Mother, to which the child listened with great interest. Mother said such games were inappropriate these days, and not entirely safe just now either.

'You see, nomads are Semites,' Mother told the child, but then he wanted to be a Semite even though the term meant nothing to him apart from the nomads. Mother was at a loss, for she couldn't know that the child's ambition in life came from half a dozen lavishly illustrated books written in a language he didn't know, and from the contents of a cupboard in an unused room. He had found it all by himself, and it contained a big leather belt, a curved sword that had a blue gleam when you drew it out of its red velvet sheath, which was set with green stones, and a shiny gold-coloured metal flask, also encrusted with stones and with a screw top, as well as a chess set which was rather shabby now but was inlaid with ivory. This cupboard with its creaking door was his secret treasure chamber for a long time, until he couldn't keep the secret to himself any more. Then Grandmother told him that the things had belonged to an uncle who was in the service of the British 'before the last war', travelling somewhere in Persia, Afghanistan or India, and who had brought them back for his cousin, who was Grandfather. The child would have liked to meet this uncle, who was said to be actually still alive, but in England, and unfortunately we were at war with England.

Another uncle, though not a real one, was responsible for the fact that the child did not like the Black Continent in spite of all the exciting pictures, and even though this uncle had given him a field flask made of real monkey-skin. Uncle Udo was fat and loud-voiced, sweated even in a short-sleeved shirt, and had a wooden leg as a memento of his time fighting in German East Africa with von Lettow-Vorbeck.[13] But even that wasn't interesting, and yet more boring were his stories, which hinged only on the cowardice of the British and the devotion to Uncle Udo of his Negroes. 'My Hereros always regarded me as a father,' he kept saying, and he had pictures in his wallet of two sons, who were in the war 'but in a safe place'. However, they looked white. Africa was as horrible as Uncle Udo, although thank God he seldom turned up.

South America once came visiting too in the shape of a dark grey, very thin gentleman, whose long nose, coming down almost to his top lip, was fascinating because it made him look like the mangy buzzard that spread what remained of its wings in a particularly empty room after an orgy devouring various pests. The child had once liked playing with the buzzard, although like the whole room it stank of naphthalene, and if you were found there you had to wash your hands very thoroughly indeed. Hence the child's curiosity about the strange gentleman, which unfortunately remained unsatisfied. The child and the domestic staff were told he was a Brazilian diplomat who was having difficulty getting home because of the war, but there were other whispered rumours. As soon as 'the Brazilian', as he was always known below stairs, opened his mouth his sharp pronunciation of the letter E was reminiscent of the Bohemian kitchen maid, and once the child listened to a debate on whether his diplomatic pass was genuine enough and his knowledge of Portuguese sufficient for him to get through. The child was suspicious. However much he looked in the books, and he could read now too, Herr Lustiger,[14] as the Brazilian was called by the child's grandparents despite his constant sad appearance, did not look at all like the pictures from the Amazon. But then Grandmother said, rather impatiently, that raffia skirts were impracticable clothing for Europe, and out of fashion even in Brazil, but Herr Lustiger would be wearing them on Sundays there. Otherwise, all conversations with him, when the child listened to them on the other side of the door, were just about making connections and getting through, and then one day Herr Lustiger had left without ever wearing his raffia skirt. The child found a long object in his empty room. But it wasn't a blowpipe, it was a walking stick. When he had unscrewed its knob, a long glass bottle fell out, broke, and the splinters smelled of cognac. Lying low, as he had learned to do in such situations, the child slunk off to the library and spent all afternoon with the four volumes about the Amazon written by Herr von Humboldt.

Sometimes Grandmother gave him a basket, with things in it for someone she knew who was in hospital. Grandmother knew everyone in the village, and most of them were women. They seemed to be very ill, for the hospital was a hut in a small wood opposite the doctor's house, and two nursing nuns looked after them. They were old, dressed in black and white, and rosaries hung from their belts. The child liked going into the wood, because the kindergarten he knew, with Aunt Minna who ran it, was there too. In the past Grandfather had built it so that women could go to work even when they had children, and when the kindergarten was over Aunt Minna cleaned the wash-room. It was at the centre of the kindergarten, for the sake of the kind of cleanliness known as hygiene, and had golden dragons spouting cold water into ceramic basins shaped like flowers. The walls had tiles on them showing fairy-tale characters, all illustrating the importance of hygiene. For instance, there was Little Red Riding Hood cleaning her teeth at a spring of water before visiting her grandmother, and the wolf, hungrily watching, had very bad teeth. Next to them were the Seven Dwarves, washing their feet toe by toe, but Snow White had only a single towel. It was all very pretty, although you knew the fairy tales anyway, and there was nothing else, but you liked the room because it was so bright.

Much more exciting was the farmyard where the child had no business, but he had soon discovered how to get there without being seen by Grandfather from his study, and he had also been quick to find out when Grandfather was coming over and he had better make himself scarce. Every

Tuesday evening a steam engine pushed a freight car into the yard, and it had to be filled up on Wednesday so that the engine could fetch it again and take it to the station, where it would be coupled to another train and be in Vienna at the right time on Thursday morning. People worked all week to fill that freight car, in the abattoir next to the stables, in the kitchen and in the nursery garden, and in the carpenter's workshop too, because the wooden crates in which everything was put ready for the freight car were often falling apart, or hadn't come back, and Grandfather swore roundly because he was short of men. There were plenty of women there, yes, but only old men, and they couldn't really muscle in, as he said. The only young men working on the farm were Poles and Russians, who did speak a little German but still had difficulty making themselves understood in the Lower Danube region, and in addition they weren't used to the way everything ought to be done. They lived 'in the camp', as the six huts with stout barbed wire around them a little way outside the village were called, and they marched off from the camp in rows four abreast every morning, accompanied by four men in uniform, all the way through the village to the entrance. Here the procession divided. Most of the Russians, Poles and Serbs marched into the factory, and a small troop came into the home farm and the nursery garden, and were fetched again in the evening. They looked funny because they wore their pyjamas all day, but Grandmother said they wouldn't do that at home, only here. One spring evening Grandfather had a conversation with the camp commandant, and the child heard a little of it, because he was allowed to take wine to the study, and then Grandfather showed him some of the rooms on the ground floor of the old part of the house, which had old gratings in front of their windows, because once some of the workmen had lived there too, but only at harvest time. A dozen Russians and Poles moved in there a few days later, 'So that they'll always be on hand,' as

Grandfather put it. They ate with the farm workers, and wore the same work clothes, and sometimes one of them kissed Grandfather's hand and said he was glad not to be living in the camp any more, but Grandfather quickly wiped his hand on his trousers and said the man had better just get his work done properly.

By now it was May, and there were all sorts of things going on. At night the child heard strange sounds under his window, and he got up on the sill and peered through the blinds. It worked really well, because the windows were open and you could press your nose directly against the slats of the blinds. Then the child saw a figure in between the runner beans, which were quite small still and consisted mainly of the poles they would climb later. It must be one of the kitchen maids, the one with the fat behind, and now she had hitched her skirt up and her behind was shining in the moonlight. And there was another figure there too, also with a bare behind, and the two of them were whispering together. The girl was holding tight to the beanpoles, and the other figure, which looked like the young Russian who was always digging in the nursery garden, came close to her behind, and then the whole thing reminded the child of what the bull had been doing with the cow on the farm the other day, which he hadn't really been allowed to watch. But what was going on down there lasted much longer and was much more exciting, so exciting that the child had to put his hand on what he called his little bunny and play with it until it felt itchy. The child couldn't remember when he had discovered this game, but it must have been back in Mother's house, because she had once caught him at it, and then she had behaved very strangely. The child remembered that perfectly: Mother sitting at the sewing machine making something which looked like a sack out of stout white cotton, and then she said, 'You're not to play with your little willy or it will turn black one day, and then it will fall off.'

The child understood that by 'little willy' she meant his bunny, and he had seen some black rabbits in their hutches in the nursery garden too, but he couldn't somehow imagine it, so he asked in order to be on the safe side, and Mother said, 'Yes, it will turn black and fall off. All gone.' And that evening the child had to go to bed in the white thing that Mother had made that afternoon, and it really was a sack which buttoned up at the back, with only his head and arms sticking out of it. 'It's a sleeping bag,' said Mother, 'to keep you from kicking about in bed.' The child had never just kicked about in bed, but later, when he couldn't get to sleep and wanted to play with his little bunny he couldn't, because the thick cotton was in the way, and he slept very badly. He hated the sleeping bag, although you could get hold of your little bunny through it in the end, if you tried hard, though it wasn't nearly as nice as without the bag. The bag grew with him, because it was always being let out as he grew, and it was a nuisance to the child in both Hamburg and Berlin. But Grandmother said it gave her too much work – as the child couldn't do a wee with it on, he had wet himself a few times – so the sleeping bag was left in a drawer, where the grown-ups soon forgot it. And the child was glad of that, because now he could not only go to the loo past the wallpapered door and two rooms further on for a wee, he could also climb up on the window sill and watch all the exciting things going on among the garden beds.

His little bunny had long ago finished itching, but the figures down below were still working away, snorting and grunting because it was so strenuous. Then they gave a final grunt, very loud and at almost the same time, stood still for a while and moved away from each other. The kitchen maid wiped her behind on her skirt and the man wiped his on his trousers. The two of them whispered for a little longer, and then the girl went through the door that Grandmother normally used to go into the park, while the man went to where the Russians slept. The child had to crane his neck a bit, but he saw him pull the grating out of the window frame, climb in, and put the grating back in place.

From now on there was something going on among the beanpoles almost every night, sometimes twice or even three times, and gradually the child came to recognize all the younger kitchen maids and almost all the Russians except for the hunchbacked, slightly older man. He liked watching through the blinds, although it wasn't quite as exciting as the first time, because really it was always the same.

The child had other favourite toys too, for instance toy soldiers, the Fleischmann brand. All kinds of uncles and aunts gave them to him, and they looked like the real Wehrmacht, with tiny insignia of rank too, but they easily lost their limbs, and then they fell apart into nothing but crumbly brown stuff and thin wire. On his birthday he had been given a whole battalion, some even came from Father in Berlin, and Grandfather joked that the child had better keep a sharp eye on them, because the Führer didn't have so many of his own left. One afternoon soon after his birthday, the child sorted out the wounded – the armless, legless, headless – for a mercy killing. Mercy killing was a term he had heard in the kitchen, and he asked what it meant. He kept hearing new words in the kitchen. For instance, one of the cooks had recently told the child, when he kept eating the strawberries that were just being packed up for Vienna, 'Carry on like that and you'll end up in the concentration camp.' Of course the child asked Grandmother what a concentration camp was, and at first Grandmother was surprised, but then she said, 'They start by beating you hard in a concentration camp, and then you fly out through the chimney.' The child thought he would like to end up in a concentration camp, because he was fascinated by the way witches can fly up a chimney, but since you had to be beaten hard first he dropped that wish. 'Mercy killing' sounded much nicer, for the priest in church talked about mercy too, and he wanted to do something nice for his wounded soldiers. He carefully laid them in a shoebox, which was soon almost half full, and took them to the nursery garden. He still had his old sandbox from when he was little at the back of the nursery garden, near an old tool shed, but it was a long time since he had built any sand castles, and he'd never felt like making sand pies. The sand did look rather dirty, but that didn't matter. Using a flour shovel borrowed from the kitchen, he dug a long grave – an uncle here on leave had once told the child's grandparents how it was done in Russia – and he stood the wounded soldiers in a row on the edge of it. Next to the grave, on the opposite side, he put the medical orderlies and the little hospital, and then he fetched a handy brick from the stack beside the tool shed, and hit the wounded men with it until there was only brown crumbly stuff left. Then the little bunny made itself felt again, and this time it itched like anything.

When the child came back to the real world he had a terrible shock, because there were two legs in coarse blue drill in front of him. They belonged to the Russian who was always digging in the nursery garden, and the Russian was smiling in a very friendly way. The child had often seen him, and recognized him because he was rather younger than the others, and his black hair was a little longer and a little shaggier than theirs. He even had some on his chest, but his smile made the child suspicious, because he had a hand inside his trousers, and they were swelling as if he had a stick hidden in there. The child cautiously asked, 'What's your name?' – 'Ivan,' said the Russian, crouching down in front of the child, but then his trousers flapped open, and out jumped a bunny such as the child had never seen before, enormous, with a big purple knob on top, dark-skinned and with a lot of black hair at its root. The child could see that Ivan was smiling, but most of all he was staring at the bunny, which was much more interesting than Ivan. Although the child was looking very cautiously, Ivan noticed, and he swayed back and forth on the soles of his feet a few times, while the bunny came further and further out of his trousers, with the child gaping at it in wonderment. 'You like that, eh? Want to see it?' whispered Ivan after a while. 'Yes,' breathed the child. Ivan glanced quickly to left and right, and then he took the child's hand and led him into the tool shed. Inside, in the twilight on the pile of old sacks, the bunny was even bigger than beside the sandbox, and when the child felt it, it was all hard. Its dark colour reminded the child for a moment of his mother's threat about his little willy, but Ivan said his bunny was perfectly healthy, and it was so thick that the child couldn't get his whole hand round it. Ivan showed the child what to do, and his eyes went all narrow. Then Ivan played with his bunny himself. The child helped as best he could, because there was room for two hands there, but Ivan's hand worked faster. Then Ivan began gasping and fell back. The child was afraid he was ill, because he was also rolling his eyes in a funny way, but suddenly his bunny spat straight in the child's face, and over Ivan's tummy too. When the child wiped the spit off his face he noticed that it tasted salty. Ivan lay on the sacks for a while, groaning, and the child felt worried about him, but then he wiped his tummy, stood up looking perfectly all right, pulled up his trousers, went to the door of the shed, looked left and right, and disappeared. As for the child, he sat down on the sacks and stayed there for a little longer, because it had been even more exciting than the way his own bunny had itched during the mercy killing. When he went back to the house, Ivan was nowhere to be seen. He didn't see him again until night, through the blinds, when he was doing gymnastic exercises with the kitchen maid. Ivan didn't know he was being watched by the child, who now guessed that all the snorting activity among the beanpoles must have something to do with the giant bunny.

Next day at lunch Ivan wouldn't look at the child, he just kept looking at the kitchen maid with the fat behind. He didn't look at the child, either, when he stood on one side of the fence watching Ivan digging on the other side. Only the day afterwards did he look at him, glanced to right and left, and then went slowly into the shed. The child quickly slipped into it after him. 'So you like me, do you?' asked Ivan. 'Yes,' said the child, but then Ivan was rather disappointed to find that his bunny was too big for the child's mouth, and made him retch and cough. However, Ivan forgave the child, who gradually got to know more about his friend. He had been nineteen only a few days earlier, and before he was taken prisoner had been to grammar school in Kiev, where he had learnt German, since two of his grandparents had been German and had emigrated to the other side of the Urals, but you had to ask Ivan questions like that before the game with the bunny, because he always went off in a hurry directly afterwards.

The child had time for adventures like these only in the afternoon, for he had started school at Easter because he and the Wittmann family didn't get on together any more. Now they met only for an hour a day, doing homework, and got on with each other better. The Wittmanns had worked hard, so you went straight into Class Two, and even there you knew it all already, and much of it better than the teacher, although of course you didn't tell her that so as not to hurt her feelings. For there were children of the servants there too, people you hadn't been allowed to play with before. They avenged themselves on the child now by calling him Hasi, alluding to part of his grandparents' name,[15] and when he once said angrily in break that he wasn't called Hasi, but he did have a *Häschen*, a little bunny, the boys laughed and said they had much bigger bunnies, they had real pricks. The workers' children were no better, particularly those of the Reds,[16] who were now Browns, and only the girls were nice to him because they didn't have any bunnies at all. And then there were the farmers' children, whom he knew already from his grandparents' visits to their parents, or when they came with their families to see his grandparents and get things to eat. Once a week the Local Party Group Leader came to school, right into lessons, and said something, but usually to the older classes. When he first came into the child's class the child was rather agitated, because Grandmother had told him not to speak to the man and to say nothing to him. The Local Group leader went on about heroism and Providence, and when he had finished he stared at the child, who had to stand up, and asked him, 'Well, and what do your people think at home?' The child said nothing, and then the teacher said, 'You must reply to the Group Leader, you know.' It was very difficult. 'What do they think?' stammered the child, but then, thank goodness, he thought of his all-purpose excuse. 'I haven't noticed yet.' The Local Group Leader did not look happy with this, but many of the class laughed, and that wasn't nice either. However, soon the holidays would be coming.

First, however, the musicians from the Philharmonic came. The child had been hearing for two whole weeks that they were coming, and he was all excited, because he had once heard them in the Golden Hall of the Musikverein in Vienna, which had to be closed now, like the opera and the theatre, because the country had been in a state of total war for some time.

Even the preparations were very impressive. Three maids and the old manservant had been working for days in the Baroque Wing, which was usually locked off, and the child saw a servant turning winches in the attic, and the maids down below took huge chandeliers out of the big linen sacks that had been let down from the ceiling. However, they weren't made of real gold but of Baroque gilded wood. The maids were soon perspiring because they had a great deal of dust to wipe off, many windows to clean, and all the flat surfaces to polish. Then red carpet was laid on the steps in the stairwell, next to the kitchen where the domestic staff always ate under the slope of the stairs, and the carpet was fixed in place with freshly cleaned brass rods, and for the first time the child really saw that all the ceilings were painted with coloured pictures, and Grandmother said those were apotheoses, and apotheoses were compliments paid by the gods to the masters of the house and the Emperor, though there hadn't been one of those for a long time now. The child recognized many of the gods from books, and the goddesses were proudly showing their breasts. This was different from Mother's house, where the walls were brightly coloured and the ceiling white, whereas here the walls were white and gold or brown and gold, and there was a great deal of activity on the ceilings. In the Small Hall below the ceilings a number of tables had been arranged in a big U-shape, and large quantities of chairs were taken out of big linen covers in another room, and they were all going to be used, first at the festive board, as the tables were now called, and then in the gallery, that was to say the Great Hall, where they were arranged in rows. At the back of the hall, which was the front this time, were the upholstered chairs, with ordinary chairs in front of them. The child was surprised to see only four music stands against the back wall, which was now the front, because he knew there were a great many musicians in the Philharmonic, and he was afraid they might quarrel over the shortage of stands. But Grandmother laughed, and showed the child the invitations, which had been printed in the paper factory, although it no longer belonged to Grandfather but was really Father's, and was being managed for him because he was in Berlin. '. . . have the honour,' read the child, 'to invite you to a musical evening with gentlemen from the Vienna Philharmonic . . .' – 'They're not all together any more,' said Grandmother. 'First they threw out the Jews, now some of the others are fighting in the war, but a few talented musicians are still left.' The child acted as if he understood, but at the end of the invitation he stumbled over *R.S.V.P.*, and Grandmother said it was a request for an answer, in French, but that didn't matter, because the phrase had always been in French, and anyway France belonged to the Reich. Then she said a few cross things about this stupid war, but she always did that.

You could tell that the great day had come because it was as busy in the kitchen as on a Wednesday, although this was Saturday. Chickens were plucked in the farmyard, and more and more baskets kept coming up from the nursery garden. The musicians from the Philharmonic arrived at midday too, but there were only four men with two cases each. One case held each musician's instrument and the other his evening dress. The child actually knew the viola player, because he had once visited them at Mother's house, and he had studied at the Academy with her. And because it was midday the Philharmonic musicians were served a wonderful lunch in the child's grandparents' dining-room, and then they had to lie down and sleep. Grandmother had put little home-made cardboard cases in their rooms full of ham, sausages and schnapps, and the envelopes containing their fees were on their bedside tables. In the afternoon the Philharmonic musicians had rested, and they were served real coffee and cake in the pavilion in the park. Then they took a quick look at the hall, moved the music stands about a little, tried the chairs, and went back to the pavilion, where they were served ham and wine. By now the festive board in the Small Hall had been covered with damask, the maids were polishing the glasses or laying the silver straight, and a great many bunches of flowers came up from the nursery garden.

The guests arrived at six. Their names were announced down below, and the child's grandparents stood at the top of the stairs. They had dressed themselves up in fine clothes; Grandmother was glittering, but Grandfather's tie was the only glittering part of him, and in the doorway of the Guardroom Hall stood the child, all dressed up too, with a tie and a silver tray of titbits called canapés, which were to give the guests an excuse to wipe their hands. The child knew many of the guests already. They had come from the country all around, and most of them had grand names. Many owned houses like Grandfather's, but without a factory attached, many had factories without such houses, some had even come from nearby towns, and now they were standing around in the Guardroom Hall, talking politely and drinking ice-wine[17] from little glasses. 'Just like peacetime,' said one old lady, although this was the middle of total war, but Grandmother told you in a whisper that the old girl was speaking about the days before the First World War. Then the doors to the Small Hall were opened, and Grandfather invited the guests to sit down. They hurried in and found their places very quickly, because their names were beside their plates. The child was sitting with his grandparents and the Philharmonic musicians at the top of the table. Then the maids served the meal. The child had learned that you mustn't eat very much in public, and his grandparents observed that rule, but the Philharmonic musicians and the guests ate avidly, as if they hadn't eaten anything for weeks. Each of them had a whole half-chicken as the main course. When coffee, liqueurs and dessert were served, the child had to go back to the Guardroom Hall to welcome the people who had come up from the village with another tray of canapés. The local teachers came, the doctors, the clerks and engineers from the factory, and so on and so forth, and they were led straight into the Great Hall, where they sat on the ordinary chairs. Then the guests came out of the Small Hall and sat on the upholstered chairs, and last came the child's grandparents with the Philharmonic musicians and everyone clapped. The child sat with his grandparents, the Philharmonic musicians sat at the music stands, and after a little crackling and rustling they began.

They played three quartets by Haydn, because they knew that Grandfather loved Haydn as if there had been a family connection between them. The child knew two of the quartets already, because the doctor, two teachers and an engineer played musical instruments too, and often came to play at the child's grandparents' house – which was why they and their wives could sit in upholstered chairs today – but he had never heard the quartets played so wonderfully before. They were wonderful instruments and wonderful musicians, and the child found everything wonderful at the time, but the Baroque hall had something to do with it too, for it increased the volume of the music, and many a *forte* passage sounded like a good organ, although the singing tone of the strings retained all its delicacy. 'It was built for this music,' whispered Grandmother in the applause between two quartets, but she and Grandfather were moved too – in the second movement of the 'Emperor' Quartet they had moist eyes and were holding hands, and 'in public' too! The guests kept quiet, hardly coughed at all – never during the music, only between movements – and only when the Philharmonic musicians put their bows down on the music stands did they clap, but then they clapped so loud that it hurt the child's right ear (he had been bending his head to the left the whole time, since he could hardly hear on that side). The guests clapped for a long time, and the Philharmonic musicians bowed and bowed, and then everyone was in the Guardroom Hall with *petits fours* for the ladies, open sandwiches for the gentlemen – the child didn't like them, because you had to be very careful how you bit into them or all kinds of stuff fell off, and then you had spots of mayonnaise on you – and schnapps for the men, Madeira for the ladies and lemonade for the child. The Philharmonic musicians stood around with the child and his grandparents, and one of them suddenly asked if they'd like to hear the 'Trout' Quintet again. Grandfather, full of emotion and slivovitz, said enthusiastically, 'With the greatest pleasure,' although Grandmother looked rather dubious. And the Philharmonic musicians said they could come back again three weeks from now.

Then Grandfather smashed his schnapps glass, and silence fell at once. In a loud voice, Grandfather invited all the guests to another recital in three weeks' time – 'we're saving ourselves the postage' – and then they left, first the people from the village, who all said thank you, then the guests, gradually, because many of them needed three glasses of schnapps before they could find their way home, and then the child was sent to bed. He was glad of that, and listened for only a little while to Grandfather and the Philharmonic musicians talking in the old music room next to his. For the first time he thought he had some idea of what Grandmother might mean when she said, 'One is someone, after all.'

Three weeks later the Philharmonic musicians came back, and their cases were much larger than before, although again they had only evening dress with them. The fifth man who came with them was a very famous pianist. He had his case carried in by one of the maids, because his fingers were so valuable that he couldn't touch anything but glasses and cutlery. As the train didn't arrive until the afternoon, the artists were not served lunch this time, only a late afternoon snack, but it was as large as two lunches. Up above the middle-sized grand piano had been wheeled out of the music room and into the Great Hall. It was the piano on which Brahms had played when he was once invited to the house by the child's grandparents, and the child watched, fascinated, as the ancient piano tuner from town fiddled around with it. First he unscrewed a board and took out almost all the insides of the piano – the child liked watching pigs being gutted too – then he worked away like mad on the felted hammers until they looked fluffy again, he pushed the 'action', as he called it, back inside the piano again, and then he tuned it for hours, but that part was boring. In the evening he was given a couple of salamis, and was delighted. The Philharmonic musicians were delighted too, because there was not only ham and sausages in their rooms but also – Grandfather had insisted on it – small wooden boxes containing six smoked trout each, on account of the Schubert. When the child and Grandmother went into the kitchen, she said, 'It's to be hoped they don't take it into their heads to play the "Ox" Minuet.' The child knew that one, because it was by Haydn. However, there wasn't as much to do in the kitchen as last time, for there was no dinner, only a buffet. In the evening the child's grandparents dressed up, but weren't quite as glittering as last time, and the child was dressed up too, but had no silver tray to carry round because of the buffet. Then the guests arrived, all at the same time, including the people from the village, set to work on the buffet straight away and ate everything. The people from the village didn't have quite their fair share because they hadn't piled so much on their plates.

The 'Trout' Quintet was wonderful, and then another piece that the child didn't know was played. Then they all stood in the Small Hall – a smaller buffet had been put out there in the meantime – the artists stood with the child and his grandparents again, and the child was allowed to congratulate the pianist and even shake the hand which had such valuable fingers. One of the Philharmonic musicians was talking enthusiastically about a marvellous Mozart octet, and said Schubert had written an excellent one too, but Grandmother looked stern and excused herself for a moment. Grandfather followed her down the long corridors, and the child stole after them. He could hear Grandmother talking to Grandfather through the closed double doors of the boudoir. The child understood only a little of it, for instance that they couldn't overdo the illegal slaughter of farm animals, and then he had to disappear quickly, because his grandparents were approaching the doors again. When they were back with their guests, Grandfather told the Philharmonic musicians that he liked chamber music very much, trios, quartets, even a quintet now and then, but best of all he'd like to hear a real, full orchestra again. In addition, it was summer now, when there was a lot of work to be done, and of course there was a shortage of men everywhere, but perhaps they might consider a couple of trios in October or November, at any rate not until after the sugar beet campaign. Then the buffet had been cleared right out, and Grandfather, looking rather depressed, said to the last guests, 'If you really must go home now, then I won't keep you.'

The summer did bring a lot of work, and the old manservant died too. Grandfather cursed, for two years ago – the child couldn't remember this, since he had been living in Mother's house at the time – his butler, whose post was known by its English name, had died too. After that a maid had to look after his clothes for him, and Grandfather said she did everything wrong, although he wore only white linen jackets in summer and pea-green cloth jackets in winter, but he had a very great many of them, and the girl never arranged them properly on the 'valet', which was a clothes stand. And now the man-servant had gone too, although he had been only fifty years in Grandfather's service and was the same age as Grandfather himself! His own father had been manservant here, and he had two sons of his own, but they had been fighting in the war and one of them had already fallen. The child was some-times allowed to play with this man's children, but they were too young to replace their grandfather as manservant. Grand-father swore, but Grandmother had said of the manservant, 'He's shrinking like Bohemian linen,' and at receptions you could see his livery hanging loose on him, and his pale, almost transparent look. The child had also noticed that the man-servant kept dropping off to sleep at his work recently, which Grandmother said was nothing unusual, the serious part was that he slept in the intervals of his work too. Then he stayed in bed, and the doctor came twice a day, and then a priest with a server. The child was allowed to watch the priest talking to the manservant and oiling him like a machine, but it didn't help, for the manservant didn't wake up, and was snoring in a funny way. The child saw him again next day, in a room draped with black on the ground floor which he hadn't seen before. He was lying in his coffin between large candles and had gone all small and grey. 'He's over his troubles now,' said Grandmother, but Grandfather was cross because he didn't have a manservant any more. He wouldn't go to the funeral either, saying, 'He won't be going to mine.'

All the same, it was a beautiful funeral. The hearse was brought from the carriage-house, black and silver with four little angels on the canopy, and Grandmother's 'Zeugerl', a small black carriage. Then the manservant's relations came from nearby villages, and were given lunch. Outside the wind band and the firemen's club, of which he had been a member, marched up and down, and when the priest came Grandfather delivered a short address and then went to the nursery garden, because it was Tuesday and the freight car would be coming in the evening. Then the coffin was put on the hearse. A server walked in front with the wooden crucifix, then came the wind band and the firemen, sweating terribly, for it was summer, then servers with the priest, the hearse, the manservant's relations, the domestic staff, with the men first because the dead servant had been a man, and then the maids, some of whom were walking very heavily. After them and in front of the people from the village came Grandmother with the child in the Zeugerl, behind the old groom. 'Look at him sitting up on the box – what a fellow he is!' whispered Grandmother, but the child didn't understand what she meant exactly. Then Grandmother put her veil up, because it was too hot for her, and after a while she pointed to one of the maids: 'Just see her, the way she's trudging along – she'll be the next.' Then they had the church and the graveyard behind them – the child had been allowed to throw a few flowers on the manservant – and tables and benches had been put up in the courtyard in front of the Baroque Wing, and Grandmother and the child went to find Grandfather. He was sitting in his study with a bottle, swearing because he had no manservant any more, and then he went down and gave the mourners a schnapps as befitted the occasion. In the evening he was cursing again, because some of them in the house had been mourning so hard that crates had been packed the wrong way. And next day he came into the kitchen where he and the child both drank their breakfast coffee. 'Bunglers!' he said, and, 'Can't even do that properly!' But Grandmother told him for heaven's sake to keep quiet. The child found out from the servants that the Führer had escaped an assassination attempt, but the child didn't think the Führer was very interesting, because his grandparents didn't like him very much.

Two days later – his grandparents had gone to see customers in Vienna – the child met Ivan again. He really liked Ivan very much, but the bunny game wasn't so exciting any more, and so the child didn't go to the nursery garden fence as often. Sometimes Ivan stood by the fence waving, but the child pretended not to see him. Now there he was all of a sudden in Grandmother's boudoir, because he had to take the African hemp pot plant that had been too heavy for the old manservant to the nursery garden. He was going to carry the big wooden container down the long corridor to the main staircase, but the child showed him the stairs that Grandmother always used, and Ivan was grateful, because that saved him half an hour's work. Then he carried the pot plant down to the door, came up, went down the main staircase to the kitchen to report that he'd done the job, and came up Grandmother's stairs again. The child showed him his treasures. There was a bookshelf in his grandparents' dressing-room, between their two bedroom doors. Most of the books were just full of words, always saying at the front that they were privately printed in editions of 300, in 1890 or 1910, but the child wasn't so interested in them, because he knew of no connection with the names of the authors – Mirabeau, de Sade, Sheikh Nefzawy, Kama Sutra. More interesting were two dozen large books below them which the child had been able to reach even when he was smaller. 'Art Photography – Artistic Nudes, For Artists Only' said the words on them, and they were full of pictures of people with nothing on, the men with large fig-leaves in front of their bunnies, but there were many more women contorting themselves and dusted with flour, which made them art. Grandmother had once allowed him to colour in the books with crayons, so now many of the figures had green and mauve behinds and flowers and elephants on their breasts. Ivan looked at the pictures, narrowing his eyes, and the child saw his bunny standing up, but he pretended not to notice. Ivan pulled the child's trousers down and took hold of his bunny, but his hand was very rough from gardening, and he squeezed it so that it hurt. Then Ivan picked the child up, sat down on the silk sofa, put the child in front of him and took his bunny in his mouth. It tickled so much that you felt afraid of doing a wee, and by way of thanks you played with Ivan's bunny, which he could do all by himself, until Ivan was gasping and panting more than he had in a long time. Then he went down to the pot plant and carried it to the nursery garden; the child tidied up the dressing-room; and by the time Grandmother was wondering about the mark on the sofa that evening, no one had noticed anything.

It was an exciting summer, because you had holidays and learned to ride a bike. It wasn't easy, for you couldn't sit on the saddle yet, and there was only one man's bike and one lady's bike. The child took the lady's bike, because then he could stand up on the pedals, but other boys laughed at him because they were riding gentlemen's bikes. They couldn't sit on them, but they stood up and rode zigzag. You tried too, so as not to be laughed at, but your knees were badly grazed afterwards. However, now you were cycling, going to see the farmers. They were almost always the same families, tenants of Grandfather's for seven generations, and the farmer himself would be a hunter who often brought game, since Grandfather no longer went hunting himself. The farmers lived in small villages on the 'upper plain', called after an Ice Age, as Herr Wittmann taught the child, and they had good rich ground, whereas the lower plain with the river, the child's grandparents' house and the buildings for the domestic staff and workers were described as being 'on the rock'. Several roads climbed up from here, so steeply that you had to push your bike, and there was the village on the left, with its church and graveyard and the Old Castle, a grey, Gothic structure with a tower where poor people had lived since the child's grandparents' house was built two hundred and fifty years ago, and there was a village on the right of the road too, from which the road went on between tall apple and pear trees, giving the road the name of Cider and Perry Avenue, and it led to several villages where large farmhouses stood side by side. Most of the land belonged to Grandfather, and so did the land beyond the villages, where it gradually became hilly, and trees grew right up to the hilltops. You couldn't see over them from below. Cattle and sheep grazed up there, and the hunting preserves were there too. Grandmother had told the child that Grandfather used to be a passionate hunter, in the tradition of his family, and there were any amount of horns and antlers lying about the disused rooms, but there had once been a quarrel with the neighbours who owned the hunting grounds on the other side of the chain of hills, and who were only Counts of some kind. Their foresters had lured a stag with fourteen tines to his antlers, of whom Grandfather was particularly proud, over the boundary with fodder, and the Count shot him. Thirty or forty years ago he had also killed Grandfather's best wild boar almost on the boundary, or even on Grandfather's side, and since then they had been at loggerheads and no longer met, even now that Grandfather had left hunting to the farmers years ago, because he was too old for it. These hills, where the child had seen his first deer and hares when he once went mushroom-picking, were those of a child's horizon, and there were hills on the other side of the river too, but they didn't belong to Grandfather, only the woods below, which extended almost to the nearby small town, and at the other end of the woods, upstream along the river, lay a hunting lodge that looked like a villa, but was now let. The woods stopped belonging to Grandfather here, but the village with the other paper factory that lay here was part of the estate too. This was your little world – to the north forest, level land beyond it, the town that you knew was important as a rail junction; hills forming the boundary to east and west; not open to the south either, for a very high hill rose far above the river there, with a gigantic Baroque church with windows that sometimes shone in the sunset light, and it had once been a Celtic shrine. But the hill, which was a place of pilgrimage, did leave a little of the horizon free, and you could see the peaks of the limestone Alps, although if you could see them clearly it meant there was bad weather on the way.

The child liked it best when he went to see the farming family to the east, in the little village in the hills. They had been Grandfather's tenants for seven generations, and had six children themselves, thank God all too young for the war, but much bigger than the child, and they were a help with haymaking at the beginning of the holidays. Since there weren't enough men around the whole village lent a hand. There would be partridges sitting on their eggs in the grass. If they were spotted flying up in time, then a little grass was left standing round the nest, but often they weren't seen, and then there were speckled little brown eggs in the nest. Grandmother had made the child a cap out of an old stocking to keep the hay out of his hair, and he collected a good dozen eggs in it. That evening Grandmother told one of the maids to put them under a broody hen, and the first chicks were hatching just as the Philharmonic musicians turned up for the second time. There were five chicks in all. They were wonderful, tiny, with yellow and brown stripes, much smaller than ordinary hens' chicks, and they didn't grow so fast, so they gradually disappeared. And then the hay was made. Half of it was taken to the child's grandparents, and the other half was put in the farmer's hayloft. Up in the loft the farmer's youngest children, Hans and Marie, gave the child another demonstration of what the bull and the cow do, and how human beings can do it a different way if the girl lies down with her legs spread. Hans also taught the child words for doing it, for it had no name at home – 'You put your pisser in,' said Hans, who wanted to be a priest one day, but he was only twelve now.

Then came harvest, and the farmers said it was only middling this year, and the children gleaned the ears that were left lying in the fields. In the heat the children turned red as the crayfish that came out of the little streams grey, and were often cooked in the kitchen at this time of year, but the grown-ups turned even redder and ate thick dumplings, drinking rough cider from earthenware pitchers. Then, back at the farmyard, the child saw the corn being threshed. A large pink container stood on the threshing-floor in the barn, connected by a V-belt to a very loud and smelly engine in the yard. The wheat was put in the container, and the grain came out into sacks on the left, while the straw came out on the right. They threshed for three days, but Grandfather said when threshing was still done by hand the straw had been better. Then the sacks were tipped out in the Baroque Wing, and the halls were almost waist-deep in grain that had to be turned over with shovels every three days.

Then, a week before school began, there was trouble in the air. The kitchen maid with the fat behind, whose name was Erika, had grown very fat in the summer, and now she was going about with a tearstained face. Grandmother was in a very nervous state too, losing her temper with the servants, and the child was sent to his room. 'The silly goose has been stuffed,' said Grandmother, and then the child heard several cars, and looking through the Venetian blinds he saw the doctor, the Local Party Group Leader, the camp commandant and a lot of uniformed men. They first rounded up the Russians who were working around the house, shouted at them because they didn't have their pyjamas on, and shut them in the truck they had brought. The child saw the sun shining on its tarpaulin, and two uniformed men with guns stood in the shade of the truck. The others were searching the rooms where the Russians slept, and they found the window grating that could be lifted out of its frame. They stayed in those rooms for a very long time, then they talked to Grandfather, very loud, and he answered them more quietly, and then they drove away with the Russians. The child felt that something was very wrong, and only after a long time did he knock on Grandmother's door. She was sitting in her boudoir, and on the little table in front of her lay various items that had been found in the Russians' rooms, Grandfather's gold pocket watch, silver cutlery, some old christening *talers*,[18] a bracelet . . . Grandmother shook her head and said once or twice, 'For such little things . . .' And she told the child to leave her alone. Everything was very quiet, even in the kitchen. Erika with the fat behind was missing too, and when Grandfather came out of his study in the evening he was walking in an odd way and smelled of schnapps. Not even Grandmother dared speak to him. Two days later Grandfather went to the camp commandant, and he had to go to town too, and a couple of days later eight more Russians came. But except for the hunchbacked man they were not the same Russians as before, and they couldn't sleep in the house either, but had to march off to the camp in the evening and wear their pyjamas all day. A few days later the child cautiously asked Grandmother what had happened, but he got few answers. Erika had gone to be disciplined in the penitentiary, she said. The child didn't ask any more questions about that, because he had been disciplined often enough himself, and he imagined that fat behind being beaten all red. In the kitchen the child was told, but that was much later, that Erika deserved a good beating for splitting on the other maids to the Gestapo, but they had denied it all. Then he asked about Ivan. Grandmother said, 'They've hanged him,' and when the child asked what that was she picked up a towel and put it round her neck. 'You have a rope put round your neck, it's pulled tight, and then you go like this!' And Grandmother made a horrible face that was so funny the child liked it. Soon he was begging, 'Hang yourself again, Grandmother!' But Grandmother didn't want to; she just growled, 'After that you're dead.' So the child said nothing, because he did understand that being dead meant you were gone, you weren't there any more, and for a long time he included Ivan in his evening prayers, where he took the Führer's place.

Then came school, Class Three, and the child was glad, because the holidays had been getting rather boring, and Grandmother was glad too. It was a longer way to come home from school now, because he liked going up over the hill and playing Indians. The older children had taught him how to make a pipe of peace out of the chestnuts that were just beginning to ripen and a twig of elder, and they said you had to pick a few flowers from the hemp field of the only farmer whose land lay on the way to school, and leave them on the boundary stone, so that they would be good and dry when you passed again on your way home. Then you could smoke the pipe of peace. The squaws were allowed to smoke it too, and it was very nice, but soon it got boring because you sometimes didn't have any matches with you, and you often coughed a lot. Above all, however, the older boys laughed at you, the ones who had taught you how to play Indians but didn't want to play Indians any more themselves. They were keen to get into the Hitler Youth organization as quickly as possible and go to the front.

Sometimes, while the weather was still hot, lessons were on the field behind the school, where there were no chickens running around under the fruit trees. Then you often had to recite poems learnt off by heart. The other pupils sat in front of you in a circle, and when the poem was over the teacher would intone:

> *He said his poem with great ease*
> *So let us have no laughing, please.*

And everyone chanted along with her. But if something went wrong with the poem, which happened quite often because the poems were not in the language that ordinary people spoke, the teacher said:

> *He said his poem without much ease*
> *So you may laugh if you so please.*
> *HA! HA! HA!*

And it went on until the boys who were being laughed at went red in the face, and the girls started crying. Then everyone was pleased.

Then Mother arrived, because she always came for her own mother's birthday. The child went to meet her at the station with flowers, and the old maidservant took the handcart for her luggage, because Mother had been in Berlin for six months. She looked very elegant, but seemed rather nervous. When they reached the house Grandfather was just coming in to welcome her in his study. Grandmother, who had been waiting down by the door, went along too, and Grandfather said, 'So will you soon have lost this war of yours?' Mother just said she was fine. The child's grandparents didn't want to hear about Berlin, so she had to tell the child all about it, but he wasn't interested either, and forgot it all again. Mother didn't look very happy, and when the child was sitting in the dining-room with the family the grown-ups looked as if they would like to start squabbling. Grandfather said something about a final victory in reverse, and then Mother turned defiant and spoke of Providence, and the child knew a final victory was needed because the people prayed for it in church every Sunday. You told Grandfather so too, and Grandfather got so angry that you had to eat in the kitchen for two days. When you were back having lunch with the family again for the first time Mother said everything would change very soon, we just had to hold out, everyone would be holding out now. Grandfather said in the Reich maybe, but not here, to which Mother said something that unfortunately you didn't understand, and then it was her turn to have to leave the table. After that Mother went away to see about her house, and since the child had to go to school he was allowed to stay with his grandparents. Grandmother said all this family strife was just too much for her. She lay down in her boudoir, had the curtains pulled, and was ill for two days. After a week Mother came back, very briefly, just to say goodbye, but the child wasn't very sad. At the station she asked the child whether his grandparents had said anything against her, and the child said they hadn't talked about her at all, and then Mother looked sad.

Otherwise not much happened, even at school. Sometimes a boy or a girl announced very proudly that a father or an uncle had fallen for Führer and Reich, and sometimes there was loud screaming and crying in the kitchen, and then the child knew that the same thing was happening at home. Once the Local Party Group Leader came to school and said the Führer loved young people because he was going to build a

new world with them, and after singing the Horst Wessel song
everyone moved out to the football field where the Hitler
Youth were exercising for the final victory. When the child
told them about this at home in the evening, Grandfather
asked if they had sung the German national anthem too, and
as they had not he said that he supposed the line about its
stretching from the Maas to the Memel didn't suit the facts
any more. He knew a lot more than the Local Group Leader,
because he often listened to talks in a foreign language on the
radio in his study, but when the child found him doing it
once he had to give his word of honour never to mention
it. That was only recently, when the teacher had said listening to foreign broadcasts was a crime, and children must
report their parents if they caught them at it. But Grandfather wasn't a parent, so the child kept quiet. Sometimes he
overheard fragments. Horthy[19] in Hungary was gone, and
the battle of Mohacz lost, not the big battle against the Turks
over four hundred years ago,[20] but one quite recently. 'Ah,
well,' Grandfather had said, 'Hungary's done for again, and
soon the Russians will be here.' But Grandmother told him
to keep his voice down, because if someone heard him it
was tantamount to undermining military strength, and she
hung a cardboard notice on his stairs saying, 'The enemy is
listening in.'

And then it was October, and shortly after that the fair
was held up in the village with the church, but this time it was
only a small fair, without much going on even in the cattle
market. At noon one day there were a number of shaggy
horses in the farmyard at home, and two tarpaulin-covered
carts such as the child knew only from pictures from the
east – yes, he had once had a toy cart like that, but made of
wood, with horses that had wheels and a wire under their
heads so that they nodded when you pulled them along, but
that was very long ago, probably in Mother's house. There
were two women sitting in Grandfather's study wearing

Grandmother's clothes, speaking a kind of German that was difficult to understand. Their name was Mahlmann, they were mother and daughter, and they came from the Petersdorf area of Transylvania. Since they told their story many times the child soon knew it by heart. Grandfather had had horses in Petersdorf which always fetched a good price, because they had won many prizes as carriage-horses. At the end of July or beginning of August, it was being said in Transylvania that the Russians would soon arrive, and the old farm manager and the Mahlmanns packed ten covered carts and took fifty-six horses, the best, to get away from the Russians. That wasn't so easy, because in some places they went the Russians were already there, and where they weren't there were rebels, and they had to take many detours. Somewhere on their trek through East Slovakia they were attacked. The looters soon found out that there were valuables hidden under the fodder for the horses in the carts, and they took away eight carts and their teams of horses. Then the women put on men's clothes, really dirty clothes to avoid rape, and brushed the horses the wrong way so that they would look bad and not be taken away. So they reached Kaschau, where the old manager couldn't go any further and had to go to a hospital, and then they went by way of Pressburg to the Lower Danube region, and it took them over two months from leaving Transylvania to reach the child's grandparents. The women wept and kept apologizing because they had lost so much on the way, including a few more of the horses, so that now they could hand over only thirty-two, but Grandfather said that didn't matter, far more would soon be lost. The women were given the room that had once been occupied by the Brazilian, and then they wept again because Grandmother had put eiderdowns on their beds, and they tried to kiss Grandfather's hand, but he didn't like that kind of thing.

The Mahlwomen, as mother and daughter were soon being called, stayed in the house and wept a lot, but when they weren't weeping they worked like men; Grandfather said each of them worked enough for three. The very next day they brushed the horses until they looked nice again, and got the stables into order; there were plenty of those, because the child's grandparents had once had many more horses. Now there were almost seventy again, the new ones looking a little thinner than the old ones, and Grandfather said it was a pity they hadn't arrived earlier because the horse manure was rather too late for the hot beds in the nursery garden now, and the women wept and started trying to apologize again, but Grandfather said he was only joking, and Grandmother told him off. In the boudoir the child saw what the Mahlwomen had brought with them. There was Grandmother's doll with its leather body, china head and eyes that opened and closed, but no hair, and Grandmother's wedding bouquet in a glass case, all dried up and squashed, but Grandmother said they could have left all that rubbish in Transylvania, the better things had all been stolen, and the child was not to say a single word about it, because the women's constant weeping was getting on her nerves, and none of this mattered any more.

At the end of October the old manager arrived from the hospital in Kaschau, but he died two weeks later, and then several more people arrived from Transylvania, many women and girls, some children and old men, and soon the rooms on the ground floor and under the roof that had stood empty so long were almost all inhabited again. The women tried to help in the kitchen, but there wasn't much to do because it was winter and total war, and the men were useless, as Grandfather said, but again that didn't matter, because there wasn't much to do in the farmyard either. No more Russians came after the end of September, and the freight car called every other week at the most. Grandfather cursed about the Christmas trade which was no trade at all, since the Viennese couldn't afford to buy hothouse-raised lettuce, and Grandmother said we could soon open a soup kitchen for the poor.

Christmas was rather different from usual too, although Grandmother said it was certainly the last Christmas, so it would be celebrated as a normal one. So a Christmas tree for the staff was put up in the big stairwell, but there were more of the Transylvanians than the staff sitting round it, praying for peace on earth. Then there was Christmas dinner, always served by the child's grandparents, and a present of an old ducat for each of the staff. The Mahlwomen got one too, and almost wept because that meant they counted as staff and not refugees any more. Then they really did cry when the staff congratulated them, and there was so much Christmas baking, but the child had realised by now that there was no love lost between the staff and the Transylvanians, even if they drank to his grandparents together. When a couple of toasts had been drunk, and the child had been allowed to sip from a schnapps glass too, because it was Christmas, one of the Transylvanian men told a good Christmas story, which went like this: Some time in the near future, the top brass are on their way across the river Jordan, and they must make their way to heaven through a swamp of lies. You sink a little further into the swamp for every lie you ever told. Hitler is already in the dirt up to his nose, but Göring has sunk only to his hips. So Hitler says, 'But Hermann, you've told just as many lies as me!' And Göring says, 'Psst! Don't tell anyone, but I'm standing on Goebbels's shoulders!' Then everyone around the Christmas tree laughed, although some of them laughed only in secret, and an uncle who always did the accounts and whom the child couldn't stand, even though he was married to a real aunt, said the war must indeed be nearly over if a story like that could be told. The child liked it so much too that he repeated the whole thing straight away, which amused all the grown-ups, but Grandmother said the child could remember the story, but he must keep quiet and not tell it to anyone until Whitsun, certainly not at school when he was asked what he did at Christmas. Then several people told more Christmas stories, but the child didn't like them so much, and then everyone said goodbye, because the child's grandparents wanted to have their own Christmas celebrations with him.

Grandmother's Christmas tree looked the same as ever, with the Angel Hallelujah on top too, but there weren't nearly so many presents under it. Grandmother had organized caviar and champagne, and she and Grandfather spooned up the caviar, and the child unwrapped his presents. There were no Fleischmann soldiers this time – 'Soon the war will be over,' said Grandfather, 'and then everything will be back to normal' – and his parents in Berlin had sent only practical things like clothes, which were boring, and a game called 'Emergency Air Raid' which Grandmother refused to play. The only package that did look like Fleischmann soldiers was from Grandfather, but there was a book in it: a *German–Russian Dictionary* of 1895, when Grandfather often went to St Petersburg. 'You'll soon be needing that,' said Grandfather, but what you need is not what you want for Christmas. Grandmother understood the child, though. Over the last few weeks she and one of the maids, and often the child too, had cleared out the unused rooms to make room for the Transylvanians, which was very exciting for the child, because he saw a lot of things he'd never seen before, like penholders which looked nothing special, but when you held them up close to the lampshade they showed the heads of famous people, or a box of little white porcelain plates which also looked nothing much, but if you held them up to the light they showed men and women doing things that the child already knew about, or old gala uniforms which had been attacked by moths, stacks of old photo albums full of pictures that had been coloured in the old way, an Eiffel Tower that was a cigar cutter, a little bicycle as a stand for a pocket watch, a wooden pug with an inkwell in his throat, huge hats with ostrich feathers, which unfortunately had fallen victim to the moths too, and evening dresses that fell to pieces when you picked them up. And there was a pair of trousers that had belonged to your great-grandfather on Grandmother's side of the family. Two fat maids could have fitted into them – he had been the heaviest man in Vienna, Grandmother said, and she had kept the trousers only because otherwise no one would believe her. There was also a wooden box full of toy soldiers that had belonged to your great-great-grandfather on Grandfather's side. All these things and much, much more were stuffed into two rooms because the other fourteen were needed again now, and for Christmas the child was given the box of soldiers, but he wasn't to play with them in front of Grandfather. The soldiers were made of metal and flat, and didn't look like the Wehrmacht, more like the soldiers in the big oil painting in the Guardroom Hall, and Grandmother said they were the army of Napoleon, but he had come to no good.

The child didn't play with them for long, because he had had enough of the war, as his grandparents also kept saying at every opportunity, even though they weren't supposed to. The winter was cold and the grown-ups cursed it, but the children were glad, because they could take their toboggans to the slope between the villages lower down and further up. They had to stamp about on the slope for a long time before they could toboggan down at top speed, and at the bottom you had to take care because there was a pond under the snow, hidden from view, but some of the children had already broken through the ice. So when you reached the bottom you had to turn sharp right, and then you often crashed into other children who were not taking the bend so sharply. But that didn't matter much, and didn't even always hurt, and suddenly there stood Mother. The child thought he must be seeing things, but it was indeed Mother in an elegant fur coat, waving. Then the child remembered that Grandmother had said a few days ago Mother would soon be coming, but she didn't know when because you couldn't rely on the trains any more. And in his study Grandfather had heard the English saying that Father wasn't in charge of the security of German air space any more, he'd never been good at the job anyway, and it was very unpleasant in Berlin now. Sometimes you saw aircraft even over the village that were not German planes, and were bombing the Göring works in Linz. Now Mother was here. The child didn't know whether to be glad, but he made out he was, picked up his toboggan and went home with Mother.

Mother didn't say much. Grandmother had a migraine and was lying down in her boudoir. Then Mother complained to Grandfather because there were Transylvanians in her room, and her bed had been put somewhere else, but Grandfather raised his voice and said if that didn't suit her she could leave at once. The child was sent out, the double doors were closed, and Grandfather and Mother squabbled. Then Mother came out, red-eyed, and told the child he was her son and must stand by her, although the child didn't know what she meant. At supper the grown-ups were silent, and it was very uncomfortable. At some point, when the maid had served coffee to the grown-ups, Grandfather said something, and so did Mother, whereupon the child was sent to his room and the double doors were closed again. Then the grown-ups started shouting behind them so loud that the child could even make out some words. Grandfather was shouting something about Hitler and 'Nazi rabble'. Mother shouted back, about riff-raff without a Fatherland and defeatists undermining public morale, and then Grandmother came out. She was looking very sad; she firmly sent the child off to bed, and she shut herself in her boudoir. Grandfather and Mother were still shouting at each other, and then the child really did go to bed. In the light of his bedside lamp he looked at the angels on the ceiling that he had first seen when he got the new lamp, and he tried to go to sleep, but it wasn't so easy. Then Mother came in. She looked exhausted, sat down on the edge of the bed, hugged the child and said they would soon be going home, and the child should be glad.

But the child wasn't glad, or not when Mother had gone. He had liked being with his grandparents, and it was ages since he'd been home. In spite of the Transylvanians it was nice here, and now all that would be lost, like the camel and Purzel. Then he remembered that they were still in Mother's house, but they weren't his friends any more, so they were lost twice over. The child had learnt that a German boy doesn't cry, but now he cried himself to sleep.

DIES IRAE

Although the child was a boy now, he couldn't remember his parents' apartment in Vienna any more, because he had last been there before total war began, and he was too small to remember. The rooms were very high-ceilinged, and it was dark, as Berlin had been dark, and cold, because the maid had turned the central heating on only two days ago, after Mother's telegram arrived, and the heating was still weak because of the war. And it hadn't been possible to clean the windows, because this was only February, and windows weren't cleaned until Holy Week. The maid's room was warm, but you couldn't stay there long because tea was served in the salon. The child didn't like tea very much since Berlin, and occupied himself with the slipcovers for the furniture that were stacked beside the big sofa, while the maid said how terrible it had all been. She was a fat old lady wearing a knitted cardigan, and was very proud because Mother asked about its pattern. Then Aunt Anny arrived. The child did remember a little about her, because she had often come visiting to Mother's house, and had a very fine café next to the Opera House, and she too told Mother how terrible it had all been. And Mother said when the war was over everything would be even worse, but the child mustn't tell anyone that, because the

Russians were already in Hungary. Then Aunt Anny asked them to supper in the café.

It wasn't far to go, and it was very dark. There was snow, but there were only a few big, dirty heaps lying about, and the tram that drove past had dark windows because of the black-out, but it wasn't exciting any more because they had already gone from the station to the apartment by tram and even changed trams once. Mother and Aunt Anny talked about their husbands in Berlin, Father and Uncle Baldi, and said it must surely be over there too soon. With luck they could get away in time, because Uncle Baldi was in the navy, which didn't exist any more, and Father was with the anti-aircraft artillery, which had no ammunition left. When they were having supper Aunt Anny complimented the child on his table manners, which he had learnt at his grandparents' house, and the women said how bad business had been since the opera houses, theatres and concert halls closed down. It wouldn't trouble the artists too much, because they had made their preparations and didn't have to fight in the war, or if they did they were only with the anti-aircraft auxiliaries, but turnover was practically zero because everyone was afraid to go out. The child looked at the Führer's picture hanging on the old brown panelling, and Aunt Anny said it had to hang there, that was the law. But not for long now, said a gentleman who had come to sit with them, and was addressed as Herr Kammersänger, Mr Chamber-Singer. Vienna wasn't safe any more, he said, and he had sent his dear ones to Altaussee in the Salzkammergut, but they weren't safe even there, because the region would be an Alpine fortress. And it would be even worse for the women, because at the capture of Kattowitz alone the Russians had violated two hundred thousand. Aunt Anny said surely that was an overestimate, but the boy thought it was a fascinating number, and asked what violated meant, but no one told him, it was something to be kept to grown-ups. The chamber-singer man said a lot more, for he

was, Mother said, a very famous man, and back in the apartment the child wrote it all down in his diary, which
Grandmother had given him as a goodbye present. His bed
was rather short, and was pushed right up against the radiator, but the radiator was cold.

In the morning the child saw round the city, because the
apartment was right there in the Vienna One district. There
was a large pile of bricks in the Neuer Markt, and Mother
said the fountain designed by Donner[21] was underneath it. In
the Stephanskirche, she showed the child a large wall. Behind
it, she said, was the famous pulpit with the carved figures of
the Church Fathers on it, and below them there was a
window with Master Pilgram looking out of it,[22] but there
was nothing to be seen but bricks, and many women were
lighting candles in front of a statue of the Virgin Mary and
praying in muted voices:

Protect us, Lady, with your cloak
And spread it over us poor folk.
Beneath it keep us safe, we pray,
Let us not die upon this day.

Then Mother showed him the place where she had sung in her
first oratorio, but there was nothing to be seen there either,
and in front, to the right, was a big block of bricks. Mother
said there was a particularly fine tomb of an emperor, not the
emperor with the beard whose portrait hung in the child's
grandparents' stairwell, but a much, much older one. Then
the boy had to pray to St Thaddeus, patron saint of people in
desperate situations. He was really called Judas Thaddeus,
but it was better not to say that at the moment, because after
all he *was* a Jew, and then there was almost nothing to be
bought in Köberl & Pientok, the delicatessen shop in
Kärnterstrasse, only things that had come from Grandfather's
estate. 'This is the last they'll be delivering,' said the manager,

'but madam doesn't have to pay for them.' Mother looked very odd, and paid for them all the same. Then there was lunch with Aunt Anny, and people were saying that Mother's house would soon be in the line of fire, and Vienna would be a fortress. Of course the boy knew about fortresses, and he imagined that it would look very beautiful, because towers would be built on all the houses, and battlements and parapets, but he also knew that there was a shortage of everything these days, including building materials, and there wasn't much time left. But when he said so to Aunt Anny – with her, he never had to wait to be allowed to speak up, because she had two children of her own, but they were at her house in the country – Aunt Anny laughed and said everything was going to be in a terrible mess, and Mother said she didn't know what was to be done, but as they had made their bed so they must lie on it. Then Aunt Anny brought out a bottle of green Chartreuse, which hadn't been available for a long time, opened it and said what did it matter now? She and Mother kept drinking more glasses of Chartreuse, but the boy didn't get any. Finally they drank to everything being all right again. Then they both cried, but that was all right because they were women.

Later they took the tram to the Südbahnhof rail station to travel to Mother's house. Mother was cross because so many trains had been cancelled, and the child looked at the winged lions standing all over the place at the station, because the line had once run to Venice, but the enemy was there now. When the train finally left he was allowed to sit by the window because it was so long since he had seen the landscape. It wasn't particularly interesting, but Vienna Neustadt, which the child remembered from the old days, had changed. You saw a lot of ruined buildings, and as the train went on there was nothing but rubble in the place where the big aircraft works had once stood. Then the train passed Mother's house, and she cried out, 'Oh God!', and soon it stopped. On the platform stood the old gardener whom the child still remembered, and who was called Herr Kottnig, with a handcart for their luggage, but there wasn't much of it. When they were walking over the big meadow in between the little river and the railway embankment, Herr Kottnig told them that there wasn't a window left intact in the attic storey because the field hospital train passed by almost every day at noon, and then the Lightnings came to shoot at it. Lightnings were low-flying planes, and while they waited for the hospital train they flew round and round Mother's house shooting at the windows. They would shoot at the chimney of the factory that belonged to Father too, and since an extra locomotive was always coupled on at the station, being needed to climb the pass beyond it, the English had shot a station master too. And a few days ago a hospital train had exploded because there was too much ammunition in it, and you could still see the damage. Not that they saw anything in the twilight, because they were looking at the gardener anyway, but Mother kept saying, 'Oh God!'

When they got home the child was given the room where Aunt Maika had been staying. It looked out on the little courtyard, but it was warm. They were all living in rooms looking out on the courtyard because of the Lightnings, but Mother insisted on sleeping in her own bedroom, where the blinds were still intact. The old maidservant whom the boy couldn't stand because of Aunt Maika and the murdered rabbit brought supper, but it was only salt herring and potatoes, and then he got into Aunt Maika's bed and thought about her and the monkey.

Next day Mother's house looked very strange. There were big wooden frames in front of the façade with the steps leading to the garden. They were new, and they were called splinter-guards. You could see hardly anything of the windows, only boards. They had been made by workers from the factory a few days ago, always working in the afternoon when low-flying planes didn't come over, and now you had to switch on the light in the rooms at the front of the house if you wanted to see anything. The boy felt proud that he could reach the light switch now if he stood on tiptoe, but nothing looked very nice. In his own room, the one with the camel, all the furniture had been pushed into the middle of the space and covered with big cloths, and dusty crates brought down from the attics when they were cleared out stood in front of America. He would have liked to look inside the crates, but he had to go to his new school with Mother. It was in the village, along the railway embankment and at the end of the big meadow, and lessons were only until eleven o'clock because of the Lightnings, and the boy didn't know anyone in the school except for Herr Kottnig's twin girls. He was teased by some of the other boys, who called him Big-Head, although his head was no bigger than anyone else's, but Eva Kottnig said they were just ignorant working-class boys and he mustn't take any notice.

On the way home, however, you had to go fast, and then you heard the air raid warning. Then you and Mother and the staff went into the big vaulted room called the *sala terrena*, and suddenly there was a low hissing sound. It got louder and louder, and was really two hisses, three hisses, very, very loud. Then there were a few bangs, and then the hissing died down and the banging died away, and then it was quiet. The grown-ups had been praying in low voices all the time, and they didn't stop until the factory siren howled. 'That's the all-clear,' said Mother, and then it was lunchtime. You would have liked to see the Lightnings.

In the afternoon the estate manager came and talked to Mother. The cows had all been disposed of according to instructions, except for two, and there were only two pigs left. The others had been sold before Christmas, and one had been put in preserving jars. It was down on the shelves in the cellar on the right now. Then he told Mother what price

the geese and ducks had fetched, how many hens were beginning to lay, and the boy did his homework. The subject was
'Why We Must Stand Together In This Hard Time', and when
she set it the teacher had said they were not to stand out in the
open because of the planes. Then the Kottnig girls came, and
they all explored the crates in the child's old room. One of
them was full of dresses and fashion magazines, and the girls
got quite pink in the face. The others held a lot of china with
brightly coloured pictures on it, wrapped in crepe paper. One
dish fell on the floor and broke. Mother came in and said it
didn't really matter, that was all old stuff. Then she looked
at the china more closely and got very angry, because it was
Augarten porcelain and older than just old, and the child
was afraid she would hit them, but Mother calmed down,
because it would all be over soon anyway, she said, and then
she cried. The child didn't know if that was his fault, and he
was glad when Mother went away again, but the games were
no more fun.

Before supper the works manager came up from the factory, called Mother Madam President, and told her about the
damage that had been done to the factory here and the other
factories, and how no one knew what would happen now,
and Mother said something about confidence and how the
tide would turn for the better, but she was very sad. The cook
was very nervous too, but the boy was glad of that.

After two days when nothing happened his brother arrived.
His brother was very tall, and was sixteen. His father was an
uncle and a famous conductor. Mother had been married to
him while she was still singing. Then she stopped singing
when the boy's sister came along. But the boy's brother's
father was still a conductor, now married to another singer.
The child knew that he had a big brother, but he hardly knew
him because he was sixteen and in an elite Napola[23] school.
His sister was fourteen, and he did know her. When the boy
was still a small child she had wanted to play with him like a

doll, and that was horrible. He hated her, just as he hated
Granny, Father's mother, although the two weren't related at
all, and he was glad his sister was in Bavaria, somewhere near
Starnberg, in a boarding school for which Mother and the
uncle who was her father paid. Once she had been to stay with
the boy's grandparents in the holidays, but he had avoided
her and saw her only at mealtimes, when you weren't allowed
to talk anyway, and he was glad when she left again. She
had always been very loud and excitable, and Grandmother
said, 'Having Liesel in the house saves you keeping a
watchdog.' In fact his sister's name was Elisabeth, after the
last empress. Well, the very last had been called Zita, but
she didn't count for either Mother or his grandparents,
because of being the very last, and she had lost the First
World War too.[24]

He was excited about his brother, and so was Mother. The
Napola didn't need him any more, and he had gone to Aunt
Anny in Vienna. She had telephoned the city office of the factories, and now he was coming back in the wood-gas-powered
vehicle that still went to Vienna to take paper there. The journey
to Vienna lasted three hours now, although it was less than
a hundred kilometres, but the trains were still less reliable,
because the front was coming closer and closer, and military
trains took precedence. They were under fire from the aircraft, of course, and sometimes so were other trains. The
child's brother had been shaving for three months, wore a
smart Hitler Youth uniform and had a dagger of honour by
his side because, he said, he had proved his worth at the
Napola school. He was very condescending to the boy, who
was still so small, and the most annoying thing was the way
he called him Hasi. It had always infuriated the boy, because
they called him that in his grandparents' village. His brother
could still remember it, even if the child couldn't remember
his brother, so he used the name only because he knew the
boy hated it.

Next afternoon, however, Stefan, which was his brother's name, and the boy went for a walk. Stefan wore a sweater under his uniform tunic because it was cold; he had his airgun over his shoulder, and he took the dagger because he was afraid of snakes. The boy knew there were no snakes around at this time of year, and no poisonous ones in that part of the country at all, but he didn't tell Stefan, because Stefan called him Hasi. There was a long hill behind the house with a lot of bushes growing on it, but Stefan said it wasn't a hill, it was a rampart from the time when Mother's house was still a castle and didn't belong to her yet. Then, when the front of the house was rebuilt a hundred and fifty years ago, they had thrown out everything left on the rampart and built ice-houses in it. Behind it were the farm buildings and the fields and meadows going up the real hill. Climbing the hill was much more exciting than going along the path from the house to the farm, and Stefan knew a lot of things. The Pope had once stayed the night in what was now Mother's house, on his way to see good Emperor Joseph, but Joseph had not been good to him, which was as well. The Pope had also said Mass in the chapel, but you didn't know much about the chapel because it was always shut up and you could see inside it only from Father's bedroom. And when you did look inside, it was just dark and dusty. Then they came to the big hill that the boy didn't know yet, and there was still snow in the ditches as Stefan told him that the final victory would come yet. They had only to go further to reach the estate that had belonged to Uncle Udo, but he had had appendicitis and was dead now. Higher up, you could see the snow on the mountains, and when they were going downhill again Stefan told you how King Henry the Fowler[25] had beaten the Hungarians at the last moment, and they were finally annihilated on the Lechfeld by his son Otto the Great. But that couldn't be true, because Grandfather's parents were Hungarians themselves, but Stefan said the Hungarians who stayed at home had been civilized by the Germans later and were really German, even if they had wrecked the monarchy, and the Transylvanians were Germans too, though they'd gone there only later. That was true, because there were Transylvanians staying with the boy's grandparents now, although Stefan didn't know that yet. Down below the barn doors were open and there were a lot of sparrows there. Stefan raised his airgun and shot one. The boy didn't approve of that, because he liked sparrows a lot, but Stefan said he was wet, and sparrows harmed the national health, just as Jews did, by eating the harvest. But they were much smaller than Jews.

It was nice really, having a big brother. Mother talked to Stefan a lot, and you liked that because then you were left alone and you could think about Grandmother, whom you missed very much. While you did your homework of course you listened, but you never understood a great deal, and then you wrote it down in the diary that Mother didn't know about. The situation was like an illness: the Russians were already in Hungary, and quite close, but once they met the German people who were so attached to their land they'd soon be sent packing back to the steppes, and in an illness that was called the crisis. And there was a miracle weapon too, but it hadn't been used yet, and when it was everyone would know it was miraculous. Stefan told wonderful stories, and Mother nodded while she knitted. She was doing a lot of knitting, because she said it calmed her nerves, but her nerves were on edge all the same and she was very impatient with everyone except Stefan.

But sometimes Stefan could get on your nerves too. Once, after supper, he came along with a metal thing that he called a pair of compasses, a measuring tape and a book, and said he was going to measure your skull. Since you were reading Fenimore Cooper, you thought he wanted to scalp you, and you didn't really know much about that yet, but he just took measurements, muttered, and wrote down numbers. Then he looked in his book, did a few more sums and said you were an Alpine type, and you must get it from your father, since Stefan himself was clearly Nordic. Mother heard this argument, came out of Father's study, and said after a while that Father was Nordic too, but the Führer was Alpine, and then Stefan had to put his things away and go to his room. Later Mother played Beethoven on the piano. When it was bedtime the boy looked through Stefan's door, which was ajar, and saw him kneeling beside his bed. But he wasn't saying prayers, he was playing with his bunny. It was much bigger than the boy's, and had black hair round it. Then you heard Mother coming, and went quickly and quietly back to your room. After that you heard Mother being cross with Stefan. Good.

Then you did see the Lightnings. They had kept away for a couple of days, and people had thought they wouldn't come back. It was soon after school. The Kottnig girls had already reached the trees along the avenue, but the boy was poking about in the ditch by the railway embankment with a stick, because Herr Kottnig had said there were Aesculapius snakes[26] in there, and you wanted to find one. Suddenly you heard the sirens from the cellulose factory and the village, and you could already hear the noise. You looked to see where they would come from, and then they were there, three planes flying in circles over the factory and over Mother's house, and there were a few bangs. The boy was still standing on the path, feeling excited, but they were flying his way, and he had been told in school that you must lie down quickly if that happened. So you lay down quickly in the ditch, the hissing made a terrible racket and you heard whistling, banging and splashing very, very close, but you couldn't put your hands over your ears, you spat out the water that had run into your mouth. Then the noise died down a little, but there were very loud bangs from the direction of the station. The boy lay in the ditch, not moving, keeping his head just high enough for no more water to get into his mouth, and he realized he was getting all wet and cold and was soiling his pants. After that he heard the sirens again, but he stayed lying there. Then Herr Kottnig came along, gasping for breath, hauled the boy out of the ditch and asked if he was all right. He couldn't say anything. As he walked along the avenue the boy was dripping wet and freezing, and Mother came running in a terrible state and said, 'Oh, thank God.' Even when you had been undressed Mother wasn't cross, although all your clothes were terribly dirty, and then the maid heated the bathroom stove and you had a hot bath. After that the maid was told to go and dust the chapel, and Mother played Beethoven for a long time. Later, the boy had to go to the chapel with Mother and say prayers. There was a little St Thaddeus on the altar, made of plaster and brightly painted. Mother had brought him from Vienna only recently, and the boy had to thank him. There were a great many painted saints behind the altar, but they were very dark and you couldn't see who they were. After supper Stefan said mockingly, 'You're very quiet today,' and you were annoyed. Mother played more Beethoven, and then she sat down on the boy's bed beside him, because he was shivering and couldn't get to sleep for a long time. Over the next few days he had a temperature and had to stay in bed, while the front came closer and closer.

When the boy could go back to school again the teacher wasn't cross because the pages of his exercise books were all wavy, in spite of being ironed, and the ink had run. Two of the village boys were missing. They lived near the station and had died in the raid two days ago. The boy generally spent the afternoon with Herr Kottnig, who was in the glasshouse preparing cuttings and seedlings for next spring, although he often said he didn't know if they'd live to see it. This year the winter was particularly long too, and the ground was still frozen down below, although it was soft on top. No, there were no snakes in the nursery garden, only a few blindworms hibernating under the hay for the rabbits, and there'd been none around Mother's house either since the two peacocks came. But the peacocks had gone long ago, and you couldn't even remember them. Stefan was always shooting sparrows in the farm buildings in the afternoon, so the boy didn't go with him when he took his airgun. When he came home there were six dead sparrows lying on the flight of steps outside the house, with the cat sitting beside them looking rather puzzled, because she knew she hadn't done it.

When he had gone to bed Stefan was heard shrieking. 'There's a snake in my bed, a snake!' He was in his pyjamas, and all pale. The boy looked. 'Oh, that's just a perfectly ordinary blindworm!' He opened the window, picked it up and chucked it out. It was still all stiff, and Stefan was looking very peculiar. Next day at lunchtime there was a beating from Mother, because Stefan had told tales, and you were not supposed to annoy him. She picked up Father's riding whip, and you had to take your trousers off, because last time you had put a cleaning cloth inside them so it wouldn't hurt so much. This time it did hurt, because Mother hit you six times, and you mustn't cry or she would have hit you more times too, and afterwards you had to say thank you for your lesson. 'I won't have it said that you're going to the bad just because your father isn't here.' You were cross with Stefan, but there was nothing you could do about it.

School wasn't functioning properly either, because a teacher in the upper class had gone missing when he went to Vienna Neustadt and was hit by a bomb there, although many of the pupils said he had run for it because he was a fervent pro-Nazi, and his wife and daughter had gone too, which was true, for if you went past his house there was no one there. Next day a window in the house was open, a pane was missing, and it looked very different inside and was a terrible mess. Some of the pupils climbed in and made even more mess, but the boy didn't join in, because it hadn't been his teacher. His own teacher was in a mess too, because she had two classes to teach now, and then all the boys and girls went to watch the old men exercising for the Volksturm civil defence, and they were sent home at ten-thirty. The boy went the long way round with the Kottnig girls, past the villa belonging to Dr Renner,[27] who had been chancellor a long time ago, had almost joined the party, and hadn't been seen for ages. He could be recognized by his beard, and he had last been seen standing outside the grander of the two inns, which called itself a hotel, reading the menu. Then a woman worker from the paper factory had come out and called, 'What are you doing there with the big brass, you belong in the Arbeiterheim inn with the workers!' But Dr Renner hadn't said anything, and you had to be polite to him. Now he was gone too, however, and the Kottnig girls said Herr Kottnig wasn't their father but their grandfather, because their father had fallen at Stalingrad.

At home Mother was very agitated, but she didn't say why, and Stefan was practising runes, because they were going to be the official form of handwriting after the final victory. Herr Rosenberg[28] had even developed new runes fitting the alphabet, and typewriters would be made with keyboards for them, but only after the final victory. Outside the quails were being killed. They lived next to the chickens, and there were still several there, because there hadn't been many Christmas orders, and now their time had come. Herr Kottnig caught them and the cook cut their throats. Then they were dipped briefly in boiling water and plucked. The cook grumbled, and the child was glad. He liked eating quails, although usually he was fond of live little birds, but quails were so stupid they didn't deserve any better and could be eaten without a qualm. But they weren't roasted, they were put in a cardboard box in cool storage.

Next day you didn't have to go to school, and suddenly the Steyrer-30 that you couldn't even remember came round, and you drove to Vienna with Mother. You sat beside her, because there were two cans of petrol and the box of quails in the back, and Stefan had to stay at home, and Mother drove a long way round several times because the proper road had to be repaired.

This time the Vienna apartment was light and all tidied up, because it was the beginning of March, and suddenly Father was there. He was wearing a splendid uniform, and you were so surprised you couldn't say anything for ages, although he spoke to you, because you had to recognize him first. Of course he looked like the photos of him that Mother had put up everywhere, but different too. 'Now we're a family again,' said Mother, and Father laughed, but he didn't sound amused. Mother hadn't told the boy that Father would be coming, although she had known, and now there was an awkward feeling. Father had quarrelled with Uncle Hermann in Berlin, because the anti-aircraft artillery had no ammunition because Uncle Albert hadn't supplied it. And on New Year's Day Uncle Hermann had assembled all available pilots and sent them to the Ardennes to annihilate the enemy, but he hadn't told Father, and the anti-aircraft people there did have ammunition and shot down a great many of the Luftwaffe. And finally the British had destroyed Dresden. Granny had died in that raid, but the boy was not very sad about it because he didn't like Granny anyway, and Father said it had really been a blessed release, since she had cirrhosis of the liver. Uncle Hermann had been very angry, and Uncle Josef, whose shoes were different heights, now had two personal astrologers. And Father was in Vienna with the anti-aircraft artillery, but stationed in Stammersdorf, far to the north on the other side of the Danube, where he was to make sure the bridges were blown up in good time. He told Mother a lot more, and the child saw the truck powered by wood gas[29] driving up down below. Then men brought in a lot of crates, and the boy was allowed to go and see Aunt Anny. The old maidservant went with him, but she came straight home.

Of course he immediately told Aunt Anny that Father was here, but she already knew, because Father had been to see her yesterday, and Uncle Baldi was somewhere near Kiel, which the war would soon reach too. Then the boy was given some goulash, and after that Aunt Anny played chess with him, but he lost three times. Next they played Halma, and then they went into town. There were hardly any people in Kärntnerstrasse, and no traffic at all. In Mühlhauser's, the big, grand toy shop, there were no Fleischmann soldiers at all now, but you didn't want them anyway, you just wanted to look in at the shop.

When you came home darkness was already falling. Father was wearing his camelhair jacket faced with leather, and was packing all kinds of things into a crate in his study, while paper burned on the hearth. You could smell it all over the apartment because the fireplace hadn't been used for a long time, and in the salon Mother was packing the silver, porcelain and figurines into another crate. There was paper lying everywhere, ready for wrapping things up. Larger items were wrapped in the *Völkischer Beobachter*, because Mother said it was the ideal size for the job. Aunt Anny was helping to pack, and she talked to the boy's parents a great deal. She had already packed up the things in her own Vienna apartment, she said, and sent them out to her house in the country, because she had a kind of feeling, and Father said he was sure she was right. The boy packed things in his own room, and when they had done enough packing they all went to have supper in the Opera Café. Father had his uniform on again, because Aunt Anny had said she'd like to see a golden pheasant[30] once more, and they didn't sit in the same place as usual but in a larger room with a piano in it. Then they had the quails. You ate a whole bird, but there were so many that some were still left over. There weren't many people there, and a man who was really a professor at the Academy was sitting at the piano, playing whatever Aunt Anny and the boy's parents asked for. In between, the grown-ups were saying it would all be over soon now, because the Russians were very close, and the waiter had to keep going down to the cellar and bringing up bottles covered with dust, because Aunt Anny thought such treasures were too good for the Russians. But the boy only got lemonade. It wasn't made of lemons, though, it tasted of citric acid boiled up with sugar. Later the chamber-singer man came too, and spoke briefly to the boy, and his name was Alfred Jerger,[31] because he gave the boy his autograph, and there were two ladies called Konetzny[32] who were sisters and opera singers. They were saying goodbye because the three of them were going to Altaussee next day, where it was safer, but they sat down because Aunt Anny had a table brought up, they finished off the quails, which were cold now, and then there were more bottles and a lady called Güden[33] who was an opera singer too, but there were no quails left for her, and the grown-ups drank, and sang in unison the songs that the pianist was playing. The boy knew some of them too. 'And when the mast goes down – no, no, we will not drown! A man who goes to sea cannot be shaken, Rosemarie. Never fear, never fear, though life may look drear.' Or: 'That won't sink the world, it will be wanted yet.' Mother said there'd never again be such singers performing such rubbishy songs. It was all very loud, and then there was champagne, and the old maidservant turned up, but she had come only to take the boy home.

Next morning Father had his uniform on again, he took some aspirin, and then his driver turned up to take him to Stammersdorf. The packed-up crates stood in the salon. Mother was very sad, she cried a little, and then they drove home. It took a long time, since Mother was driving through the villages because the Trieste road wasn't safe. There were uniformed men beside the road between Mödling and Gumpoldskirchen, and Mother had to show her special

permit, because you weren't allowed to drive a car now without one. At home, Stefan had shot a squirrel and was very
proud of himself. The boy was sad because he felt sorry for
the squirrel, and he wasn't even allowed to be cross with
Stefan for it. He buried it in the garden. He couldn't dig deep,
because the ground was still very hard down below, but the
squirrel was a very small one anyway. Very late in the evening
the wood-gas truck arrived with the crates from Vienna, and
they joined the others in the boy's old room.

A few days later the boy heard that Vienna had been badly
bombed. Half the Opera Café was gone, three-quarters of the
Opera House, the whole back part of Heinrichshof, the
Burgtheater, and so on and so forth, and the building with his
parents' apartment in it too. It wasn't entirely gone, because
the back rooms, he heard, were still standing, the ones looking out on Führichgasse, although the façade had collapsed,
but in front, looking out on Tegethoffstrasse and the
Albertina,[34] everything was in ruins. There had been a great
many people in the cellars who thought they were safe there,
and now they were all dead, including the old maidservant.
The boy was sorry.

The next few days were very boring because school was
closed, more than a week before the real Easter holidays, and
the weather was so bad that you couldn't really get out of the
house. Sometimes the Kottnig girls came, but they wouldn't
join in any games that weren't allowed, and Stefan was practising runes. Mother had told him not to go into the village in
his uniform. He had muttered something about defeatism,
but he had to do as she said, although he still kept the dagger
of honour stuck in his belt, even in the house. Both boys were
bored, so they made up their differences and squabbled only
over games of ludo because Stefan always wanted to win.
The grown-ups were all very nervous. Mother had been to
Vienna for two days to see Father. Now that the apartment

was gone she had stayed at Aunt Anny's in Gusshausstrasse, but Aunt Anny herself had left too, for her house in the country, and the Opera Café was closed. When Mother came back she was very sad, and said we would probably have to leave as well.

On the morning before Palm Sunday Mother took measurements everywhere, and then the works manager came, and Mother gave him the measurements. Then some grown-ups came and talked to Mother, who was standing beside a stack of the *Völkischer Beobachter*, packing. The Local Party Group Leader had poisoned himself and his family, they said, and so had the doctor. And the Russians were already in Styria, and in the Burgenland, and they had flattened the Führer's Berghof[35] with their Lancaster bombers. That hadn't been broadcast on the official radio, but they'd heard it over the forbidden radio which everyone was listening to now, because you couldn't believe what the official radio said, and the antisocial rabble was scenting the morning air, and was there a place left in the wood-gas truck, said the works manager from another factory, because he wanted to get out too. Mother said all this was rumour, she wasn't going to run for it, and then the workers came with the first crates. Then the works manager from the other factory and Mother talked for a while longer, and when he had gone Mother said he was a fool because he had once pronounced the garden as a Patri-Zier-Park and not a Patrizierpark, as if it had something to do with the word *Zier*, ornament, instead of the word for a patrician, but no one understood what she meant. There was only soup and a sandwich for lunch, and then the cook, Herr Kottnig and the mother of the Kottnig girls all came along, and the boy was told he could either help and not stand around in that stupid way, or go to his room. Stefan was already in his own room because he'd said something about feeble cowards, and had quarrelled with Mother, and he had to stay there for an hour drawing runes.

Herr Kottnig put a ladder up against the wall and took the pictures down. The boy was allowed to help dust them, because many of them were very dusty on top, and then they were put in crates which always fitted the largest, and wooden slats, sawn to size in advance, were put between the pictures, with crepe from the factory a little way upstream. Many of the pictures were the same size, and then you didn't need the slats. Once Herr Kottnig fell down, ladder and all, and ripped the yellow silk wallpaper, but Mother said that didn't matter, and you could clearly see where the pictures had been hanging, because the wall was darker there. Most of them showed ancestors of some kind, and a particularly big picture was of a canal in Venice. Mother said it wasn't a Canaletto[36] and was really a Bellotto. So they went all through the *piano nobile* except for the corner rooms, because the pictures were stuck to the walls there, the four continents now known to be five in the child's room, and in the other a beautiful landscape full of birds that came from Japan. You had never seen many of the pictures so clearly before, and there was a Waldmüller[37] in the dining-room showing dinner time in an almshouse. Then more crates were brought, and everything standing around was packed in them. A Meissen china Harlequin got broken during the packing, but Mother wasn't cross and just left it where it was. The grown-ups didn't talk much at all, but brought things along and packed them. But they left the bust of Hitler in Father's study because it was made of plaster and only looked like metal, and the photograph signed by the Führer himself stayed put too. Then you went to join the Kottnig girls picking palm catkins. They were for Palm Sunday, and were nothing to do with cats but were branches with round furry things hanging on them, and they didn't grow on palm trees but on the willows by the works canal.

On Palm Sunday you couldn't go to the procession of palms, because Mother said no one was to say the top brass were crawling to the cross now, and instead the packing went on. But the Kottnig girls went, and they said not much had happened, because people were frightened, and the working classes didn't go to church anyway. Those people lived in the labourers' houses on the other side of the works canal, and most of them were women and children who worked in the factory. When the boy was walking down their street in the afternoon, because a Lightning was said to have crashed on the other side by the river, a woman called after him, 'Hey, bet you're shitting your pants now!' But his pants were clean and he didn't feel as if she meant him. And there wasn't a Lightning for him to see either, because it was the first of April. So he went another way home, where no one could call after him, and as he wanted to get his revenge on Stefan he told him there was a nest of snakes in the nursery garden, but Stefan didn't go to look.

Later you played with the gramophone that had been found in a cupboard and was too big to be packed. Mother had said you could have it, and a couple of records too. It was a big oak box called a Polyphon, it had a handle at the side and two doors in front and a wooden cavern inside. If you closed the doors it wasn't so loud. The child had learnt to work a gramophone from Grandmother, and if you turned the speed regulator it always sounded different. There was a nice disk which went, 'How about a nice little walk in the country? After you, Herr Franz! No, after you, Marie!' You were just learning it by heart when Stefan came in and said it was by a Jew called Hersch Kohn, but it said Hermann Leopoldi[38] on the record, and Mother, who had come in because of the quarrel, said it made no difference now, and then Franz Völker[39] sang the Volga song on a specially big record. When he got to 'Have you forgotten me all that way off?' the gramophone ran out of breath, and you had to wind it up again hard.

At supper the whole house looked quite different, and you ate with the servants' cutlery, because the silver had been packed. There were still a few empty crates in the salon, but they were for the glass. The plaster Führer on the chest of drawers in Father's study and the signed Führer on the desk had disappeared; only the photo frame was left. There was a lot of burnt paper in the fireplace, and Herr Kottnig had made a bonfire behind the house and was throwing paper and a great many books on it. Mother went through all the rooms, and then she cried. Then she played Beethoven for a long time. Later a friend whose husband ran the ironmonger's in the village came and said she'd heard that the SS were going to come and blow up all houses that had a white flag hanging out of them, and the Russians would rape all the women. Then Mother sent for a bottle of sherry and told you to go to bed. She had said the bedroom doors must be left ajar, so you could see Stefan playing with his bunny. You went in and wanted to watch, but Stefan quickly put it away and was very cross. Then you said you wouldn't tell on him, and gave him the word of honour of a German man. Stefan said the boy was not a man yet, but he was very excited, and you could clearly see where his bunny was. The boy reached for it, and Stefan didn't stop him. His eyes went all narrow. But after a while he took the bunny out of the boy's hand, worked on it very quickly, twitched and gasped, and then it spat. When Stefan got his breath back he said, 'Bet you can't do that yet!' So you said yes you could, but then he looked quite different and said it was dirty and Mother mustn't know. So you told him you really had nothing against him, and you had to stick by him because he was your big brother, and then you went back to your room. Later you had to go and do a wee. On the way there was still a light on in the salon, and Mother was sitting on the sofa. She was sitting all sideways with her legs stretched out so that you could see her knee-length pink knickers, and she was snoring very loud. There was a second bottle of sherry on the little table, half full, and the other one was empty. One glass was still full, one had fallen over, and

the table was sticky with sherry. Since Mother was still snoring, the boy tried the sherry. It was sweet, but he liked the
flavour. Then he drank another glass, and refilled it and put it
back where Mother wouldn't notice anything. But she was
snoring. When the boy went to his room he noticed that his
legs felt wobbly, but that could be for all kinds of reasons, and
then he quickly went to sleep.

Next day Stefan helped with the packing, and Mother was
surprised that there were no quarrels until the afternoon.
There wasn't much to do on the top floor. There was spare
bed linen there, a cupboard full of spare nightshirts, and
Stefan wanted to play with Father's hunting rifles, but Mother
wouldn't let him, because she never wanted to set eyes on a
gun again, and she closed the cupboard and put the key in her
apron pocket. They had been in the cupboard the whole time
before, but Stefan had failed to notice them, so now he was
annoyed. Then Herr Kottnig brought in the first radishes and
fresh chives, and there were open sandwiches with 'spring
topping'. You cut up an egg on your bread, then added
radishes, then chives, piling it as high as possible, and when
you bit into it you had to be terribly careful or it would all fall
off. Stefan had piled everything very high, and at his second
bite it did all fall off, and there was laughter. When you bit
into your own Stefan tugged you by the ear, because these
were the first radishes of the year, and everything fell off, you
dropped the bread too, and the pair of you were quarrelling
as usual.

Then two men you had never seen before came and said
they must speak to Mother. You had to go out, but you heard
it all. They were wearing loden coats and armbands with red,
white and red stripes, a pattern you'd never seen before, and
they told mother they were from the Ostmark Resistance,
and the Ostmark was going to be Austrian now, and they
were taking over here. Mother said in a very loud voice she
knew all about them. One had been an informer for the

Gestapo and the other a Socialist, nothing wrong with that, but she didn't see why he had applied for Party membership. And the Gestapo informer had better look out, because she knew the names of all the people he'd denounced, and they were not Resistance men either, just arseholes – a word you weren't allowed to say yourself – and if they liked she would go straight to Dr Renner. She said a good deal more, and then the men went away again saying she'd better watch out herself.

Mother was very worked up, and Stefan said she'd behaved like a true German heroine, and that was the right kind of war-time morale, but then Mother got even more worked up and shouted at Stefan that the war had been well and truly lost long ago, he just didn't understand it yet because his brain was addled by all that Napola crap, by those stupid fanatics, those puffed-up golden pheasants (she meant the big guns who went around in smart uniforms), they'd made our bed for us and now we must lie in it. Then she slapped Stefan's face, said she was sorry, and burst into tears. You were glad you had to go to the village to fetch nails from the ironmonger's for the crates.

Stefan had just stood there all that time saying nothing. Only out in the big meadow did he say, 'Then I suppose I've lived for nothing.' Then he fell silent again. There was a lot going on in the village, because all kinds of people were on the move with all kinds of heavily laden carts, all going upstream, where there was a spa resort. But they weren't going to take the cure, they were getting away from the Russians who would come to the village anyway, either down from the pass or along the plain and then going all over the place, but they were already everywhere as it was. And people were everywhere too, from Vienna Neustadt and even from Hungary and the Burgenland, as Uncle Max in the ironmonger's told you. A linen cloth was hanging from a pole outside his house, and almost all the other houses were similarly adorned, sometimes only with pillow cases. His wife, who had been to see Mother yesterday, said, 'Better a Russian on your belly than the roof on your head,' but you didn't understand that. She had a terrible lot of children, and two of them had frozen to death on an expedition into the mountains, but that didn't matter, because Uncle Max said he only had to look at her and she fell pregnant. There was dreadful confusion on the road, horse-drawn carts, ox-drawn carts, wooden tractors with trailers, and people with handcarts which they had to pull or push for themselves, and everyone shouting crossly because the others wouldn't let them get by. You had never seen anything like it before, and Uncle Max was kept very busy because people kept coming in when something was wrong with their cars and now they needed iron spare parts. 'It's like stuffing sausages,' said Uncle Max, looking out, 'and pretty soon the Höllental will burst.' You had heard that this valley was far up in the hills by the river, but you'd never been there yourself.

Stefan and the boy stood in the road for a little longer to watch all the hustle and bustle. Whole families were sitting on the carts, on bundles, crates and cases, bellowing, while people from the village boarded up their windows, and there were no candles left. The boy thought it was all exciting, but Stefan said, 'This really is the end, then.' When they went home the boy carried the bag of nails. Stefan clenched his fists, and you could see he was thinking. Sometimes he said something, but all you could make out was 'unworthy' and 'running away from it'. At home you told Mother all about it, and she kept saying, 'Dreadful, dreadful', and then Herr Kottnig came and nailed up the crates.

The Wehrmacht arrived on Tuesday afternoon. They consisted of some men, a jeep and a truck. The jeep and an officer came first. He talked to Mother at the entrance to the yard and said they couldn't get any further today because of all the refugees, and could he and his men camp on the lawn in front of the house? Mother said no such thing, they could stay in the house, and then the officer whistled, and along came the truck and twenty-seven men got out. They all had uniforms like the Fleischmann soldiers, but they were very dirty, and were carrying their steel helmets at their belts. Stefan led the way, and they trotted over the yard and up the servants' staircase to the *piano nobile*. It didn't look nice any more, because there were crates everywhere, and only the furniture was left and the carpets that were too big for the crates. Mother asked them to carry the crates out of the salon and the dining-room to the yard entrance, and she told the cook to heat the bathwater, but the officer said he'd do that for himself if someone would just show him where the firewood was, and then Mother told Herr Kottnig to catch the chickens. There was a great to-do because of all those soldiers.

Mother told the officer she was very glad they had arrived because it was beginning to get rather unsafe here, with all that riff-raff around. Stefan stood there looking like a title photo from the *Wiener Illustrierte* printed in sepia, but there weren't any more of those because they'd been used up for packing. Later Stefan told the boy he was surprised that the Wehrmacht hadn't blown the house up, because there was a 'white flag' hanging on the corner between the front of the garden and the entrance to the yard, but it was only a sheet on a stick, and we had plenty of sheets. Then the soldiers had their bath. They had only a short bath, because then it was the next man's turn, and the corridor between the bathroom and the salon was all wet, but Mother wasn't cross. Instead, she talked to the works manager who had come to say that the wood-gas truck was gone, no one knew where. Mother was terribly annoyed by that, but the works manager said he had sent a message to another factory, 'I went to the very top,' he said, and they still had their truck, and it would come as soon as they could get through, because the trek, as all the confusion on the road was called, was still blocking everything.

After that the boy watched the cook killing chickens in the yard. She put each bird between her knees, plucked a few feathers from its neck, cut its throat with a knife, and the blood was caught in a bowl on the ground. The farm hand at his grandparents' had killed chickens differently, cutting off their heads with a chopper on the chopping block. Once, when the child was watching, he let go of one, and the headless chicken fluttered high, high up on the old agricultural implements, and then the man had to fetch a ladder to retrieve it. That was probably why the cook held the chickens between her knees, but when she took a gulp from the bowl between two birds and licked the blood off her lips with her tongue the boy thought it was disgusting and went back into the house.

The soldiers hadn't carried all the crates out, they just moved most of them up to the wall and sat on them. Some of them washed their singlets in the bathroom and hung them on lines slung from the picture-hooks in Father's study, and some heated the stove, because Mother had said there was no need to leave any firewood over. It was very hot everywhere and smelled like a laundry room, since the windows couldn't be opened properly because of the splinter-guards. It was very hot in the kitchen too, because the cook was scalding the chickens and some of the soldiers were plucking them. Then you went with Herr Kottnig to fetch a lot of bottles from the wine cellar, and there were potatoes and rice boiling on the stove and the chickens were roasting in the oven. Stefan was with the soldiers in the salon telling them about the war, but they laughed at him. The officer told Mother they were from Swabia, they'd come down from the pass and were supposed to go on to Vienna, which was sure to be encircled and would be declared a fortress, but they really didn't fancy that plan any more, and would probably try to make their own way home.

Then the chickens came along, on everyday china because

the good china was all packed up, and the soldiers opened their mess-kits and helped themselves. The cook brought in the everyday napkins, and the boy was allowed to serve them wine in their canteen mugs. There were far more chickens than soldiers, but that didn't matter, because they had tins into which they stuffed everything that was left over. The Wehrmacht men had not been directly on the pass, but a little below it, in the second line, but when the fighting really got going up there they had made off, seeing that fighting was pointless now anyway.

When the child wasn't refilling mugs with wine, he went to his room to write it all down in his diary. So he caught sight of Stefan sitting in his own room, but not doing anything, just crying. When he went in Stefan was very angry and said he wasn't to tell Mother, but you told him you'd learned the hard way, by being beaten, that a German boy doesn't cry, so Stefan was to some extent reassured and said it was bloody hard to witness the decline of the West,[40] but he would fight to the bitter end. Then he wanted to go back to the salon. You told him he'd better wash his tearstained face so as not to be laughed at, and you wrote it all down.

Now Stefan had been pouring more wine, and the noise was getting quite loud. There'd never been so many people in the house before, and Mother was walking up and down among them all in a very odd way. Sometimes she drank to the soldiers and laughed, sometimes she hurried out into the corridor and cried. One soldier laughed at Stefan's dagger of honour and said he was a butcher in civil life himself, and that thing would be no use at all, and Stefan went back to his room in a bad temper. Then it was the boy's turn to pour wine, and the officer shouted that after all these years of crap and dirt they'd never have dreamed the war would end so well, now they just had to make their way home, three cheers for their noble hostess, and everyone gave three cheers, but Mother had gone out into the corridor again. When she came

back the officer said something to her in a very quiet voice,
and smiled, but Mother was very angry, and Herr Kottnig
came and placed himself between the two of them, and then
the officer apologized. After that you were sent to bed, and
you were told to lock the door this time. When you told
Stefan the same he was sitting in his room, drawing runes.
You had to make your way around the middle of the room,
because he had laid his Hitler Youth uniform there, with the
airgun and the dagger of honour crossed over it.

Although there was so much noise, you got to sleep very
quickly after writing in your diary, but you woke up again at
four when there was more noise, because the Wehrmacht
were starting out for home. But because you weren't allowed
to leave your room before six in the morning, you lay there,
and never saw them again.

On Wednesday the trek had died down just a little, but still
the wood-gas truck didn't come, and Mother was very nervous. The works manager kept coming to tell Mother where it
would or would not be by now, and the boy stole around the
house in case he could see it coming. There were funny faces
at the front of the house over the basement windows, called
masks, and there was an iron clamp too that had fallen out of
the splinter-guard. When you hit the nose of one of those
masks with it, the mask crumbled, and now the face looked
like an ancient classical statue in a book. You did it to another
two or three classical noses, but then you stopped because you
just might get told off. From a small rise in the ground you
could see a long way over the road to the other side of the
river, and there were still a lot of carts, although the works
manager said the torrent of refugees would gradually slacken.
But Mother said that was not a good sign, because then the
Russians would soon be here. Herr Kottnig and the cook
were dragging crates from the salon to the yard entrance, so
that there could be a quick getaway when the wood-gas truck

arrived, but the soldiers had mixed them all up and now no one knew what was in which crate, although Mother had said the more valuable ones should be at the front. But the lighter crates were left in the house, because they could be quickly carried out.

Stefan was drawing runes, and said he was writing a will with them, but you couldn't make anything of it, and he had to read it aloud to you. The German nation, he said, had been completely softened up by Jewish influence and the Führer's long rule of peace, and would run away at the first real test instead of staying put like Henry the Fowler in defiance of the enemy and ill fortune. He cursed Providence for having been born so late, so that he could only see the end of the nation, but it was a well-deserved decline, and it would serve everyone right if the steppes and the Bolshevist Jews took over the German lands and ushered in times of shame, misery and degeneracy, because people hadn't fought hard enough for the Führer's great vision. He had nothing to reproach himself with, for the blood of heroic ancestors flowed strongly in his veins, and so he was bearing witness, for future generations, to the last heroic struggle and the downfall of the Germanic race. Then he put all this in one of the empty wine bottles left by the Wehrmacht, corked it up and left it on his desk for future generations. The boy said he thought a letter in a bottle really ought to go in the water, but Stefan said it would get caught up in the turbine gratings in the works canal, and the river was a very long shot because it didn't have enough water in it, and anyway that pack of riff-raff lived there now, which was why he didn't like to go there any more. Then things got boring again, and the boy asked if Stefan wouldn't like to play with his bunny, but Stefan said there was no time for that in the middle of these stirring events. But then he got very odd and restless, and the boy had to leave the room. After that Stefan went out to shoot sparrows, and the boy was unhappy about that. He hoped that he,

Mother and Stefan would flee into the wilderness, which is full of snakes.

Later the works manager came and said it was certain now, absolutely certain, that the truck would be coming tomorrow morning, but Mother had her doubts and lost heart. Then she went into the chapel and talked to St Thaddeus, and there were fewer vehicles on the road, probably because a very strong wind was blowing. Then the works manager came back and said it was all clear with the truck, he had managed to telephone even though you couldn't reply on the phone any more, but at four in the morning the wood-gas truck would be heated up, and the works manager from further upstream would get away in it with his family too. His own family, said our works manager, was in the Tyrol with his parents, which was a good thing, because the Yanks or the Tommies would go there. Then Mother played Beethoven for a very long time, weeping now and then, and in the evening supper was the cold chickens left by the Wehrmacht. You had already got all your things together, and it was ages before you could get to sleep, because you'd never been in flight before.

On Maundy Thursday everyone woke very early and waited for the truck to arrive. The boy already had his coat on, and was going back and forth between the big pendulum clock in the drawing-room and his old nursery, where you could look through a crack between the Venetian blind and the splinter-guard and see down the avenue. The Eye of God stood above the clock-face. It was linked to the pendulum, and kept looking to the right and left, but still the wood-gas truck didn't come. Stefan was in his own room; Mother, in a state of nerves, kept going all around the house. The works manager came to say that the truck had set off, but the roads were all chock full up there, so it would be a little while before it arrived. Mother kept pacing up and down, praying quietly.

Then the boy finally heard the sound of an engine, and

cheered. Mother said, 'Thank heaven!' and went to the window, and then she cried, 'Oh, for God's sake!' Then she grabbed the child's hand and shouted to Stefan, saying the Russians were coming, but when she shook at the handle of his door it was locked. Mother went on shouting, and then she ran across the yard with the child, past the icehouse and into the bushes. That was a good hiding-place, because you could look through the trees lining the avenue and see right down to the level crossing, without being seen yourself. Three tanks stood there, engines running, but they didn't look like German tanks. Part of the road beyond the river could be seen, and a great many vehicles were going along it, but this time in the opposite direction. Then people went up to the tanks, and the front tank turned its turret back and forth, and you couldn't hear anything but the tank engines.

However, suddenly they started moving over the level crossing and into the avenue. Mother said quietly, 'Oh God!' and moved slightly to the left with the child. You couldn't be seen at all here, but you couldn't see anything either except the entrance to the yard. Then a couple of shots were heard, and the sound of the tanks grew louder. One of them came round the corner and turned its turret towards the yard entrance. It was so close that you could have thrown a stone at it, but Mother was lying on the ground, peering cautiously over the roots of the bushes. The tank was a strange shade of brown, like the Führer's uniform, and it had a red star painted on the front. Mother pushed the child down on the ground so hard that the diary in his coat pocket hurt him, whispering to him to keep still. Six soldiers carrying guns came round the corner, and two more got out of the tank and went into the house. They stayed inside the house a very long time. The tank was rattling noisily, and Mother and the child kept so quiet that a blackbird came very close and almost hopped over the child's hand. Mother was trembling, praying silently, and it was beginning to get cold, because by now sleet was falling. But the Russians were still inside the house, and you could hear shooting in the distance. After a very, very long time two Russians came out of the house. There were two men with them who pointed to the farm buildings. But the tanks were making such a racket that you couldn't hear what they were saying. The men went back into the house, and the Russians got into their tank, which just stood there and went on making a lot of noise. The height of the sun suggested it was midday when it suddenly began moving again, first back and forth, then away round the corner. Its rattling could be heard for a long time, but you stayed where you were because the other Russians hadn't been seen coming out yet, and there was a lot of noise inside the house too. You and Mother had crawled a little further to the left, where there was a small dip in the ground to crouch in.

At some point, much later, Herr Kottnig came running round the corner, calling over and over again, 'Oh, madam! Oh, madam!' It was some time before Mother called back quietly, 'Yes, I'm here.' Then Herr Kottnig came along, calling softly, 'This is terrible! This is dreadful!' Mother asked if the coast was clear, and Herr Kottnig said, 'Yes, but . . .' Then Mother stood up and went down to him, walking in a rather odd way, because it was very cold now, and Herr Kottnig said a great deal to Mother, sometimes in Czech because he came from Bohemia, and Mother looked worse and worse and kept on saying, 'Oh God!', just that, and then she called to the boy. At first he couldn't stand up properly, and then she cried, 'The house is on fire!' Now he knew where the smoke was coming from. They had already seen it, but he had thought it was the boiler being lit, and then they went down to the house.

Herr Kottnig was supporting Mother, and they went along the avenue. When they reached the front of the house smoke was billowing out of two windows, and you could see flames around the splinter-guard of one of the salon windows too.

But the grown-ups weren't looking at that at all, they went on down the avenue, and Mother said you weren't to go any further, so you watched the fire around the splinter-guard growing and spreading. Then there was a crash, and smoke came out of another window too.

The grown-ups had reached the middle of the avenue, where they were examining a heap of fabric lying at the side of the drive. Suddenly Mother began to scream and wail, and she fell down. Herr Kottnig tried to help her up, but Mother screamed and fell down again. Then the Kottnig girls' mother came over the level crossing, called something too, and ran back to her cottage. Mother was still screaming, a little more quietly now, but still louder than the crackling in the house, and then Frau Kottnig came back with a bottle and gave Mother something to drink. Meanwhile the boy was watching the fire, which warmed him too. Now there was smoke coming out of all the windows on the *piano nobile*, the floor where the main rooms were, except for the windows of the two corner rooms, and the splinter-guards in front of four windows were burning too, with flames going right up to the roof. The fire was beginning to get noisy. Frau Kottnig took Mother into her cottage, and Herr Kottnig came over. He said the boy must be very brave now, because something terrible had happened. Well, anyone could see that.

Then the works manager arrived with a few old men whom the boy had seen before, at fire-fighting practice, and they were pulling the cart with the fire-hose behind them. The child would have liked to watch them putting the fire out, but they simply stood there staring at the flames, and Herr Kottnig said he and the boy had better go now. A little way off, in the middle of the path, lay a wrecked airgun, which was Stefan's, and on the left was the heap of sacks which had made Mother scream so loud. Herr Kottnig got in the way, so that you couldn't see it properly. But a leg was sticking out of one side of the heap, with a shoe on it, and the boy asked: 'Is that Stefan?' Herr Kottnig said: 'No,' but the boy was cross and wanted to go and look at the heap, and then Herr Kottnig said: 'Yes.' When the boy asked more questions Herr Kottnig said Stefan had gone to meet the Russian tanks, wearing his Hitler Youth uniform and carrying the airgun, and he was only a child, 'but you don't see that so well from a tank', and they had shot him, and then the tank ran over part of him too. No, it wasn't the Russians who had set fire to the house. 'That was our own people.' They had come along directly after the Russians, looting the place while the soldiers stopped for a break at midday, and then they had set the house alight, and the Russians did nothing to stop them but just drove away again. By now Herr Kottnig and the boy had reached the Kottnigs' cottage.

Mother was sitting beside the stove there, she jumped up and hugged the boy as if she hadn't seen him for ages, and then she shed more tears and had to sit down again. Then the works manager came in and said there wasn't much that could be done for the front of the house, but they'd make sure the yard and the rest of the building stayed intact, those parts were better built too, and then he offered Mother his sincere condolences. That made Mother weep even louder, and the boy was sent into another room with the girls. He sat on the edge of the bed saying nothing, while the grown-ups talked in the kitchen. Then Herr Kottnig went out to the avenue with a spade, and Frau Kottnig made coffee with milk.

The child didn't know what to think, so he just went on being a good boy for a long time, and suddenly the wood-gas truck arrived. It drove past the cottage, over the level crossing, into the avenue, and stopped there. The grown-ups went out of the cottage, taking the children with them. Herr Kottnig talked to the driver, pointing this way and that, and the house was still burning, but the fire was only coming out of the windows and the roof. When the children reached the truck several grown-ups were already standing there, talking to each other, the works manager, the other works manager from the factory upstream with his mother, his wife and his daughter, and you couldn't make out what was going on. They hadn't been able to start sooner, said the other works manager, because the wave of attackers was coming over the pass and they had had to wait for it to go by, and he was the one who had given the driver the order to wait, so he took responsibility, after all, it was his own factory's wood-gas truck, and he had to be responsible for his family, even if Mother was president of the company, and he was very sorry, but they must get a move on now because it would soon be dark, the Höllental road was jam-packed; they all had to get away before the second wave of attackers arrived, and he said a great deal else too.

Stefan had gone, although his gun was still lying there, and Herr Kottnig, who had simply walked away from the argument, was digging in the meadow. He said it was very hard going, because the ground was still frozen underneath, and there was a long sack lying behind him tied up with two other sacks to make a narrow package, and that was Stefan. Then Mother called Herr Kottnig, and the wood-gas truck drove up the avenue. The grown-ups were still arguing because the other works manager didn't want to take the crates standing in the yard itself, only the crates at the entrance to the yard, and Mother said he could do that only because she was a woman, and she went on crying. Meanwhile the works manager, Herr Kottnig and the fire-fighters loaded crates into the truck, which was already quite full, because the other works manager had a great many crates of his own, and then the truck turned, not an easy thing to do because the fire-fighters' equipment was in the way. Then the women got into the back of the truck, and the other works manager got into the front of it, and the truck moved off. The boy went over to Stefan with Herr Kottnig and the works manager. The truck stopped, the boy got in the back, and the sack with Stefan in it was lifted up. It was stiff as a board. The women from the other works had put mattresses on their crates and were sitting on them. Mother and the boy sat on crates to the left and right of Stefan, who was dripping out of the sack. The works manager wished them all luck, Herr Kottnig kissed Mother's hand, the boy looked back briefly at the burning house, then the tarpaulin was let down and lashed in place, it was dark, and the truck drove off.

You didn't know where you were. The truck was jolting, shaking and droning, sometimes it swayed so much that you almost fell off your crate, and you did fall once, almost on top of Stefan, and you badly needed to be excused, only for a wee, but the truck wouldn't stop. After you had told Mother a few times she said you'd better try doing it between the tailgate and the tarpaulin, and you did find a space where it worked if you stood on tiptoe, but only for a minute, because then the truck jolted again and your trousers got very wet. The truck did stop sometimes, but you couldn't get out, except once, when it was dark. A woman stumbled over Stefan and screamed for a bit, and then you went to sleep on your crate again. Then you were woken up, and Mother said you'd arrived.

The tarpaulin had been taken off the truck, and the driver and the other works manager were down on the ground, he was saying the boy and Mother must hurry because he had to go on to the Upper Danube. You got out, still feeling very stiff, then the crates and Stefan were unloaded and put on the ground, and the truck drove on. Mother said it was just after four. But the truck had started out just after four, and it wasn't so dark then. You were outside your grandparents' iron-barred gate, which looked like a row of spears, and it was closed. Mother knocked on the window of the lodge-keeper's family, and after a while the old man opened the gate, and you and Mother went into his living-room. Later you were woken up again. Then men put the crates on a handcart, and they put the sack with Stefan in it on the bier from the chapel, and you went off to your grandparents. You followed the bier with Stefan on it, Mother was crying, and you could see the men's nightshirts showing under their coats. Grandmother was standing inside the door of the house, with a cap on her head and a coat over her night-dress, and you went into her boudoir. She said the whole house was full, and while Mother talked to her she helped the boy out of his coat, and he was allowed to lie down on the little sofa. He recognized his coloured blanket again, and that was reassuring.

When you next saw Grandmother it was midday, but you had a high temperature so you could stay in bed. Sometimes you saw Mother, sometimes the doctor, once even Grandfather; you were given hot lemonade, but made from preserved lemons; you had to drink tea which tasted disgusting, like quinine and codeine, but nastiest of all were the hot compresses from tummy to throat; they were supposed to do you good, but you sweated badly under them. By the time you were able to get up again Stefan was in the graveyard, and Mother was living in the library, because there were so many people in the house, and the Russians were outside Vienna. Grandfather said they would probably stay there a while, because they'd want to celebrate Russian Easter, which is a week later than ordinary Christian Easter, but you hadn't had any Easter presents this year, and no Easter eggs either.

There were indeed a great many people in the house, because as well as the Mahlwomen several families from in and around Vienna had come. They were all friends or business acquaintances of the child's grandparents, so they were very old people, and they had brought their daughters, daughters-in-law and grandchildren with them. It was very crowded now at the long tables where only the servants used to eat, because so many chairs had been squeezed in, and a bench too. As usual, the child's grandparents sat at one end, at the corner of the table, eating soup from the same plate, while the boy and his mother sat at the other end, but in between there was considerable confusion, because some of the children were still very little, the result of their fathers' home leave from the front. When they came on leave the soldiers always left their wives with babies, to keep the womenfolk occupied until they were back. Now the children were small, and their fathers were away. When they weren't eating, the grown-ups often quarrelled because there were only a few lavatories and because water had to be carried, and now and then some of it spilled and really ought to be wiped up at once, but of course it wasn't, or because a child had fallen sick with something or other and infected another child. Grandmother said all this was really getting on her nerves, and she spent a lot of time in her boudoir and would send the boy off to his grandfather's study. After a while the boy's grandfather sent him to join Mother in the library, where she sat beside her crates knitting. There were not six crates now, only four, because during the flight the driver had failed to unload two, and those were the crates with the most valuable things in them, so she was sad about that, and about Stefan too, and then she in turn sent the boy away again. But it wasn't very nice out of doors, it was April weather, and muddy, so he hung around the house and listened to the strangers quarrelling. One of them was very nice, she was seventeen and was called Mimi. He got on well with her, and she said Vienna would soon fall, because the Russians had almost reached the Danube Canal. And a bomb had fallen in the village too, she said, probably by mistake, dropped by a squadron flying towards Linz. It had hit the tailor's house and killed the whole family except for the tailor himself, who was sitting in the village inn at the time and hadn't heard the air raid warning.

Some of the younger men came back from the war. They were tired, dirty and cheerful, and wore not uniform but what Grandmother called 'scruffy civvies'. The gardener was glad to see one of his sons among them, and so was Grandfather because now 'there was a real man in the house again at last'. He was called Herr Mandi, or rather his name was really Hermann, but that was better left unsaid these days, and he hadn't been called after Uncle Hermann anyway but got his name earlier, during the First World War, so you didn't really have to say Herr to him either, just Mandi. He was gigantic, almost a head taller than Grandfather, very broad, and one of his children was a year older than the boy, one was a year younger, and then there was another little result of home leave from early in the war. You knew them, but they lived on the other side of the nursery garden, and you really saw them only when they brought something to the house and were given sweets. You didn't know Herr Mandi at all, and now he was telling your grandparents how he and some comrades had made off from Hungary by way of Styria. He didn't wear his 'scruffy civvies' any more now except for working in the garden, and in fact they were his old uniform with the military badges taken off it. The son of the factory electrician had made off too, but he had a wound and was sick in bed at his parents' house. Then the gardener's younger son arrived too, after making off from Yugoslavia. He was a little shorter than Herr Mandi, and not married yet, but Mimi thought he was very good-looking, and the whole family were so happy that they went up to the church and lit a candle to the Virgin Mary.

The grown-ups were saying that Vienna had fallen and the Russians had already taken St Pölten, but now they wouldn't advance any further, instead they would wait for the Yanks, who were already in Bavaria and the south. There was terrible confusion in the town on the other side of the great forest, because there was a column of refugees there too trying to get away from the Russians, as well as a number of Wehrmacht units who wanted to get to the Upper Danube, which the boy's grandparents still called Upper Austria and which was soon to belong to the Yanks. The Wehrmacht was said to be going upstream along the river and making for Upper Austria too, but on the road beyond the other forest, so you didn't hear much about it. Just once some soldiers did come, the parents of one of them knew the boy's grandparents, and the soldiers wanted to buy civilian clothes. Grandfather gave them some, much too big for them, but they were happy enough, and since they couldn't pay money for them they left two large cans of petrol, but they had to take their uniforms away too. They left them on the riverbank near the drive up to the house, where they were found next afternoon. The lodge-keeper's grandchildren were playing war with them, and their father, who had made off from the Wehrmacht himself, caught them at it and gave them a good hiding.

It said on the radio that the Führer had fallen, in fact had killed himself first, and so had Uncle Josef and Aunt Magda and their children, so now the Ostmark would be called Austria again, as people had secretly been calling it all along, and Dr Renner whom you knew, Dr Renner with his beard, was the new government. And the servants told you that the doctor up in the village had killed himself and his family, and the senior teacher had hanged himself, which was a good thing. There wasn't any school anyway, and everyone was saying they didn't know what would happen now. Aunt Minna of the kindergarten was in trouble too, since she lived with her brother. He was feeble-minded and a Nazi, which is why he had gone to sit outside the house at night and couldn't be brought indoors until he was frozen. The boy happened to be sitting in Grandfather's study, reading one of Stefan's magazines with an article by Frau Ludendorff, which said that the people behind the Jewish conspiracy and the Bolsheviks were really the Tibetans. He knew about them from Sven Hedin's[41] books; they lived in the deserted Himalayas – and just then in came Herr Mandi with the Local Party Group Leader.

You knew him, although he didn't wear an armband now, but you sat quietly there in your corner, and he was almost a head shorter than Herr Mandi. He greeted Grandfather with a 'Grüss Gott', which you had never heard him say before, and said he had a wife and a daughter, and no offence meant to Grandfather, he was sorry that now he had to ask him please, for Christ's sake, to help him. Grandfather said, 'By all means,' looked in one of his desk drawers, and gave him something that looked like a little pistol and was ornamented with mother-of-pearl. Later, Herr Mandi said it was a lady's revolver, but now Grandfather told him to take the Local Party Group Leader out of the house and through the gate, because he didn't want any trouble here. After a while a shot was heard, but Grandfather wouldn't let the boy look out of the window, he was cross because he had forgotten that he was there and sent him off to Grandmother in the kitchen. She was sitting there in her little nook, a glass box with curtains; she could see everything through them, but no one could see her. However, Grandmother sent him away again too. Mother had locked herself in her room, and in the garden they told you that Herr Mandi had gone into the village to see the Local Group Leader's newly widowed wife. He came back with her in the afternoon, and she had brought a wheelbarrow to take her husband home, but yet again you weren't allowed to watch.

Later some men with red and white armbands came to see Grandfather. Listening at the door, the boy heard Grandfather say they could run their republic without him, he hadn't accepted office under the monarchy either, and he just wanted the state, any state, to leave him alone. Then one of the men said he didn't have to be afraid of the Communists, and Grandfather said even louder that he should damn well hope not, but those poor fools the Commies would be well-advised to be afraid of Stalin, and when the men went away and the boy asked Grandfather what poor fools he was talking about,

Grandfather laughed and said he meant the Communists, he could deal with them all right, having survived so much already.

Later that evening you were allowed to watch Frau Philipp and Frau Luftensteiner, the two old seamstresses. Grandmother had given them the old flags and a few worn linen sheets. They were making them into new flags, as required by the new government, and these flags were wider than the old ones because of the strip of white linen in the middle. It was taken out of sheets which had already worn thin, but could still be used for white stripes in the flags. On both sides of these stripes came the old flags, ripped apart lengthways to make them into Austrian flags instead. There were dark semi-circles on the red parts of the new flags, and next day they were hanging from the house and at the gate. As for the round pieces of cloth with the swastika printed on them which used to be in front of the dark red fabric, they went into the shoe-cleaning things.

At lunch Grandmother told the guests the country was liberated now, and if they really wanted to pay something they could, or alternatively they could take a look at freedom. Herr and Frau Wittmann were worried because the Russians were coming, and they were on the Südmark committee. That was an association dating back to the monarchy which organized German school books for the German schools in Transylvania, but Grandmother said something else had intervened, and the Südmark had turned brown as crap. Later a man with a red and white striped armband came and said he was mayor now, and had the lists of all the Party Comrades, and Grandfather said he'd simply inherited them from the Local Group Leader, or he'd have had nothing. Then he said it was all right for the Socialists to come back and the people in the factory to be an ordinary bunch of employees again, but the boy didn't know what he meant, and Grandfather wasn't going to explain, because he said he ought to be glad not to know about all that nonsense, and he would experience enough of it anyway.

Several families in the village were packing their things because they wanted to go to Upper Austria, where the Yanks would be coming, and Herr Mandi said now the Nazis would find that the weather had changed, but the weather was good, and there were snowdrops, daffodils and liverwort in flower. Later Mother slapped your face because you hadn't spoken properly. 'You stammer,' she said, but it wasn't your fault. Grandmother said later you ought to be careful how you talked, but you were. Only it was rather difficult sometimes.

People said the Socialists and Commies from the factory had celebrated the first of May, but you couldn't go and watch because Austria was liberated and everyone was waiting for the Russians. Grandmother said the house had been cleared, but you never knew, and the women practised hiding to avoid being raped by the Russians. They dressed in thick layers of clothes, and the child wanted to know how you played being raped, but Grandmother said it was no business of his, because he was still too small, and she was far too old. Under the big kitchen table with a shelf for the saucepans under it, there was a trapdoor leading to an old ice cellar. A ladder was put up in the cellar, and a small table with a few Hindenburg lights was taken down. The younger women climbed down there with a camp bed and a couple of mattresses, because of the Russians, but they hadn't arrived yet.

They didn't come until 9 May, a day before Ascension, but you couldn't see them, you had to go down to the ice cellar with Mother and the younger women, and then the men pushed the kitchen table over the trapdoor. Then you didn't hear anything for ages, and then there was a lot of loud noise for a while, and the women prayed in low voices. There was a bucket in a corner where you could wee, and the women had to wee in it often too. And there was a jug of lemonade, and rolls with sausage and cheese, but the women ate almost nothing and just jumped nervously when things got loud again up above. Then they prayed yet more quietly. The boy was bored, and lay down on the camp bed behind the women's backs.

When someone woke him up the trapdoor to the kitchen was open, and the little light was burning. Otherwise it was all dark. Grandmother said it had been very bad. The Russians had rampaged around the whole house, and there was no estimating the extent of the damage yet because no one had looked. They had left the women alone, but they'd taken several watches, and they had wreaked particular havoc in the wine cellar. Tomorrow the regular army of occupation would arrive. Then you would have to go down to the cellar again, but Herr Buchlar, who had been around for ever and had been manservant since the old manservant's death, would put a cable down there to give electric light. Mother said she had lost one child to the Russians already, and the boy was to sleep in the cellar for safety's sake. After supper his bedclothes were taken down. Herr Buchlar installed a light with a switch, put something called a commode there instead of the bucket, and then you lay down to sleep.

When the boy woke up it was dark, and he couldn't find the light. He had to wee, and was afraid he'd been forgotten, but then he found the light and saw the room and the commode. You had to sit on it or you couldn't aim straight, but there was only another bucket inside. Then he lay down again, but he left the light on, and soon the kitchen table was pulled away above him, and in came Mother, the young women and breakfast. The boy didn't say much, because you were supposed to keep quiet, and Mother had said he mustn't stammer. Up above there were sometimes loud noises again, but not as loud as yesterday, and there wasn't as much praying.

The kitchen table was pushed away again, and there was only a little light in the kitchen, but that was because of the blackout over the windows, since it was only evening outside. When they were all sitting in the kitchen, Grandmother said a few hundred Russians had taken up their quarters in the Baroque Wing, but their commanding officer was fairly civilized and even spoke some German. He had told Grandfather to lie in bed and pretend to be ill, because when the commanding officer's own commanding officer came he had better say he had something infectious, or the whole house would be requisitioned. When the boy asked what that meant Grandmother said, 'Taken away from us', but he didn't understand that either, because after all, the house was still here. Mother said she didn't trust the Russians and the boy was to stay down in safety for a few more days. Then she went off with the women, most of them unmarried, and you sat in the kitchen with Grandmother. She kept sighing and said if she'd known she would have to go through this kind of thing she'd have hanged herself first. She made the boy an egg dish, scrambled eggs, because there was a little fire burning in the stove, and Mother brought some books so that the boy wouldn't be bored. Grandmother said she was sorry for the little one, staying down there, but he wasn't hers, and the boy said he wasn't little any more. Then Herr Buchlar tidied up the space down below, and you had to go down again.

Later, the boy didn't know how long he spent down there. Mother said it was a few days, Grandmother said ten or fourteen, but it was a very long time. In the evening Mother and Grandmother always came down, because then there was blackout in the kitchen, and Herr Mandi and Herr Buchlar pushed the table back. Then you got a hot meal, but you didn't really want to eat much. Mostly you read. There were a few books that Stefan had been given by Uncle Rudi, who was a real nephew of Grandmother, a bookseller and a camp commandant, which was why Grandmother couldn't stand him. He was imprisoned later because of the camp, too, but in Germany. He stayed there afterwards, and you never met him.

But the books were interesting. One was called *Christoph the Soldier*, but that was set in the Thirty Years' War. Another was about the Banat[42] region of Central Europe, from where all those Germans had come six months ago, but in the book they were only going there because Prince Eugen had just taken it from the Turks. *Adventure in Saratov* by the Young Generation was very nice too. It was about a German family who had brought civilization to the Russians, but the Bolsheviks wanted to kill them for it, and a brave girl with a horse had to rescue them. You read several such books, but they bored you because you couldn't be as brave as the children in them, for you were sitting on the camp bed in front of a little table under the lamp. Even the cat who used to like sleeping in your bed with you wasn't there. Just Mother and Grandmother, Herr Buchlar and Herr Mandi. That wasn't enough people.

Then, a few days after his birthday, the boy was allowed out of the cellar again, and Mother told him not to stammer, but he didn't notice when it was happening because talking could be very difficult at times. Mother always rapped him on the head when she thought he was stammering, so it was best to avoid her. Outside it was still May, and when it was raining Grandmother teased him. She had told the child that rain in May made people grow taller, and you wanted to do that, so you ran through the rain out behind the house with nothing on, but you didn't grow. So now you sat indoors while it rained, and you still didn't grow.

But you mustn't spend very long out of doors, because the Russians were in the Baroque Wing, and you saw their motor vehicles on the garden borders that were left uncultivated. It was forbidden to go close to them, but of course you looked. There was a door in the farmyard through which you reached the nursery garden, but it also took you to the other side of the Baroque Wing, where there were no motor vehicles and the Russians did their washing. They wore long johns, even though the weather was warm.

The first Russian you saw up close was the commandant. He came to see Grandfather, who was in bed, and said he could get up, everything was all right. But Grandfather was genuinely ill now, because it was hot and he had nothing to do, so he was running a temperature and had constipation.

In the farmyard the younger men were exhausting the stocks of the wine cellar underneath the child's grandparents' rooms. It was very large, and hewn out of the rock, but now it smelled extremely strong because everything in it was broken. Herr Buchlar said that at first the Russians had acted almost like human beings, and just got drunk, but then one of them had found the new wall, with a barrel placed in front of it on purpose, and all the silver hidden behind it, and then they were so happy that they smashed everything, the barrels and the racks of bottles and even the reserve stocks. Now the wine had to be pumped away. It stood almost half a metre high at the front of the cellar, and almost a whole metre at the back because the cellar was deeper there, and the wine, which was no longer either red or white, came out through the pipe and down the drain. Herr Mandi said the fish would be stinking drunk today, because it all flowed into the river, and when he could go down into the cellar with his boots on he quickly called all the others, because there was still a Russian down there. The boy saw him later, lying in the yard, doubled up under a sack. The men said he must have slipped and drowned in the wine. Then the commandant came, looked at the Russian, took a chain from his neck and a few other things, and said he had been one of the stormtroops, but not a real Russian, he came from far beyond the Urals, and he'd have him taken to the huts. There were Germans from the Banat living there now, people known in the village as Bana Germans, because *bana* meant bones and they didn't have much more than that, but it was where the workers from the camp had slept before, and there were several Russians buried nearby already, soon to have a heroes' memorial put up to them. Herr Mandi had found a little more silver beside the Russian too, but he didn't tell the commandant that, he only told Grandmother, who was not pleased that you had seen the Russian.

When you told Mother about all this she said you were not to stammer, and she would give you a smack on the head every time you did. Frau Wittmann agreed that that was the best thing to do, and school was going to start again too.

There were two new teachers, a man and a woman, and the head teacher was Fräulein Unterreiner, who was very small and old as the hills. Everyone was afraid of her, because she'd already thrashed the whole village, and the Nazis had retired her. But she was very nice to the boy and said it wasn't surprising if a Nazi brat stammered, that was God's punishment. Then you found out that things hadn't really been the way they were at all, because those people had been the Reich Germans. It was nothing to do with the Austrians, which thank God we were again, and we weren't speaking German any more, we were speaking Austrian. It sounded the same, though.

There were two tailors in the village now, and they had plenty to do, because all the men wanted Styrian clothes to wear, except for the workers from the factory who were working-class Aryans. The Nazis were fetched for some kind of work by the Russians every day, though they said they hadn't been Nazis, they'd been in the Resistance. It was all the same to the Russians, and the man who fetched them was known as 'God sees everything', because that was what he always said. The village children told the boy that the Russians would drive around the villages shouting out loud, 'Adolf! Adolf!' or 'Hermann! Hermann!' If a child came running they took his parents' livestock away, and the children were soundly thrashed by their parents for having names like that. And in the house, the boy heard that Uncle Hermann had been arrested in Zell am See. He had been in hospital because the Führer had persecuted him so badly, and he had to take no end of morphine, but the Yanks were not sympathetic. Grandfather said that in the case of most people, one man was a crowd of riff-raff in himself, and Grandmother said they'd better build a roof over the village to complete its conversion to a brothel, because the women whose husbands had fallen in the war had all taken up with the Russians now, some of them for no more than a loaf of bread. But she wouldn't tell the boy just what she meant by that.

The Russians always had to be back early in the evening, and the commandant had a key to the front gate. But there must have been another gate too, one that no one knew about, because once, when you needed to pee in the night, you saw people among the beanpoles again. But no one from the house was there, and you couldn't see what was happening very well, since Mimi and her parents were sleeping in the room with you too. They hadn't gone home yet, because their house was all shot to bits, and they couldn't repair it. In the daytime you could sometimes see the Russians when you went to the Wittmanns, where you did your homework, because they were living above the Russians on the other side of the Baroque wing. The Russians often went through the village too, because they had taken a great many bicycles away from the people there. They just threw them away when they were broken, and the smith repaired them. Sometimes he could do a proper repair job, sometimes he made a new bike out of several old ones, and the villagers came to him to buy their bicycles back. Once a Russian asked the boy if he'd like a bicycle too, but you knew it wasn't his to give, and you were afraid Grandfather would tell you off.

Grandfather's nerves were all on edge anyway, because no business was being done these days. Not much had been grown in the nursery garden or in the fields anyway, since it couldn't be sold, and the Russians would only take it anyway. But people did come from Vienna to buy bacon or sausages.

An uncle who managed the estate was in charge of that. Mostly he didn't sell them anything, saying there was nothing available. And he didn't accept money, because it wasn't worth anything, or silver or rugs either, only old gold coins and sometimes stamps, which he collected. Sometimes a pig was killed, but only at night so that no one would notice, and the pigs were kept in different sheds so that no one would know where they came from. Sometimes Grandmother said that if she'd known it would all turn out like this she'd have killed herself in good time, and indeed she said so very often, having plenty of reason for it. Then Grandfather said we were lucky really, because our Russians were half-way civilized. There were other houses where they were doing much, much more damage.

Later the boy found out why. When the Nazis came Grandfather had hidden some Communists and helped them over the border. Although he couldn't stand the Communists he hated the Nazis even more. Now the Communists were back, and they had told the Russians in Moscow to be polite to the child's grandparents. But Grandfather and Grandmother were still kulaks and boyars, so the Russians invaded their house. They had something against kulaks and boyars, and they shot all the oil-painted ancestors through the head. Grandmother laughed at that and said it served the ancestors right, even if they didn't feel it any more, but she was cross too, because the wall behind them was ruined and you couldn't get silk wallpaper to match any more. Sometimes Grandmother seemed a little strange. Once she said she had been through the end of the world three times already, the end of her own world twice and now the total end of the world, but the world was still there. Perhaps she just hadn't noticed, but when you told her that she said you were a stupid boy.

ALMOST NORMAL AGAIN

Not far from the entrance to the child's grandparents' house and the factory stood a house that belonged to Grandfather, and was really an inn. It had last been run by an old lady whose husband died before the war, and when the boy was still small she closed it and moved to live with her daughter in the nearby town. Grandfather didn't want to rent it out to anyone else, because there was a war on, and the Russians preferred the Baroque Wing, where they had more space. The boy knew the house because he'd sometimes been into it with one of the domestic staff to open windows and let fresh air in. On the ground floor there were the public rooms, extra rooms, a kitchen, three lavatories and two rooms for the staff, up above there were a few more rooms, and two that were known as the Small Hall and the Large Hall, but even the Large Hall was smaller than Grandfather's study. There was furniture standing around everywhere, so dusty that you weren't allowed to touch it.

Now you were to move in there with Mother, so that she would have a way to earn her living, as Grandfather said, and a fat cook went with you. She was a little older than Mother, and her mother had been Mother's wet-nurse. While the house was being got ready the boy went on sleeping in

Grandmother's boudoir, although there was more room in his grandparents' house now, because almost all the families had gone home again. But the nursery was now occupied by Grandfather's sister from Transylvania, whom he couldn't stand and who couldn't go home, because the Romanians couldn't stand her either, and she in turn couldn't stand her daughter-in-law's family.

One day before the holidays began, her son turned up. He didn't look good, and he himself said he was in a bad way too. He'd been accepted into the SS because he was from Transylvania, and he'd ended up in Prague. They had made him walk barefoot over broken glass there, and then let him go home. That wasn't easy, because he had his blood group tattooed under his armpit,[43] and although he had torn all the marks of rank off his uniform, proud of them as he had once been, he was made to take his shirt off in every village, and then the villagers thrashed him. On his way he met a man who was trying to get to Austria too, but this man came from Theresienstadt and had his number tattooed on his left forearm. He watched Uncle Walter being beaten up a couple of times, and then he felt sorry for him and tattooed a number on his left forearm too. After that Uncle Walter had only to push his shirt-sleeve up to his elbow, and people left him alone and even gave him food. He had parted from his friend in St Pölten, because the other man's family had been gassed, and Uncle Walter was looking for his own. He had come to see Grandfather, his uncle, only in order to find out something about them, so at least he was reunited with his mother. Aunt Hermine was glad to have him back, but she herself didn't know about his wife and children, who had last been heard of with his parents-in-law. Perhaps they were in Styria, where they had distant relations. Uncle Walter stayed a few days, was given fresh clothes and underclothes, and then he went on to Styria.

Mother was very sad because she had to move to the inn,

and the boy's sister was dead. That had happened some time ago, when children were evacuated to the country and she was in the Allgäu, but Mother had only just heard about it, and now she had Elisabeth's things back. She had been just fifteen, and when the Yanks arrived she had bitten her capsule of cyanide, 'so as not to be raped by niggers', she wrote to Mother. Mother wept bitterly, which the boy didn't really understand, because Liesel had been dead for quite a while now, and she'd been very silly when she was alive. The boy didn't really like her at all, and Liesel had relished his dislike and needled him whenever she could. Now she was dead, and Mother said, 'I have no one left but you.' Which wasn't a good thing, because you always got beaten when you stammered.

Since it was the holidays, you helped get the inn ready. Your grandparents' carpenter repaired the windows, and he had some dark green pre-war oil-based paint left. But there was no good paint for the walls, and Herr Mandi had to whitewash them with lime and skim milk, cursing while he did it. The maids rubbed the floors up afterwards and dusted the furniture, and the boy polished the glasses. Suddenly the kitchen stove wasn't good enough any more, and the stove-fitter came from town to install another one. That was very interesting, because he brought some new tiles too, saying they really belonged in a bathroom. But he put back the old firebricks and iron parts of the stove, and then everything was dustier than ever. The boy found a picture of the Führer in a corner of the attic, and Mother said that would come in useful and stuck a picture of Dr Renner over it. You could get those quite cheap now, and you were supposed to have one the way you'd been supposed to have the Führer before. The red, white and red flags[44] with red semicircles on them came from Grandmother and Grandfather. They were needed because orders to put out flags came quite often now. When it was all ready the boy's grandparents came to see the house.

Grandfather said it all looked a little slovenly, but that suited the village, and Mother was sad because she had taken so much trouble.

Then a man came from town and said that many of the glasses at the inn didn't have the official calibration mark on them. Mother said that was because they dated from the Biedermeier period, her parents had given them to her and it would be a shame to spoil them. But the man said they must have the calibration mark, and it was all the same in the eyes of the law if she didn't have the money to buy cheap glasses. Then the glazier came, bringing a machine with him. It looked like a sewing machine, but with a ring wheel on top. The boy had to pour water over it, and Mother poured water into the glasses up to the point for the calibration mark. The marks on the glasses did look very ugly, but it was the law, and then the boy had to polish the glasses again, because they were crystal.

Mother said business was going reasonably well. Seven people from the factory came to eat lunch, because they lived too far away to go home. They weren't really workers, but clerks, so they were socially above workers but paid less for lunch because they had a subscription. When the shifts changed at the factory one worker came with a wooden carrier to fetch what the others had ordered. There wasn't much, mainly just sour cider or perry made from apples and pears by a farmer up in one of the villages and brought down. If you added raspberry water to it, it was called Almdudler, and the boy was allowed to taste it. He secretly tasted the cider too, when no one was looking, and when he was once asked why the level had gone down he took to adding water when he had drunk some. And Mother made a drink called Sparkling Ambrosia out of citric acid and sugar. If you added plenty of water it tasted very nice on hot days, and people liked it because they couldn't get sugar. But Mother had sugar. She bought it from her parents, who had laid in two thousand kilos a week before the war began. Sometimes the boy saw her take a big piece out of the sugar sack and stuff it in her mouth. She glanced to right and left first in case anyone was looking, but the boy didn't like sugar himself.

If she had nothing else to do, Mother sat with her round knitting needles and the Wehrmacht yarn that the boy had had to tease out for her until it was very thin, and she knitted lace tablecloths. They had holes of different sizes, and Mother said it was a much quicker method than bobbin-work. When a tablecloth was finished, it was pinned out flat on the wooden lid of the copper in the laundry room and starched. Then it was rolled up in paper. She made one almost every week.

Three workmen came every afternoon. Mother said two of them were members of the works committee, but they had to work too, and one was a Communist. They drank cider and now and then schnapps, played cards, and watched to see when Mother would begin her knitting. Then one would say, 'Madam Managing Director, I'd like an A!' Cigarettes were available again, but they were on the ration, except for cigarettes sold separately, and there was only one sort of those, called A. When Mother had knitted another few stitches, the next man said, 'Madam Managing Director, I'd like an A too!' And when Mother had knitted a few more stitches it was the third man's turn. They did this two or three times every afternoon, and Mother said they probably thought it was an amusing game.

Once Frau Wittmann came too, and Mother said she didn't think smacking the boy around the head was going to help him stop stammering. Frau Wittmann said Mother must just be stricter, and the boy felt very uncomfortable. Mother said it would hurt her too, but it was for the boy's own good, and if he was caught stammering now he would be smacked on the bare behind. When she did that Mother took the ox whip, which was long and thick and made from the dried pizzle of an ox. It hurt a lot. Once the boy found the ox whip and tried putting it in the stove. But it wouldn't fit in properly, and was found. There was an extra beating for that, and then you had to go into the room next to Mother's that she called 'the quiet room', and you mustn't cry, or there would be more smacking because it was good for you, and afterwards you had to say thank you.

The boy didn't like any of this, and tried to say as little as possible, but he was sometimes caught stammering all the same. Once he was so scared on the way to the 'quiet room' that he soiled his pants. Mother noticed, of course, because you had to take your trousers down to be smacked, and when the afternoon shift changed in the factory and the workers were going in and coming out, the boy had to stand outside the house holding his dirty trousers. Some of them just passed him, some looked quickly and then looked away, and some laughed and teased him.

When Frau Wittmann came back Mother said she was having a terrible time with the boy, he was soiling his pants, and he'd been clean at the age of one. Frau Wittmann said she couldn't help there, but perhaps Mother wasn't being strict enough, and there were always problems with boys who didn't have a father around. And when it came to boxing a child's ears it was a pity to miss your aim. So Mother was stricter than ever, but that did no good either, and soon the boy had to stand outside the house in his soiled trousers again. Next day Grandfather came, and talked to Mother in a very loud voice. The boy might be her son, he said, but she was his daughter, and she would discredit the whole family with her Nazi methods. It was unacceptable to have people gossiping about a member of the family, and if he heard any more about it she would have to leave this house. Mother said she didn't know where she could go, and Grandfather said that was all the same to him. Then he went home to his own house and slammed the door very hard. He hadn't said a word to the boy, who could see, all the same, that Grandfather was cross with him. They were allowed to stay on at the inn all the same, but the boy didn't have to stand outside it any more.

When school began again the grown-ups got a new thing called an Identity. It was a pale, printed card, you folded it down the middle between the Russian side and the side in the teaching language, it had the same number on it twice, and the parish stamp twice. It had to go in a pass with a photograph, so that the occupying forces would know who you were. And in school you didn't learn in German any more, you learned in the teaching language.[45] But it was just the same, and you heard that different words for crap were used by people who wanted to sound German and people who were Austrian.

Everything that had once been German belonged to the Russians now, but not Father's factories. Because a man had come who had sat at Father's desk when Father went to the war, so that Mother would sign a document saying that he owned the majority of the shares, and the Russians had believed him.

Mother went back to her old house with her new Identity, and the boy stayed at the inn with the cook. Bottled beer had recently become available again, and a worker fetched it for the midday and evening shift. It was never more than a few bottles, because there wasn't much to do at the factory either, and a couple of workers could keep it going. The boy hated one of them, who always mentioned those dirty trousers, but he had to be nice to him too, in case the cook told on him to Mother.

The second day that Mother was away, the boy had to get married after school. Elke was new, fair-haired and fat, and the biggest girl in the school. She spoke a very funny kind of teaching language, because her parents were Sudeten Germans. She could wrestle any bigger boy to the ground too, but then she was over twelve, because she'd had to stay down a class three times. Their homework was a composition on 'Why I am Glad to be an Austrian', and Elke asked the boy if he could help her, because he was German himself too. They walked back from school by the upper path, because Elke lived in the upper village, so they passed the little jungly wood above the old football field, which was beside the deserted house whose owner had died in Russia and was now empty, without any windows left. The jungle contained only a few trees, but there were a lot of bushes and a great many things that people didn't need any more: broken bedsteads, a burnt-out truck and two tractors, but they had all long ago been plundered for spare parts and were rusty. You weren't really supposed to play there, but that made it more interesting, and most of all the boy wanted to see Elke's crack, because he had heard that it was much bigger in older girls.

Elke said she wouldn't show the boy her crack unless he married her, which made it right and proper, and if he didn't marry her then she would thump him. She also told him how weddings are held, and then he had to look for some flowers. There was still a little withered sorrel growing nearby, and they walked round a tree three times with that. Then Elke said the words the priest usually says in church, and when she had finished she added, 'Amen, and now take your clothes off.' She took her own knickers off too, and you were just looking at her crack when suddenly there was a noise among the bushes and a strange man came out and stood in front of them. You were very scared, because you were afraid he might tell on you to Mother, and you didn't know him, and he was laughing. All the same, you didn't like him, because he had only two teeth and was very dirty. However, you couldn't run away because your trousers were still down. Then the man said something, unbuttoned his own trousers and took out his bunny. It was very large and had a very pungent smell, and Elke looked at it with interest too. 'This is good for little girls,' he said, and then Elke had to lie face down over the wrecked tractor with her legs dangling. The man bent over Elke and put his bunny between her legs, and the boy pulled his trousers up again. Then the man straightened up, spat on Elke's bottom and his own hands, rubbed his bunny with them, and said he didn't want to hurt Elke. But then he pushed his bunny into Elke's bottom, and Elke cried, and screeched 'Ow!' and said she was going to die. The boy got into safety, but he didn't go too far off, because it was interesting, and the man had a number like Uncle Walter's on his arm. Then Elke whimpered, 'Faster! Faster!' and the man grunted and then calmed down. After a while he moved back from Elke, wiped his bunny on some leaves and went away. Elke was still lying there with pale slime gleaming on her bottom. The boy asked if the man had hurt her very much, but Elke said no, he hadn't screwed her bottom, he'd screwed her cunt, and she knew all about that and the boy wasn't to give her away. Then she went home, and so did the boy.

Next day she was going to keep the boy company again, but he didn't want to walk with her any more when he saw the man in the jungly wood. Elke went on, though, and she and the man talked to each other.

That afternoon Mother arrived with Herr Kottnig and several suitcases. Herr Kottnig said he didn't want to let her drive back on her own, and she had cried a lot on the way without even noticing it. And the old cook had hanged herself, he said, because she had been put in prison as a Gestapo informer, but the boy didn't mind that. Then they went to see Grandmother, and Mother told her story. She had been to the workers' houses with Herr Kottnig and a policeman. She saw things of her own hanging outside one of the houses, and recognized them by the monogram. Then they went into the houses and took out anything that Mother could prove had belonged to her, and at some point a car came along with Russians in it, and they arrested Mother because she was

accused of being a German spy. Herr Kottnig and the policeman went with her, but it all took a very long time, and
Mother had to spend the night at the commandant's HQ, but
not in a cell, in the commandant's room. Mother put on all
the layers of clothing she had with her, but she got to sleep in
the end, and in the morning she saw the commandant asleep
on a sofa on the other side of the room, and he had put chairs
covered with blankets between them. Then she and Herr
Kottnig and the policeman went back to the workers' houses,
but she didn't find much more. Herr Kottnig still had
Mother's really big suitcase with him, containing things he
had found in her house, and you took everything on to
Grandfather and Grandmother's house, where it was all
unpacked. She had found some of the silver too, but all mixed
up, so that only nine place settings could be assembled, but
she had two cases full of table linen back. Grandmother asked
if it had been worth the trouble. She herself had almost no
silver left, she said, only what had been hidden in the smaller
niche in the cellar, but she could live with that.

Next day Herr Kottnig went home. Then Elke was absent
from school, and the day after that Fräulein Unterreiner came
into the classroom with the local policeman and a detective
superintendent. Something very bad had happened to Elke,
she said, and all the children were to say anything they knew
about her. But the boy didn't say anything, because he didn't
want to stammer, and he had promised Elke not to give her
away. That afternoon the boy heard at the inn that the former
concentration camp inmate who had been living in the empty
house had disappeared, and the day after that it was all in big
print in the newspaper, on the front page, but the concentration camp inmate wasn't found, and the boy was afraid of
being killed by him because he knew something, and he didn't
go near the jungly bit of wood any more.

The whole school had to go to Elke's funeral, walking in a
line three abreast. It was very solemn, and the priest said,

'She died in protecting her innocence,' but the boy was afraid of the concentration camp inmate for a long time after that.

Early in October a young man came looking for Mother. He was a farmer's son from the Ennstaler Alps, and he brought her a letter from Father, who was in hiding there, because it was in the American zone of occupation. Mother packed some things in a rucksack for Father, and went with the farmer's son. After a few days she came back and said Father was all right, but he had to stay in hiding, because the British were looking for him. Then the newspaper reported that Elke's murderer had been found. He was the son of a haulage contractor from the nearby town, and had killed three other girls too, and he was only nineteen but he had been in Russia, where he had learned to do such things. All the same, he was going to the gallows, because it was the death penalty for murder. The concentration camp inmate was found too, hanging from a tree in the Buchenbauer-Höhe region, where no one was allowed to go because of foot and mouth disease. A letter from him was found in the empty house too, but it was a long time before anyone could read it, because he wasn't just a concentration camp inmate but a gypsy too, and it wasn't read till it reached police headquarters, but then it was all in the newspaper. He had been the first to find Elke's body, and he was afraid he would be blamed. And so he had been, but now he was innocent again, so he had hanged himself for nothing. He was buried outside the graveyard wall, because he was a suicide, and the boy was glad he didn't have to be afraid of him any more.

In your free time you had to make lavatory paper because there was none of the real sort available. You used old newspapers and cut them up, but not the Austrian National Party's newspaper because it used a funny sort of printer's ink which would have given you a black behind. The *Volksstimme* was the best, because Mother said that was what people liked to feel on their behinds, and you always took four sheets at a time and rubbed them soft so that they would wipe better. You did that with every sheet yourself before wiping your bottom, but now you had to prepare the paper and soften it for other people, because Mother said that kind of thing showed the quality of a really good restaurant.

The inn was used as a polling station, because people were supposed to go and vote for the Communists. They had set up a soup kitchen in the factory, with potatoes, root vegetables and canned horsemeat, and people were supposed to be grateful for it. The Nazis couldn't vote, because they weren't democrats, but the other workers weren't grateful either and voted Socialist. The villages higher up had turned black,[46] and the Communists were drinking as if they had won the election. Grandfather and Grandmother had to come and vote too, and Grandfather came back in the evening to hear the election results, and he told one Communist that the whole bunch of brown Nazis had divided neatly into black and red.

Mother went to see Father again, wearing his winter shoes, because he didn't have any, and the snow had fallen very early. She came home in thin fabric shoes and was so ill that she had to spend a day in bed. Then it said in the newspaper that the Americans had arrested Father because the British wanted him. Mother was very sad and knitted even more lace tablecloths, and the boy had to tease out a great deal of Wehrmacht yarn for them. But his grandparents said Father was only getting what he deserved, and then the boy wasn't allowed to go and see them any more.

Just before Christmas Aunt Anny came from Vienna. She had re-opened the half of the Opera Café that was still standing, though the other half was in ruins, and she had got hold of some bituminous roofing felt to keep the rain out of the rest of the place. Uncle Baldi was still in prison too, although not because of the war, he was in prison because of the Nazi putsch against Dollfuss, which was so long ago that this was the first time the boy had ever heard of it, and Dollfuss had been shot at the time, but not by Uncle Baldi. Aunt Anny took Mother's tablecloths back with her, saying she would sell them to the Yanks in the Opera Café, Americans were very keen on anything to do with the Nazis.

On Christmas Eve you were allowed to go and see Grandfather and Grandmother again with Mother. This time the Christmas tree was in the salon next to Grandmother's boudoir, and the Russian commandant had come too, with his family. He had two daughters. Nina, the elder, was a blonde beanpole of a girl, and Nuschka had wild hair and was the same age as the boy. Neither of them had ever seen a Christmas tree before, and their mother said that the family had almost starved to death during the siege of Leningrad. She didn't speak such good German as her husband, and when she was stuck Grandfather helped her out with the Russian he had learned in St Petersburg. The girls spoke no German at all, although you would have liked to talk to Nuschka, but they liked the Christmas tree a lot, and they gave the boy a wooden doll with several other dolls in it. It was Russian, said the commandant, and you would always find a surprise inside. Your grandparents gave you a toy truck made of real tin with a little crane on top of it, but you only had time for a quick look because the Russian girls were playing with it. Then they began quarrelling with each other, and Nuschka hit Nina on the head with the truck so that the crane broke off and the truck was spoilt. The commandant's wife slapped them both, and the commandant said he was sorry, and then he invited everyone to celebrate Russian Christmas with them, on the afternoon of Epiphany Day.

On Epiphany Day the boy entered the Baroque Wing again for the first time in ages, but it looked quite different now. The Russians ate in the dining-room where there was a big iron stove by way of a kitchen, with its pipe sticking out of a window, and the walls close to it were covered with soot.

The Guardroom Hall was full of camp beds, and one of the big battle paintings showing soldiers of different nationalities fighting had been all cut up. But Grandfather laughed and said at least they'd left the Russian soldiers intact, and they couldn't be conquered any more now that their enemies had been eliminated, in this case by the use of a knife. In the gallery, that's to say in the Great Hall, there were more camp beds and Grandfather's upholstered armchairs, but they were very dirty and dilapidated now. There were Russians sitting on some of them, but most of the Russians were doing war exercises in the park. Then you went into your great-grandparents' apartment, which you hardly knew at all, but it was clean because this was where the commandant lived. Some toys that you still remembered were lying about in the salon, and the Christmas tree was there too. It was a lovely tree, with a great deal of surgical cotton wool on its branches to imitate snow. Then the first candles were lit, and the cotton wool began to burn, and so did the tree. The commandant's wife flung a window open, and the commandant picked up the tree and threw it out of the window. The whole room was full of smoke, and Grandmother quietly told the boy that this was the Russian way of celebrating Christmas. The commandant told Grandfather that he was sorry, this wasn't the way he'd envisaged things, and you went to the window and looked at the tree burning down below. But it didn't burn for much longer.

There was a lot to do at the inn now, because a ball was held there almost every week. Mother said people needed to catch up on some fun again, and the orchestra rehearsed on weekday evenings in the spare public room. There was a small piano in there, on which Mother sometimes played Beethoven, and now the piano stool was occupied by Fräulein Hebauer, who was not in her first youth but had a huge bosom and also, apparently, the affections of all the Russians. One of the tailors played the violin, Herr Mandi played the trumpet, his father played the clarinet, and there were a few other people with instruments, but the most interesting was Herr Engelsbrunner on percussion, because that was good and loud. The orchestra had to learn a great many new pieces, because a lot of what they knew already was banned now. The day before the ball, the hall was heated with stoves that burned wood-shavings. They came from the factory saw-works, which were in a hut, and the boy was allowed to prepare the stoves; large, black tin cans open at the top and with a hole down below. You put a stick into the hole, shov-elled in the wood shavings, and had to keep pushing them down so that they would get firm. Then you could pull the cans to the house by their sticks, but you couldn't carry them in yet. Just before the ball, several village women came up to be waitresses. Herr Buchlar came too, although he was really a groom, to help at the bar, but Mother said he always got drunk too early, and when the time for the ball came the boy had to go to his room at nine-thirty and lock the door, because this was no place for him.

They all wanted to have balls; the huntsmen, the firemen, the workers, the savings clubs, and they all came to Mother because her hall was the largest in the village. Sometimes the boy had to go to one of the villages higher up to get schnapps from a farmer, but he wasn't to let himself be caught at it, because there was foot and mouth disease up there. The farmer sometimes came bringing the schnapps himself, but he wasn't really supposed to do that either. And sometimes large preserving jars came from town, full of the little fish that had always been called Russians, but now they had to be called just small herrings.

The Russians came too, and if both they and the villagers got drunk there was always trouble. At the huntsmen's ball, after preparations to decorate the hall really nicely had been going on for days, an NCO started firing his revolver all round the place, leaving holes in the walls and unfortunately in the windows too, and then the commandant had to come. He shouted at the NCO, took the revolver away, and tore pieces of cloth off his shoulders in front of everyone, but they had been sewn on again next day.

Of course the Russians weren't supposed to bring weapons to the balls with them, but most of them ignored that rule, and as soon as it got late you heard the trouble starting. Once a Russian was very drunk quite early in the evening. He went into the kitchen, wanting something from Mother, but she picked up a very long kitchen knife and walked towards him, saying, 'You bastard, don't you dare.' The Russian thought about it for a while and then left the kitchen again, but Mother sat down and cried. Later the commandant came, threw the Russians out – this was at the firemen's ball – and wanted the orchestra to play a march to reward him. As the Badenweiler March[47] was the only one they knew, they played that, but the commandant didn't recognize it, because the ensemble for the evening was a salon orchestra who played it as a slow foxtrot.

In the village higher up, the cinema was showing movies again too. There had been a cinema since Herr Fallbauer gave up farming, decided to sell drinks and converted his barn to a picture-house. But he was a Nazi too, so the Russians had closed his cinema. However, people wanted to see films, even the Communists did, so it was re-opened, and the long tables in front of the screen were covered with fresh paper. There were always film shows on Saturdays and Tuesdays, and a Saturday matinee too, to which the boy was allowed to go. Frau Strohinger, the postal official's widow, was in charge. She sat in the booking office before the show, and then behind the projector in a little box at the back of the hall. The projector had its little ways, as she said, and wouldn't wind back automatically any more, so she had to wind each roll of film back by hand, and in the intervals the Fallbauer family served drinks. Graser the master tailor also sprayed the cinema with Flit from a chrome spray, to improve the quality of the air, because everyone was smoking hard just to show they could afford it, although most of them smoked home-grown tobacco raised by the women in their vegetable gardens, and the Flit also helped to kill insect pests.

The sound playback on the projector had gone wrong too, so Graser the master tailor had to tell the stories of the movies. He had notes from the film hire company with everything on it. But the films were always very much longer than the notes, and they didn't usually say what happened at the end, so then Herr Graser would look at the screen and just go on telling the story, and people often laughed at him. Fräulein Unterreiner was always at the piano, and no one laughed at her, because she had smacked almost everyone in the village and they were all afraid of her.

The screenings the boy was allowed to watch were always the first ones, and the new film would only just have arrived that morning from town in its tin cans. Sometimes Frau Strohinger got the rolls mixed up, and Herr Graser told her it didn't matter. He was right really, but the audience complained if THE END came up on screen when a film had only just begun. When Fräulein Unterreiner was at the piano her back was bent like the shell of a tortoise, because she had trouble with back pain, and in between searching for the right keys she looked at the screen to see the picture and get the music right. She always stuck to the same system with her pieces, as the boy found out only when he went to the cinema once with Grandmother. It was a Russian film, and the military men were preparing for a battle, and Grandmother said, 'Oh, my God, here comes "The Maiden's Prayer" any moment now.' Sure enough, when the cannon puffed out smoke, there it came. In the interval, Grandmother told the boy about Fräulein Unterreiner's repertoire, which had been around since before there were any talkies: in silent films she played 'The Mill in the Black Forest' if the movie was about forests and nature, for mountains she played the 'Archduke Johann Yodel', for plains and deserts it was the 'Hungarian Rhapsody', for water 'La Paloma', for love scenes 'Träumerei', and she could also provide the 'Dance of the Japanese Lanterns', the 'Radetzky March' and the 'Blue Danube'. 'And when people are killing each other she plays the "Maiden's Prayer".'

So she did, although if there was a lot of action in the film she often just played a few bars of each piece. But you could recognize it, because it was always the beginning she played. And Graser the master tailor said what the people in the film were saying. If two of them were looking at each other, it was usually, 'Darling, do you love me?' and if they were looking angrily at each other it was, 'Darling, don't you love me any more?' and then Fräulein Unterreiner would sometimes say, in a very loud voice, 'Idiot!' and the audience laughed, because that was what the Tsar of Russia had said to Napoleon. But they also laughed when the boy said something, so that wasn't bad.

The boy liked going to the cinema. He could go every other week if he was good, and the films were lovely. There was *The Jungle Book* with the famous Indian actor Sabu – he even got to hear the whole of 'The Mill in the Black Forest' several times in that one, and the beautiful 'Blue Danube' when the monkeys were on – and *Blood over Nagasaki* with a lot of lantern dancing and the 'Maiden's Prayer'. But that wasn't because of the Yanks' atom bomb, which everyone was supposed to deplore now, it was a story about missionaries nailed to the cross, and before the film the priest said it really had been like that once, and then he had an argument with a Commie who said it was clerical propaganda. *Hamlet* with Laurence Olivier was good too, because there was an argument between Fräulein Unterreiner and Herr Graser, who couldn't read what she had written down specially for him, about to be or not to be, and everyone laughed. But best of all the boy liked *The Thief of Baghdad*. When he was watching it he didn't even hear Fräulein Unterreiner. It was as if Sabu was hovering over the whole world in the hair of the genie from the bottle. First there was a bit of the 'Mill in the Black Forest', then a bar of the 'Lantern Dance', a very quiet passage from the 'Hungarian Rhapsody', and then she stopped playing. The audience was worried in case Fräulein Unterreiner wasn't well, because she'd already been given several liqueurs, but then came the 'Roof of the World' and the 'Archduke Johann Yodel', and they were all laughing again.

Sometimes the boy met Nuschka, and learned to say *da* and *nyet*, but mostly they could only look at each other because they had nothing to say. Then, just before Easter, the commandant and his family came to say goodbye. He and most of his men had been ordered home, because Austria was liberated now, and his wife Nina and Nuschka cried a lot because, as the commandant said, they would never have it so good again. He gave Mother several bottles of army vodka, and next day he and many of the Russians left.

But the others stayed on in the Baroque Wing of the boy's grandparents' house, and unfortunately their new commandant spoke hardly any German, so Grandmother often got cross. There were fewer of them, but they did more damage. Stalin had said the Austrians were now liberated from Hitler, so the Russians must provide for themselves. Now that they couldn't take any more cattle from the farmers they had to go hunting in the woods with their machine guns, which annoyed Grandfather very much even though he didn't hunt any more himself. And they had to cultivate their own fields. They did that in the boy's grandparents' park behind the Baroque Wing. There was a huge grassy meadow which had once been the bowling green, and they ploughed it up. The Russians borrowed Grandfather's implements to do it, and they were all wrecked afterwards, because the turf was a hundred and fifty years old and had always been kept rolled flat. And where there was no turf they had to blow up the roots of the trees they had felled in winter for heating, and then they planted all sorts of things. But Grandfather said nothing would come of it, because the soil was so poor, that was why it had been made into a park, and neither Stalin nor the fertilizers they were taking from him and the farmers could do anything to remedy that.

After Easter men from the factory came to the inn to put the skittle alley in order. It was behind the building and was rather decrepit, because there had been no men around to play skittles during the war. The skittles and the bowls were in the attic, but the alley was outside, and the tiled roof leaked. That was the first thing to be repaired, with bituminous roofing felt, and then the decorative carving was removed to make it all look modern. There was no paint either, so the remains of the old paint were burned away with blowlamps; all the wood was oiled to keep pests away, and when the sun shone on it it stank, all summer. Finally the floor of the long hut was stamped flat, and boards were placed down the middle. You weren't allowed to tread on them. The far end of the hut, as seen from the house, was wider to take the skittles, and had a wooden floor with marks painted on it showing where to place them. On the left was a small bench from which you could see only the skittles, and you had to sit on it when the bowls came down the alley to avoid being hit by them. Then you had to put the bowls in a groove so that they would roll back, and you set the skittles up again, to the accompaniment of catcalls. The bowls were made of hard wood and were very heavy; the skittles and the boy had a tough time with them.

The men came to play skittles on Sunday, whatever the weather. When it rained and was cold they sat at a table in the hut. The boy had to act as skittle-boy because the men were guests, and bought drinks. Sometimes he got something when they left, ten groschen or occasionally even fifty. A youngish man called Emil who occasionally came during the week too once took the boy aside and told him he could earn two schillings on Sunday. Then he gave him a long string with a loop which the boy was to put around the skittles. The boy practised, and it worked; all the skittles fell over. On Sunday he arranged the string so that it wouldn't be seen, and when Emil started the bowl rolling down the alley he sat on his bench and took the end of the string. When the bowl came closer he pulled the string, and all the skittles fell down. But the men laughed, because the bowl hadn't reached the skittles yet, and Emil wouldn't give him those two schillings in the evening.

Mother had to go to the city to get a passport, because she wanted to go to see Father in prison in Nuremberg. The city authorities said they weren't responsible, because Mother had become a German when she married Father, and there was no Germany any more. The boy was a German too, even though he had been born in Austria when Austria still existed, and they said she and the boy had better go to where Father came from. The Russians were there too, of course, but otherwise they knew no one there; the people they had once known didn't live in the place any more. Father's sister was in neutral Sweden, a female cousin was in Bavaria where the Yanks were, and the men were all dead. But that made no difference to the authorities, for they were Austrian.

The boy was always being made to feel that the Austrians couldn't stand the Germans, because only recently they had all been Nazis together, and now the Austrians didn't want to have been Nazis. The boy himself was a German from the Reich, as people kept telling him. He was once allowed to go with Grandmother when she took Herr Buchlar and the carriage called a Zeugerl and went to the village higher up to see the Kratzberger family, Bakers and Confectioners,

and Frau Kratzberger said, 'Ah, here comes the little German.'
Grandmother said that he was her grandson, and advised
Frau Kratzberger to hold her tongue and go take a running
jump, and then she got back into the Zeugerl with the boy
without taking any refreshment, and the boy didn't get
the ice he'd been promised either. And the stout chimney-
sweep came into the inn once and told Mother she wasn't
a real Austrian woman, just an immigrant, and 'us folks
don't fancy that'. Mother sighed. 'Yes, yes, I dare say I ought
to be called Wopravil.' That was his own name, and he said
no more.

But Mother was very sad about being a German, and Aunt
Anny came from Vienna to comfort her, for she was in the
same predicament, except that Uncle Baldi wasn't in prison in
Nuremberg but somewhere else. Aunt Anny had sold all
Mother's tablecloths and took the new ones she had knitted
with her, but before she left she and Mother went to talk to
Grandfather, and Grandmother was there too. Grandfather
knew the Interior Minister's secretary, who was a Red and
had hidden at Grandfather's once, and after a few weeks Aunt
Anny and Mother became Austrian. First Mother had to go
into the city to something called a tribunal,[48] where she was
given a blue card saying that she was incriminated only to a
minor degree because she hadn't joined the Party until August
1938, when Austria had ceased to exist. Aunt Anny had
brought Mother lots of money for the tablecloths, and she
bought herself a passport with it and went to see Father. But
the boy wasn't allowed to go with her.

When he was alone, with only the cook to look after him,
the communists had a festival called International Kirtag Tree
Meeting. The boy knew what a real *Kirchtag* was, a church
day, the festival of a church's anniversary, and he knew the
Commies didn't like mentioning church, but he had never
heard of a Church Day Tree, and was very interested to find
out, particularly as the Kirtag trees were to meet outside the

inn for the festival procession. The band started playing very early on Sunday morning, and people were so thirsty that the boy sold a lot of beer. But only the Commies from the village and some people from outside were there, because the other villagers were in church, where there was a service at the same time. Then a top Commie made a long speech, while the boy looked at the Kirtag trees leaning against the wall. The Commie talked about the French Revolution, and the glorious Russian Revolution when trees of freedom had been planted, to show the nobs what was what, and this glorious tradition was now being revived in a proper proletarian way with the Kirtag trees. But they weren't trees really, they were long poles with embroidered ribbons on them, most of them red, and they were friendship gifts from other Commies in other villages. Later, young men wearing funny belts took them and stuck them in leather holders in their belts. That way they had their hands free and could twirl the trees to make the ribbons fly. That wasn't so boring, but they didn't twirl them for long, they went on up to the village with the wind band and the other Commies. The boy had to stay behind and wash glasses.

At midday he went to have lunch with Grandmother, who said the whole thing was an invention of the Commies who were trying to ingratiate themselves with the people.

That afternoon the boy went up to see the festivities. There was a large picture of Stalin on the platform with the band – he knew about Stalin – and people were very drunk already. Later a fight got going. Two men at a table began it, and then more and more people joined in the scuffle. The boy retreated a little way and saw glasses flying through the air, and even a bench, but then unfortunately he had to go home because he was to have supper with Grandmother. When he had told them all about it Grandfather said perhaps the Commies would adopt old Austrian traditions after all, because a good fight was part of every Church Day festival, but they'd have to get rid of Stalin first.

Grandfather had put out flags that day too, but only because he had to.

When Mother came back from Nuremberg she was very sad and said Father's prospects were poor. A few days later Aunt Anny came from Vienna and said the tablecloths wouldn't sell so well now that Mother had been assessed by the tribunal as incriminated only to a minor degree, which meant that the Yanks wouldn't pay so much. But why didn't Mother try giving a song recital? There would still be people around who remembered her as a singer, and just now everything from the distant past seemed interesting. Aunt Anny took away the few tablecloths that Mother had knitted since she was last here, and before she left she opened a Russian can of lobster that she had brought with her, and Mother stirred egg and oil together to make it a thick creamy sauce.

Mother seemed very odd over the next few days. Even in the morning she was going mi-mi-mi and la-la-la in all different notes, sometimes it sounded like gargling, but she said it was voice exercises. In the afternoon, when there was no one in the inn, she gargled up and down scales, and then she sat at the piano and sang to it. One song was about a virgin who was to hear a maiden's pleas, it wasn't the 'Maiden's Prayer' but an 'Ave Maria', although it sounded very similar and seemed to go on for ever too. She sang many more such songs. In one her peace was gone and her heart was heavy, in another she said she had come here a stranger,[49] but she hadn't been a stranger when she moved into the inn, and in the evening she put slices of cucumber on her face to make her skin more beautiful.

One day she went to see Grandmother and came back with a great deal of grey material which she called silk crepe, and the dressmaker came too. And a few days later a gentleman arrived from Vienna – the boy had met him before in the Opera Café – sat down at the piano after their meal, and what Mother did with him was called Schubert. They did

Schubert for three days; you could hear it even when you were doing homework. It was very nice, but it kept making you think of other things, and afterwards you poured beer for the guests.

Next day they went to Vienna in the morning. The dress had come the day before. It was long, and had a full skirt, and the dressmaker had had to make a lot of alterations over the last few days, but Mother didn't put it on, she packed it in her case, and at the rail station she told the boy to cross his fingers for her hard. You heard from Grandmother later that Mother was going to give a song recital at the Musikverein, though not in the Great Hall, which the boy remembered, but in a smaller one, and he was rather disappointed.

Three days later Mother came back without the pianist, in a very cheerful mood. Besides the dress she had a poster with her, with her name on it, and it was in the newspapers too, because the song recital had been sold out. One paper wrote about 'an unhoped-for return', even though Mother had prac-tised so long, and praised her 'soft soprano', though it was rather too loud for the boy. He had to read the reviews out loud, and Mother waited to see if he would stammer, but it was never very hard to keep from stammering when he was reading aloud, and one paper said Mother had 'the sound of shellac' in her voice, but Mother wouldn't explain that, she just said it was very unkind.

Mother said she was very pleased with the outcome, because perhaps she would go back to singing and be rid of the inn that way, and in three weeks' time she was going to give the recital again in the nearby town. The printers did a new poster, saying some of the things out of the papers she had brought home, though not the bit about the sound of shellac, and the pianist came again the day before. They rehearsed all afternoon, and then Mother ironed the dress. Grandfather didn't want to lend his car, and the Steyrer-30 had been stolen, so a man came from the village with a

Wehrmacht jeep and petrol coupons. Mother drove to the town for her recital in it, and the boy was allowed to go too.

There was a big hall above the café near the Rathaus, where the town's artistic events took place, and the recital was there. Advance ticket sales had been very good, the fat woman from the café said, and she looked at the cash desk takings for the evening and said people were starved of culture, it was so long since they'd had any, they were grateful for anything. The boy sold sheets of paper with the words of all the songs that Mother was going to sing, for ten groschen each, and then the lights went out except on stage, Mother came on with the pianist, and people clapped. Then they moved their chairs about, and the boy saw his grandparents coming in and sitting down very inconspicuously at the back of the hall.

The people clapped after each song, sometimes more and sometimes less, and then Mother bowed and bobbed a little curtsey. In the interval the boy went to look for his grandparents and found them down in the café, and they told him not to give them away to Mother. Then Mother sang again, standing inside the curve of the grand piano. When she had finished, Grandmother and Grandfather left before the lights in the hall came on. People clapped for a long time, and Mother had to sing two more songs which she called encores, but the boy's grandparents weren't there any more. Afterwards Mother stood around with a lot of people, and the boy was supposed to say something too, but he found it difficult, and Mother said unfortunately he wasn't very bright. Then they drove home in the jeep, and the boy didn't say any more.

Mother gave several more recitals, one of them even for the Yanks in Linz, which had once been the Führer's town but now belonged to the Americans. In Enns, on the border between the Russians and the Yanks, you had to get out of the train because it was a Russo-Austrian train and show your ID.

Then you had to wait for the American-Austrian train, because the occupying powers didn't share a train timetable. There was a barracks near the station where they had Coca-Cola. The boy had already heard that the Yanks drink nothing but Coca-Cola, but it was brown, tasted terribly sweet, and was funny in other ways too. Outside the barracks a GI was handing out chewing gum. He said, 'Try that, this is culture,' and a grown-up translated it for the boy, who didn't understand. However, he was curious about chewing gum, because he'd heard a lot about it. He and some others had already tried the resin of an apricot tree because he had been told that it was just like chewing gum. However, chewing gum turned out to be a strip of something called Juicy Fruit, and tasted very odd at first. Then it tasted of nothing at all and stuck to your teeth, two of which were wobbly because you still had your milk teeth. Spitting it out was difficult too, although you had seen how the GI did it. The boy had to fish the gum out from between his teeth, and then he secretly put it on the window of the train, in which they were now sitting. But some of it stayed sticking to his fingers and then his trousers. Thank goodness Mother saw nothing, because she was sitting directly opposite him but was looking out of the window, although there was nothing nice to be seen.

There were a lot of factories on the right, factories that Uncle Hermann had given the people of Linz because they were the Führer's followers in his own city.[50] But they weren't called after him any more, because the Austrians are never grateful, as Mother said, but were called things like Nitrogen Works and VOEST,[51] and red smoke came out of one chimney, but that meant nothing, since the Yanks didn't like the Russians anyway, it had always been like that.

The rail station had been a present from the Führer too, and Mother said it showed. There were a few cardboard notices up in the station concourse with something about

Mauthausen written on them, but you weren't to look at those, because it had been a concentration camp and no one wanted to know anything about it. There was a big open-air café on the left-hand side of the high street, where you had lunch, with fried mushrooms, a rarity, because at home there wasn't any oil to fry them in and mushrooms could be found only in the fields, but not everywhere. However, the Yanks wanted to show that everything was better with them than with the Russians, so you could find anything in their zones. The main square was very handsome, and you were almost run over by a tram, because it was driving right through all the people. There were two big buildings on the Danube, one on the right and one on the left, erected by the Führer when he was planning to retire to Linz some day and inhabit the whole of the bank of the river, but only these two buildings had been finished, and the hall where Mother was going to sing was in one of them. Then it suddenly turned dark, and Mother and the boy thought there was a thunderstorm coming, although there hadn't been a cloud in the sky. But then it became impossible to see the Pöstlingberg on the other side of the Danube between the Führer's houses, and several people coughed. A man said that it wasn't a storm, it was an outlet valve leaking in the Hermann Göring Works; it had been like that ever since the works suffered bomb damage which hadn't been properly repaired. Such things never happened under the Führer, he added, but now that everything was Austrian you got this kind of mess almost once a week. He said a lot more, because he was rather drunk and a native of Linz, and he'd been an 'illegal'[52] too, but Mother didn't know him, and she was worried about her voice, so she and the boy went into a coffee-house, where there was much less smoke, coming only from people's cigarettes.

This time the hall was only half full, and the boy didn't have to sell programme notes because a man in Styrian costume was doing that; the boy had to sit at the back and be good. In the interval the concert promoter came over to Mother and said he was sorry about all the empty seats, but she'd been off the stage for seventeen years, and people didn't know her any more. They might still remember her in Vienna, and in her local town near the inn people would have come just because she was the daughter of the boy's grandparents, but the people of Linz had their own tastes, so he would have to reduce the fee slightly. Mother was sad and sang only one encore, but after the recital a man came and told her a singer had dropped out of his production for the Salzburg Festival, and would she like to take her place? Her voice was reasonably good, and it was only a small part. Mother told the man she had once sung a much larger part in the same opera, but one must be content with what one could get, and she said yes. Then they spent the night at an inn where the bedclothes were not clean, and went home next morning. But this time there was no American Coca-Cola and no chewing gum, because they were going to the Russians.

At the beginning of the school holidays Mother was rehearsing her part industriously, and the boy poured beer and learned to hold the bottle of carbon dioxide properly. That wasn't very easy, because sometimes only froth came out, and sometimes none at all because the carbonation fitting was very old and had its defects. Then you went to Salzburg with Mother. There was Coca-Cola in Enns again, and a piece of chewing gum that you picked up, but nothing happened on the border between Upper Austria and Salzburg, the train just went through because both places belonged to the Yanks. You left Salzburg immediately too, in a bus to Mattsee, where you were going to stay. But you didn't stay in Mattsee itself but in Ochsenharing, with the Zinnhobel family. Herr Zinnhobel was a cheerful man and 'something in local government', and in summer he rented out the upper part of his house. A lot of people there did the same, and musicians from the Philharmonic usually came to stay with them. Mother knew one of the musicians, who had put her in touch with the Zinnhobel family, and Mother said it was good value. Next day there was an expedition to Salzburg, where Mother met a lot of people she knew but hadn't seen for a long time. Stefan and Liesel's father was there too. He was a very famous conductor, and very friendly, but now he couldn't conduct because of being a Nazi, which made him sad. His wife was a singer, and she couldn't sing either, but she didn't mind so much about that. And then there was a very much more famous conductor with a bald head rimmed by hair, who couldn't conduct now either and whose name was Furtwängler.[53] His wife said it was very unjust because he had helped a great many people, and that was the only reason he had agreed to be general music director, and an old gentleman said she was right. He could conduct because he was Jewish, and was called Bruno Walter.[54] The most famous of all, however, was a very old gentleman who came from Garmisch,[55] and whose son led him by the hand. His moustache and his wineglass shook, although was no older than Grandfather, who only sometimes shook, but when he came in everyone stood up because he was so famous. Mother was going to sing in his opera, and he was very nice to her and said she had been his best Sophie, although her name was Stefanie. And he told the others that he thought the ban on conducting was ridiculous, and here was someone like Karajan[56] jumping into the breach, who had been an even greater Nazi, but cleverer, and this got him so agitated that he upset the contents of his wineglass over his suit. The party occupied two tables outside the Moser Weinhaus, where the street was rather wider opposite the Festspielhaus, and the tables were covered with paper like the tables at home, but Mother said this was like being on Parnassus. The boy said nothing so as not to stammer and shame his mother.

Then Mother had a rehearsal, and the boy stayed with Stefan and Liesel's father because his wife wanted to watch the rehearsal too. When you asked something, he said, 'Hello, so you stammer!' but he didn't mind and took the boy off for a walk to show him round Salzburg. First they went into an open-air café called the Café Tomaselli, and you had a glass of raspberry water with an ice cube in it. You'd never seen anything like it before, and you were given another because the waitress knew the gentleman. Then you saw the Residenz Fountain, which had a square all to itself, and was very tall, and there were horse-drawn cabs in front of it, and the horses had left droppings everywhere. You could see only half the cathedral, because a bomb had hit it behind the high wall. There was a lot of wood for *Everyman*[57] in the forecourt, but people left it alone, because it was going to build two platforms, one for the actors and another for the spectators. Then you went into the Franciscan Church, which the boy liked very much. Stefan and Liesel's father said he didn't really care for churches except in Salzburg, so they went to St Peter's Church too and saw the tomb of St Rupert, but it was empty because he was a saint. The boy wanted to see the churches, because you could wish for something in every one of them when you entered it for the first time, but you mustn't tell your wish. The boy always wished for the same things: to be grown up, because he'd heard that you didn't get beaten any more then, and not to stammer.

Then you saw the graveyard of St Peter's, which looked like a village graveyard, but it was up against a rock wall with a castle above it. The graves were very short. The boy had heard something at his grandparents' about graves where people were buried in a crouching position, but Stefan and Liesel's father said the people here were buried in the perfectly normal way; we'd be climbing over their feet, but it didn't hurt them now. There was a long text on the side of one tombstone about a soldier, which the boy had to read aloud. It listed all the battles the soldier had been in. He had been badly wounded a couple of times, and then mortally wounded, but he had always fought on, and Stefan and Liesel's father laughed and said even a hero's death today wasn't what it used to be. And as the boy hadn't stammered he promised him an ice on a stick in the wooden dairy behind the Festspielhaus, and his wife and Mother were already sitting there because the rehearsal was over. The dairy was nice, with some tables in front of it, but the ice was only frozen raspberry water, and you could suck the red out of it.

The grown-ups talked about Father, and Stefan and Liesel's father said the most sensible thing would be for Mother to divorce him, but Mother got very angry and said maybe divorce was his speciality, but she was no character assassin, and anyway she was too old to start again as a singer. Then she lowered her voice, because some other people she knew came along, and they were all saying how bad things had been, but now they must look ahead to the future with courage. Then Mother consulted the timetable, and the bus went back to Mattsee, where there was smoked sausage with oil and vinegar for supper.

This was at the Steiner inn and butcher's shop. There were two of these, one half-way from Ochsenharing, the other in the village square, near the church and the lake, and that was the grander one, because it had a couple of tables out in the square. If there were no rehearsals, and Mother wanted to be grand we ate down there, although the cooking wasn't so good, because of the high society you saw. One day a very large car drove up, and a stout married couple got out, leaving their driver in the car. When they entered the café garden the gentleman saw Mother and came over. But Mother did something that the boy recognized as a court curtsey, and then the gentleman asked if she was in the clear again, and Mother said well, she could travel on. That was because she had been a fellow traveller of the Party. Then the man's wife came and shook hands with Mother, and Mother bobbed another curtsey. But they only said good day, and the couple sat down at a reserved table in the corner and ordered roast chicken. People looked at Mother and the couple, and whispered, and Mother whispered to the boy that the man was King Leopold of the Belgians, but the Western powers had made him abdicate because he was too friendly to the Germans, so now he was only an ex-king, and the woman wasn't his wife but his mistress. And while the people were still whispering, and the exes were drinking beer – he had a large beer, she had a small one – a jeep arrived with an old man in a funny traditional costume, and all heads turned because he was the Crown Prince of Bavaria. He didn't say anything to Mother, but sat down with the exes, ordered roast pork, and Mother said he wasn't having an easy time either, because he'd been in the Party. Mother said you saw high society in Mattsee. But the boy was most interested in the lake.

There were three lakes in Mattsee: the Mattsee itself, the Trumer See and the Graben See, but that one didn't count, because it was dug out of the moor. There were two moorland bathing places too, where people could lose weight, but they weren't doing good business, because few people were fat these days. The Trumer See was large, and only a little way from Ochsenharing, and the boy often went there when Mother was in Salzburg, because he wasn't really supposed to go. There were reeds and the water was very shallow, and had shells in it. The boy hit many of the shells with stones, hoping to find pearls in them, but there was never anything but slime, and there were horseflies around that looked like ordinary flies but had a nasty bite, and came from the cows. The bathing beach was on the Mattsee. There were fewer horseflies there, but a great many children of Philharmonic musicians, and the Philharmonic musicians' wives looked after them because the musicians themselves were in Salzburg. Gerda became his best friend. Her father was a horn player and had been in the SS, but nothing had happened to him because he was a good horn player, and people weren't angry with the other Nazis in the Philharmonic either, because they were the pride of Austria. There was only one man that nobody could stand, because he had been in the Resistance, and Resistance workers were anathema to all true Austrians. But the Philharmonic children were mostly normal and made a lot of noise. When they couldn't go to the bathing beach because it was raining, they played on the first floor of the Water-Lily Café. It was a large wooden building between the lower Steiner inn and the bathing beach, and up above there was a hall that wobbled when you jumped about on the floor. Down below the mothers drank weak imitation coffee. They said it was the worst coffee ever known, but they drank it because then they were rid of the children playing upstairs. It rained a great deal, mostly on Sundays, as mother said, because that was when the outdoor performances of *Everyman* took place. If it didn't begin to rain until the scene where Everyman is eating and drinking and making merry, the performance was cancelled, the spectators didn't get their money back, and the actors had time off. But if it had been raining all day everyone moved to the Festspielhaus, and that wasn't so good, because the audience missed the cathedral square, and the actors had to perform all the same.

You were allowed to go to Salzburg to see Mother's dress rehearsal, but you saw her only briefly at the beginning of the second act. Before that a middle-aged woman had some kind of relationship with a younger woman, only the younger woman wore trousers so that people wouldn't notice. Later she had a relationship with an even younger woman, and towards the end of the opera she was a proper woman after all for a while, and went to a tavern with a fat old man.[58] Then she was a man again, and right at the end all three women sang nice and loud, but Mother wasn't in that scene. People were saying that the conductor had lost his place twice, which was why the première had to be a great success.

You didn't see that première, but it was said to have been very good, and Mother didn't come back until very late at night. But the reviews said nothing about her, except that Sophie was now the duenna.[59] Mother tried to explain that to the boy, but he didn't understand, just as he didn't understand why time should be 'a strange thing'.[60]

Then you were allowed to go to Salzburg with Mother again. Aunt Anny was at the Café Tomaselli, and Mother gave her the boy's little case, because she herself needed a little relaxation. So in the afternoon you went back to your grandparents. She asked a lot of questions on the way, and the boy was rather nervous, but Aunt Anny didn't say he was stammering. She told him that Mother had studied music at the Academy, and she had once been famous. She herself had wanted to be a singer in the past, said Aunt Anny, but she had given up that idea when she inherited the Opera Café, and art was not to be depended on.

The last year at primary school was boring, because you already knew everything they were teaching. There was a new teacher who was still very young. All the same, he had been in Russia, but when Austria was liberated Stalin sent him back, and now he was a teacher and this was his first job. He was very nice, but after a few days he wasn't there. Fräulein Unterreiner came into the classroom and said he had a perforation of the stomach, and we must pray for him, and then an older lady came as the new teacher. She hadn't been allowed to teach before because she'd been high up in the Bund Deutscher Mädel[61] organization. But she only stayed three weeks, not even until the nice teacher was buried. He had died in the hospital in town, and his mother wept a lot, because her husband and her other two sons had died in the war, and now she had no one left. The next new teacher was a probationary teacher, although he was quite old, but he was a Socialist. When he had been going to begin teaching the

Cock's Tail-Feathers militia,[62] now called Austro-Fascists by the Commies, threw him out of school, then the Nazis and the war came along, and so this was his first class, but he was very dull. All the same, he took you on a nice expedition to another village some way from your own, one where you weren't supposed to go because of foot and mouth disease. In fact the expedition only almost went there, because there was a forest to the left of this village where the Evil Trench stood. A witch had once made it when the Turks came, and they all fell in with their horses and died. While the children played hide and seek up above the trench, the boy explored it with another boy, hoping to find Turkish weapons, but there weren't any, only a spring of water with three fire-salamanders around it. They were very pretty, but you knew you mustn't touch them because they gave you warts. Then the teacher up above was getting annoyed, because he had already called a couple of times but you hadn't heard him.

Then the old electrician's grandson died of a brain tumour. His name had been Hansi, and he was a year younger than the boy. Herr Mandi told everyone at the inn, where he came to drink a lot because Hansi's mother was his sister. It was terrible that Hansi had died, said Herr Mandi, but the child had no brain left, and then Herr Mandi fell down in the puddle outside the house left over from last time it rained. The boy had to take him home, and they were all crying there too, because Hansi's father had fallen at Leningrad, and now his mother had only one little boy left. The boy was allowed to go to the funeral with Grandmother in the Zeugerl, right at the end of the procession of mourners, but when it reached the graveyard he and Grandmother stood right at the front, and Hansi had a very small coffin. When the priest was going to speak Hansi's mother began screaming out loud, saying she had done everything for her child, she even let the Russians have their way so that he would have a better life some day, and her father told her to keep her mouth shut. But she wouldn't stop, and shouted something angry attacking the good Lord too, so the priest walked a couple of steps away to avoid having to hear. Then the doctor came to give her a morphine injection, and Grandmother took the boy back into the carriage, because she thought all this was terrible. The boy didn't tell Mother anything about this, because he didn't want to stammer, although he wasn't getting thrashed for it so much now.

Mother's nerves were in a bad way in any case. At the end of September she had given another song recital in Vienna, but not many tickets had been sold, and she sometimes said her time was over. Then she had gone to see Father in Nuremberg again, and came back in a very sad mood. The boy could visit Grandmother more often in the afternoons now, but she usually sent him to the nursery garden, because she had a headache and wanted to get the business on its feet again. Grandfather said it was very difficult, because people in Vienna had no money, and the Russians had wrecked his freight car, and the livestock had to be built up again. There was no selling any timber either, although a lot of wood was needed for reconstruction, but the Russians had wreaked havoc in the woods, and reforestation was very difficult, even if there was no need to fear damage caused by game browsing on young saplings any more.

There was a lot to do at the inn even before the ball season, because the fire service was organizing a vintage celebration, although only wild vines which didn't even have grapes grew in this area. But one of the firemen had relations in the Wachau,[63] and they took the fire engine there and came back with a few crates of grapes and a large tub of liquid called Storm. The boy didn't know what that was, but it turned out to be new wine still fermenting, which made you drunk and gave you diarrhoea very quickly. The Storm was decanted into jugs and large bottles, which mustn't be closed or they would explode, and a huge bunch of grapes was made with the contents of two crates, tied together with string, and attached to a broomstick, because it was supposed to be the grapes of Canaan. It was hung from the big chandelier in the hall, and the boy was to sell the smaller bunches of grapes from a table. In the evening the waitresses, the orchestra and the people arrived. The orchestra had learned a new piece, and they sang it so often that the boy knew it by heart that very evening.

Lieserl, come here, the coast is quite clear,
Your mother is sleeping
No birds are still cheeping.
Lieserl, keep still, hear the cricket so shrill,
Who wants, for his part, what I want from your heart.

They knew a couple of Swiss songs too. Swiss songs were very modern now, because Switzerland had been neutral and was doing all right, but the boy thought the words were very silly. Then the broomstick with the bunch of grapes was let down lower, so that people could snap at it with their mouths, but two young lads knocked their heads together and began scuffling over it. Then more people started scuffling, and the boy sat at the table with the bunches of grapes he was supposed to be selling and watched. But some people fell on the table and the bunches of grapes, and the whole thing toppled over. When the boy moved away he could see that people had some of the grapes all over their clothes, and had picked up the others to squash them in the faces of the people they were fighting, and then the orchestra stopped playing, and it was just very noisy. Later the local policeman came, and the police from town too, and next day Mother said there had been a lot of damage done because a great many glasses were broken, but the people who were fighting denied it, although the boy had seen them perfectly clearly. The lavatories were all stopped up and filthy, because the Storm had got into people's guts, and Herr Mandi had to come and work on the plumbing for a long time. Then he and the boy went to see Grandmother, and when he told her about it she said genuine riff-raff didn't need any Russians to organize a genuine fight at an inn.

People began to worry about Fräulein Unterreiner. In the summer the cinema had got proper sound. Now the films sounded quite different, and Fräulein Unterreiner wasn't needed any more, but she was sad because she missed the money, and a teacher earned very little. She wasn't needed at the school any more either, because the provincial schools inspector had decided to retire her, even though she was only seventy-six. Her successor was already at the school, and taught the first class. He was quite young, and people said he was a nitwit, but he had the right Party membership book, the black one. The authorities up above thought that was good, but the workers down below didn't, and Fräulein Unterreiner still came to school every day, because she wasn't going to be thrown out until Christmas. But just before All Saints' Day she fell over the grave of the very old priest when she was going to tend it, and broke her pelvis. Now she had to stay at home, but the pupils saw her every day, because she had her bed moved to the window so that she could see if they were all going to school like good children.

Mother had gone to see Father in Nuremberg, because he was in a very bad way, and she came back a week later, cried a lot, and even prayed now and then. People were rather nicer to her now, and the three workers who came in all the time didn't send her off to fetch every single cigarette any more, but ordered them all at the same time, and usually the boy brought them the cigarettes. There were far more available now. The A and even the B brands were gone, there was only the C. And of the 1, 2 and 3 varieties only the 2 was left, which was expensive and smoked by white-collar workers, and the 3, which was for the blue-collar workers. Then there were Donau and Sport brands, but they were for high-class folk. People mainly bought 3s and Cs in the café, and the boy fetched them in packets in the afternoon from the tobacconist's in the village street. It was run by a war widow, and in fact all the tobacconists in Austria were run by war widows by decree of Empress Maria Theresia.

Then the butcher's son and daughter were both getting married, and the double wedding was to be held at the inn. The tables in the Hall were extended, which was necessary, because days before the wedding more meat and sausages than the boy had seen for years began arriving. The cold storage room was crammed with it all, and the day before sausages were being sliced and laid out on large platters all the time. The ovens were full of roasts too, and Mother said it was a really swanky tradesmen's wedding. There were over a hundred guests, and the orchestra, and many people had brought bags with them to take sliced and roast meat away, but all the same there was a lot left on the platters. When the tables were cleared away up above, and people were dancing to the orchestra, a lot of them came down to the bar to drink walnut schnapps because they'd overeaten. Some of them threw up, and many were unwell because they weren't used to all that butter and meat. And there was so much left in the cold storage room that Mother was able to sell it for a long time after the wedding.

A few days later the boy saw his first Schlurf.[64] He had heard a lot about Schlurfs already. No one had a good word to say for them. They were supposed to be filthy dirty and let their hair grow long, whereas a good Austrian must have the nape of his neck neatly shaved in the German fashion. And they were said to grease their hair with Russian margarine, to be obtained in the USIA shops that belonged to the Commies. No one wanted the margarine because it had such a strong, fishy smell. The Schlurf that the boy saw was a boiler fitter from Vienna who had work to do in the factory, where something had gone wrong. In fact Herr Karli Vrskosil wasn't a boiler fitter yet, but just an assistant because he was only seventeen; he ate with his master at the inn for a week and slept up in the maid's room, because there wasn't any maid to sleep there. But he was a Schlurf, because he had his hair down to the back of his collar, and it didn't stink of fish, he used brilliantine, but that stank too. He was very funny and friendly, but people called, 'Schlurf!' and 'Yuk!' after him. He didn't mind, he was proud to be a Schlurf, because it was modern. He liked listening to the jazz the Yanks played on their radio station too, and the boy smoked his first cigarette with him round behind the skittle alley, so that Mother wouldn't see. It was a real Yank cigarette, a Chesterfield that he had brought from the American zone of Vienna, but it tasted of nothing except smoke.

Then, one morning, the curtains at Fräulein Unterreiner's windows were closed, and you heard in school that she had died in the night, and everyone would get the day off school for her funeral.

In the evening the Krampus came.[65] St Nicholas had come earlier, looking like a bishop with a beard. He was the old porter. He had a Krampus with him too, who looked like a devil with a sheepskin turned inside out, but it was his wife. You could tell by her coat. The Krampus had a rod to threaten children, a chain to rattle, and a sack into which she was going to put the boy, but she didn't, because his grandparents employed her husband. The year before there hadn't been any St Nicholas, and Herr Mandi was the Krampus. The boy had watched him rehearsing, but he didn't tell Mother, so as not to spoil the fun, and Herr Mandi didn't have a sack with him because of Stefan, since Mother didn't want to think about him. But now there were many more young men in the village, and they all wanted to be Krampuses so that they could hit the girls. The girls liked it, because when the Devil came for them they could have a good time with him, as Grandmother put it, away from the road, but first the Krampuses had to make a lot of noise in the road, the louder the better. There were many Krampuses out and about, and sometimes one and sometimes several came into the café to have a beer, so that they could make more noise after it. They took their beers into the spare room, because they had to remove their masks to drink, and no one was to recognize them. But the boy knew almost all of them by their voices when they ordered the beer. In the night the Krampuses from the village up above were said to have scuffled with the ones from the village down below, but he didn't see any of that.

On the day of Fräulein Unterreiner's funeral Mother was dressed all in black, lit a candle even in the morning, put it in the window and wept. The boy was surprised that she was so sad about Fräulein Unterreiner, but when he told her so she cried even more, and then he went to school, because this time he couldn't go in the Zeugerl with Grandmother; he had to go with his class. The school walked to church in rows three abreast. The church was so full that the children had to stand, because Fräulein Unterreiner had taught the entire village, including the wind band, which played, and now she was lying up in front in a coffin with bits of silver all over it, under a large wreath of paper chrysanthemums. The priest delivered a long address about Theresia Unterreiner, a virgin who had been wedded to Christ and the village, and she was a shining example to all the village men, women and children, for they could see today that the church was much too small for them all, so they ought to donate to make it bigger, as Fräulein Unterreiner had wanted. Then the mayor of the village up above described the way that Fräulein Unterreiner had tanned the seat of his pants, and he sobbed, and the mayor of the village down below said the same, even though he was a Red, and looked as if he were going to cry, and the boy thought they had been lucky, because he always had to take his trousers off before he was beaten. Then the church choir sang, the wind band played, the organ squealed, the servers and priest walked around, and it was very solemn. Some of the women began crying, some of the men went out of church to smoke a cigarette, then the wind band had to leave the church to walk at the front of the procession to the graveyard, and the firemen came along too. The Zeugerl carriage with Herr Buchlar and Grandmother was standing outside, because Grandmother didn't like going into the church, and then Fräulein Unterreiner was put on the hearse, which had four horses harnessed to it this time. Since so many people had come it all took ages. As usual, Grandmother brought up the rear of the procession.

Fräulein Unterreiner was buried in the grave of the very old priest, on top of him, because the grave belonged to the parish and she had none of her own, and then the district schools inspector, who had been one of the Cock's Tail-Feathers himself, spoke too, and the boy's legs began to ache. The priest spoke again as well, and when it was all over the school could go home, and the boy joined Grandmother in the Zeugerl. When he told her how sad Mother had been about Fräulein Unterreiner, she sighed and said it was about Father, who was being hanged today. Then she looked at the watch hanging from a chain round her neck and said he had probably been hanged by now, and you were to have lunch with her. Herr Buchlar stopped outside the inn and went in to tell Mother, but the cook said she had gone out. Over lunch Grandfather was worried because no one knew who owned the majority of shares in the factories now, since Father's had been expropriated, and Grandmother said it was just as well that no one knew for certain, or the Russians would have confiscated everything as German property and given it to the USIA. Later you went home from Grandmother's, and soon Mother came back. She had been for a walk in the forest, she looked very tearstained, and she put a new candle in the window. But the boy went to his room and thought about never seeing Father again.

What had happened to Father was in the newspapers a couple of days later, not on the front page, but all the same, people talked about it because they talked about everything that was in the papers. There were a great many newspapers in Austria, and the café had to have those that were obligatory because of politics. There was *Neues Österreich*, which belonged to the occupying powers, was neutral, and published news of all the parties, and people thought it was dull. The *Volksblatt* was black, and published articles by conservatives and clerics. The socialists had their *Arbeiter-Zeitung*, and the Commies had the *Volksstimme*. And they all had to be in the Thonet-designed newspaper holder and hung side by side on the wall. People always read their own parties' opinions, since they wanted to know what they ought to think, and they liked best a weekly paper called *Echo der Heimat,* which was a trashy rag, as they said themselves. That was the one that had most about Father in it, and how it was a disgrace to the whole village, although he had never lived there.

A lot of people spoke to Mother about the article, usually not in a friendly way, because she often cried. Once a man came from town saying he wanted to see what a criminal's widow looked like, and Mother got angry and told him to nose about in his own shit and go away. But the man sat down, grinning, and said Mother was a woman, and he could beat her any time. Then Mother went into the kitchen with the boy, and told him to fetch Herr Mandi. When you came back with Herr Mandi, the man was still sitting in the bar, although he hadn't had anything to eat or drink, and Mother talked to Herr Mandi quietly in the kitchen. Then Herr Mandi went into the bar and told the man to push off. But the man shouted that he was an Austrian and a democrat, and he could sit where he liked, even in a criminal's house, and then Herr Mandi punched him in the face, and hit him a bit more and dragged him out of the house. The man shouted that he was going to fetch the police, and Herr Mandi told him to do just that, and sat down in the bar in case the man came back. But he didn't, and nor did the local policeman, and Herr Mandi was given two beers.

People spoke to the boy about Father too. At first a few of the working-class children teased him in class, until the teacher told them not to, and then he took the boy outside the classroom and told him he didn't have to come to school next week, because after that the Christmas holidays would begin, and by the time they were over everything would probably have died down. That annoyed the working-class children, and on the way home, just below the upper village, near the Franz-Josef-Jubilee linden tree, the biggest boy snatched his school bag off his shoulders. He was so big because he had stayed down a year at school twice, and then he and the other three played football with the school bag, shouting, 'Nazi boy! Nazi boy!' Then a man whom Mother always called the top Commie came out of the barber's shop, took hold of the big boy and slapped him a couple of times. When the others ran away, he shouted after them that they were even worse than the Nazis. The boy picked up his bag, and the top Commie told him he couldn't help it about his father. At home Mother was annoyed to see the dirty school bag, and when you told her all about it she said the top Commie would be a nice man if he wasn't the top Commie.

Then the *Echo der Heimat* reported the incident of the man Mother had had thrown out, because he was a journalist, and there was something about Grandfather in it too, because he was Mother's father. Then for the first time in ages Grandfather came to the inn again, bringing a man with him called an advocate, and they talked to Mother for a long time. Much later the boy heard that the journalist had been sentenced to two weeks in jail, but that was only because

Grandfather had telephoned the government in Vienna, and they had telephoned the judge. But the paper didn't publish anything else about the family.

At Christmas you went to your grandparents' first, once the present-giving to the staff was over, and the Christmas tree in the salon looked smaller than before because you were bigger. The new Russian commandant wasn't there either, because he had no family and Grandmother couldn't stand him because of what he had been doing to the house and the park. Grandfather said nothing would turn out well again; Grandmother said they had been able to sell only half a freight car full of things in Vienna, and Mother said nothing. Then Grandfather said the staff were eating him out of house and home, and he would let them gradually die off and not replace them, not even by children of the present staff. They would get a plot of land instead where they could build houses of their own, and see how they could fend for themselves. Then Grandmother and Mother sighed, and the boy didn't understand, because he had often heard the grown-ups say, 'This is the end' before. His grandparents gave him a hundred schillings for Christmas, but it dated from 1927, and was a thick, heavy gold coin, worth much more than the new schillings. Those weren't worth anything, said Mother, a tankard of beer cost two schillings fifty today, and you could have got three for that money before the war.

The ball season was even faster and more frantic this year than before, although no Russians could come, and only a few people came anyway. Mother had bought cheap glasses, so that the good ones wouldn't get broken straight away, and people made full use of that fact. Mother said they often dropped the glasses on purpose, saying they were wet and had slipped out of their hands. They had handles, and the drink inside had always been finished when they were dropped. Always by the same people. Mother said they would have to pay for the glasses, but many of the waitresses didn't keep an eye open and charge for breakages at once, and the boy always had to sweep up the broken glass. Sometimes not all the members of the orchestra were there, and then Fräulein Hebauer sat at a table breaking glasses. She could do that without paying for it because one of the older waitresses was her sister, and always closed an eye to it. When the boy was having to sweep up broken glass under the table, he looked up through the slats of the bench and saw that Fräulein Hebauer had no knickers on, and she had a big, dark crack. They called it a cunt in the village, but the boy had never seen anything like it. When he asked Herr Mandi about it later, he said that Fräulein Hebauer was always a fast worker, and that made you sooty, like a locomotive. All the stones on the railway embankment were indeed sooty and dirty, but you would have liked to hear Fräulein Hebauer whistle, because then the locomotives always let out white smoke rising into the air. At ten o'clock the boy didn't have to sweep up any more glass but went to his room instead, and after that there was usually a lot of noise, because the fighting happened then. Glasses were broken during the fighting too, and Grandmother said she thought it was the only way the village people had of expressing their feelings.

They expressed them most at the huntsmen's ball, because that was the grandest. The place was being decorated for three days beforehand, and fir trunks with the bark still on them were brought into the hall – they had been cut down in summer, because of bark beetles – and some crates of fresh moss from the forest. The firs and moss were used to make the façade of a beautiful forester's house in the Hall, up against the orchestra wall. A girl cut out of the front page of a newspaper was looking out of the window, and lower down she had a figure where two old cushions had been stuffed under her blouse. Antlers and stuffed animals, called trophies by the huntsmen, were arranged all around the house. It looked very beautiful, although the Hall was extremely dirty by the time they had finished decorating it, and the floor had to be polished. The boy was told to grate up some Hindenburg lights – there were still several cartons of those left – with an old kitchen grater, and if they were scattered around the parquet floor it would be nice and smooth as soon as people started dancing on it. But no one danced for very long, because when the orchestra stopped for the first interval Frau Engelsbrunner started fighting Fräulein Hebauer, who had been fucking Herr Engelsbrunner, or so his wife shouted anyway. Until now the boy had only seen men fighting, or girls, but the women were very impressive, tearing at each other's hair and clothes and trying to scratch one another's faces. Then some of the men tried to intervene, but that didn't make the women stop, or perhaps it was the very reason why they didn't stop, and the boy had to climb on a chair to see, because so many other people wanted to watch. People laughed because the men couldn't separate the women, but they came up against the forester's house, and first it wobbled and then it fell on the orchestra with a big bang and broke apart. Some of the musicians had been sitting under it, but they were all right when they emerged from the forester's house. They just had some scratches from the nails in the beautiful decoration, and put sticking plaster on those later. But the double bass and the percussion were wrecked, so was one of the violins, and the French horn and slide trombone were all twisted. There were a lot of feathers from the stuffed birds lying about, and a very large set of antlers was broken because it had been on top of the forester's house, and the huntsman who owned it was very upset because apparently it was a royal stag. People shouted angrily for a while longer, and the two women stopped fighting and wept. They were taken out of the Hall through different doors, and the local policeman came, but the ball was over. Mother was very upset, because it was only nine o'clock and she would have to pay the waitresses for the whole evening, although no real business had been done, and the huntsmen didn't want to pay for the damage because they had no money, on account of a lot of people wanting their entrance money back. There was arguing for a long time down in the bar, because apparently someone had been putting a hand in the till for the evening's takings, and the policeman said they should all go home now. At ten Mother closed the inn and said there would never be another huntsmen's ball here, and the people went off to other inns, who got her business now. But for once there was no fighting at the firemen's ball, and next Wednesday was Ash Wednesday, and then the ball season was over.

That was not good for the boy, because Mother had more time for him now, which wasn't easy because she was so changeable. Sometimes she was very nice to him, saying he was all she had, even hugging him, but then she would push him away saying he had been stammering. He was taking the greatest trouble to speak very carefully, but he could seldom please Mother. Sometimes she asked out loud what she had done to be afflicted with a boy like this, but only the boy himself was there and he didn't know the answer, so he preferred to go to his room and pretend to be doing homework. Once Mother came into his room unexpectedly and saw that he wasn't doing homework, but looking out of the window at a siskin building its nest in some ornamentation on the skittle alley which had been overlooked when it was renovated. Mother was very cross, and now you had to do your homework down in the spare room, where she often sat at the sewing machine when there was nothing else to be done. You acted as if it took you a long time to do your homework, so as not to have to do something else. It wasn't entirely easy to do that, because the homework was too simple. Sometimes Mother noticed, and then you did have to do something else, and it was a nuisance.

For instance, there were the chestnut trees behind the house by the skittle alley. Gravel consisting of round white stones lay under them, and a few tables and chairs were put out in summer on this gravel, which was so expensive that it always had to be kept clean. But the chestnut trees weren't clean, and shed mess all the year round, so you had to keep raking the gravel. It wasn't easy to keep it clean, because first the buds of the chestnuts opened, and then sticky brown sepals fell which stuck to your feet and were very uncomfortable. But even if you wore wooden shoes to rake the chestnuts they were no better, since you could remove the sticky stuff from the soles only with a knife, which was very tedious. The cat sometimes brought these sticky things into the house too, but if they were found the boy was always blamed. Then the flowers fell, and at least they weren't sticky, but they were very difficult to rake out of the gravel, and then came the little green chestnuts with bristles that pricked your feet. It was only when the chestnuts were ripe that they did you any good, because then you could put them in bags and sell them to the huntsmen, who fed them to the game that was very thin on the ground now because of the Russians. That had been done at your grandparents' house when the war was still on, but the boy was left with only the shells to clear up then, while the servants' children sold the chestnuts. In that respect some things had improved, although many of the grown-ups said it was no better now than in the war. But autumn was still a long way off, and until it came the chestnuts were nothing but trouble.

Sometimes Frau Prankhofer came in the afternoon. Her husband had fallen in the war, and her son used to go to secondary school in town by train every day. But last autumn he had been picking up scrap metal near the school – you could get a lot of money for it – and he had been blown up. Now Frau Prankhofer was on her own, and she often came to see Mother and drink a quarter-litre of wine or so with her. The women would talk about the change of life and hot flushes, which the boy didn't understand, and sometimes Mother said it was a shame about Frau Prankhofer's boy, who had turned out so well, while she had nothing but trouble with hers. Sometimes Director Sattler visited too. He was works manager of the factory now, but he was called director, and he was married to a much older wife, who had brought money into his household. He was stout and usually drank cognac, although it said brandy on the bottle, and then the boy had to go to his own room, because Mother sent him away. The Director always came to the spare room the back way, and Mother closed the inn so that no one could see him. But the boy saw him when he went out by the back way again, usually after an hour. Mother said that was no one else's business.

A little while after Easter, Mother altered an old suit of Grandfather's to make a new one for the boy, because she was going to send him to a famous boarding school, and he had to look good for the entrance exam. It was thick, dark fabric, very old, dating from before the First World War, excellent quality, as Mother said, but it was still a long time until the entrance exam, and the boy perspired when he had to try the suit on. But Mother said it was all the material she had, and she meant well. There was nothing you could do about it.

When it was the boy's birthday he was allowed to visit Grandmother, whom he hadn't seen for a long time because there had been no interesting funerals, and she didn't go out for anything else now. She gave the boy a beautiful red silk tie of Grandfather's, which went well with the black suit. You could tie a tie all right, since you always had to wear Father's altered ties on Sundays, but this was your first grown-up tie. Grandmother said that would annoy the habit-wearing pissers, and when the boy asked what she meant he found out that he was to go to a boarding school run by monks. Grandmother always knew everything, because twice a week the cook had to tell her what was going on at the inn, but the boy hadn't known he was being sent off to the monks, and they were black monks who hated red, although they wore red garments themselves for many Church festivals. When the boy got home Mother took the tie away from him because of that, saying it wouldn't do for the entrance exam, and she would give him a grey one of Father's, which was elegant too. But the boy was sorry about the red tie, because it had been really lovely.

The entrance exam was a little while after Whitsun, and not much fun, because you had to get up very early to go to the station. You had to change trains in town, and then you went on in a real express. It was called an express because it stopped only at every other station, but even so there were three of them. The carriages were exciting, because they were first-class carriages, although you were travelling third class, but they were very old, with no corridor, only doors to the world outside and seats full of holes with the springs sticking out of them. The sun was shining, the suit was very hot, and when you sat on a spring because Mother happened to be looking out of the window the suit stood up to it. You got a brief glimpse of the Danube, and one station later was the boarding school. It was huge and yellow, and you could see it a long way off. From the station you had to go along an avenue past the town, with the office building, and then up a great many steps. Mother had to stop twice to get her breath back, and the boy was told that the boarding school was also a very famous monastery. Only a little way in, you went up a few steps to the right, and then there was a spiral staircase on the left, and a long corridor full of fathers and mothers and boys waiting for the entrance exam, most of them very excited.

Then two priests came in – they were called Fathers, but they looked like priests – all in black, but with an extra piece of black fabric hanging in front and at the back of their robes. This get-up was called a habit, and now the boy understood what Grandmother had been talking about when she said habit-wearing pissers, but he knew he mustn't say so now. They talked to the mothers and fathers and to Mother, and then the boys had to go into two rooms to take the entrance exam. An old Father supervised it, but it was easier than in school, you just had to write something to dictation and do a little arithmetic. Drawing was what the boy most enjoyed, because all you had to do was draw anything you liked. Since he was in a monastery the boy drew the prophet Jonah, and as he had plenty of time he drew him twice, first with the whale eating him, then with the whale spitting him out again. In the picture where he was being spat out the prophet's face emerged from the whale, and you could see the prophet's legs in its jaws and the prophet's behind between its teeth. The Father said the drawing was 'original', because the other boys had just drawn flowers or trees, and one of them drew a tank, red, white and red for Austria, with a gun mounted on the back. When you were asked to explain your drawing to the Father he said, 'Oh, so you stammer,' and some of the boys laughed. But you passed the entrance exam. Everyone passed, even one boy who had written 'Digdation' because he came from the Forest quarter and wanted to put on airs, for Grandmother said the clerics never let a groschen get away, although they had more than enough ducats. Ducats were gold coins, and you couldn't buy anything for a groschen, but she said that later, and now you had to go with Mother to see Father Columban, headmaster of the school, in his office. He congratulated Mother on your passing the entrance exam and took a payment from her. Then you had to go a floor higher to see Father Coelestin, who took more money and gave the boy a number. He was head of the boarding house, and very fat. He told Mother he'd soon cure the lad of that stammer, and then you went down the steps to the town, where you got an ice because you had passed the entrance exam, and the train home didn't go until much later.

Soon after that your time at primary school was over, and you had to sit for a class photo. The teacher joined you all, and said something about his children and how he was proud of them, though in fact he didn't have any. The others would now have four years of secondary school, then some would get apprenticeships, and the farmers' children wouldn't have to study any more, they could work at home. Two houses further on there was a wheelwright's with a big workshop where nothing was going on, and the girls practised office work there almost every afternoon. The more important girls held pieces of wood and pretended to be telephoning all the time, and the others had to carry pieces of paper about, or put water into empty bottles, making out that it was coffee. But the boy knew from his grandparents what a real office looked like, and he knew that the real bosses seldom did their own telephoning. They had employees to do that. But the oldest girl said when she was a real secretary it would all be different, because she'd chase up the boss. Yet she was in Class Two at secondary school and had stayed down a year, but that didn't help the boy, because he was one of the nobs that no one listened to, and sometimes, when he was walking along the road, a working-class boy threw horse dung at him and then hid quickly so that his parents wouldn't hear about it. But you had learned from your grandparents never to tell on anyone.

Then the Brazilian suddenly turned up again. You still remembered him, although you had really forgotten him, but he looked almost the same. But Herr Lustiger hadn't come from Brazil, he'd never got there, only as far as Shanghai. They'd had the war there too, war with the Japanese, and when the Japanese weren't around any more he went back to Bohemia to take charge of his factories again. But Herr Gottwald[66] had taken them over, saying they belonged to the people now, and so here was Herr Lustiger coming back to see the boy's grandparents. He was very sad, even though the war was over, and Grandfather said he couldn't help him. Then Herr Lustiger went to America, but not to Brazil, to the USA, and he gave the boy a little golden Star of David on a very thin chain. But Mother took it away from him because he was a Christian. Much later a postcard came from Herr Lustiger in Philadelphia, but you could hardly read it for all the Russian rubber stamps on it, and the postage stamp had been cut off too. That didn't matter, because you didn't collect stamps, and the Star of David had been much nicer, but it was gone.

Mother was gargling scales again, because she was to sing in Salzburg that summer, and altering a pale blue garment on the sewing machine, which she called a beach dress for the Mattsee. The boy looked forward to the Mattsee, but he was badly beaten because he had done something wrong with the bottle of carbonic acid by the beer tap, and now there wasn't any to make the beer fizzy. Only bottled beer could be sold until new carbonic acid came from town, and by then the beer in the barrel would have gone sour. Mother said the boy wasn't coming to Salzburg with her. At first he was rather sad, but then he thought about going to see the farmers, in the woods and everywhere he couldn't usually go, because Mother wouldn't be here. However, a day before she left, he was to go with her after all, and that was good too, because of the Mattsee.

This time there was no chewing gum on the border between the Russians and the Yanks, and you had to pay for the Cola, because the Commies weren't in the government any more, and the Yanks didn't have to put out so much propaganda against them. It was a pity, really, because they were the only place you could get Coca-Cola, it wasn't even available in the bars of their zone of occupation, but they sold it at a very high price, and Mother said their propaganda wasn't worth that much.

Stefan and Liesel's father was in the dairy behind the Festspielhaus, with a younger man called Herr Wagner,[67] whose grandfather was a god to many people, but he was banned now. However, Herr Wagner said all that would soon be over, and then all the good people would be needed, because it would be back to what it was before, only a little different. Then an old man came by who wagged his chin and was called Klemperer.[68] He stopped and said this was all he needed, and the grown-ups looked at their glasses and said nothing.

Later, Mother told the boy that Herr Klemperer was not a nice person, and it was wrong to listen to other people's conversations, that was why no one could stand him. And Stefan and Liesel's father said after a while, but by then Herr Klemperer wasn't around, well, now all the Jews who'd been forgotten would be back, and Herr Wagner said nothing. Then he was told he ought to insist at the denazification tribunal that his grandfather's certificate of Aryan descent wasn't quite kosher either, and he could ask for reparations now, but he got angry, saying he was not of Jewish descent, that was just a Jewish invention because to the Jews all men of genius had to be somehow Jewish, and when the boy asked quietly what that meant he was told it was nothing to do with him, and he'd better not join in other people's conversations. This time he didn't see much of Salzburg, because the grown-ups were in a bad mood, but Herr Zinnhobel was waiting at the bus stop in Mattsee, because they'd announced their arrival in advance.

Next day, however, there was trouble by the big linden tree at the bus stop near the junction of the road to Salzburg and Ochsenharing, and right behind it was a big old farmhouse with a little metal plaque saying it was the first hereditary farmhouse in the Salzburg area. There was a bench in front of it where the big boys were sitting and smoking, as was expected of them. The bathing beach had closed, and you were waiting for Mother, who was coming back from her rehearsal by bus. The big boys were practising blowing smoke rings. One of them told the boy he could blow smoke out of his eyes too, he just had to look at him very hard. The boy looked, but then the other boy pressed the cigarette into his leg above the knee. They all laughed a lot, but it hurt, and was sore afterwards so that you couldn't go bathing for days, and then the weather turned bad. Herr Zinnhobel had seen what happened, and he told the boy to think nothing of it, it was just the Salzburg sense of humour.

A few days later you went to Salzburg to eat noodle soup with beef in the Peterskeller. It wasn't really a cellar, but a big cave in the rock with people waiting on tables, right next to the cemetery and the Festspielhaus. The soup had just been served when there was a lot of fuss at the table next to yours because some people were arriving. Three of them wore Styrian suits, because they were official Austrians, and the smallest had a moustache like the Führer's, but he was the Austrian chancellor. He ordered a dish of sausage, ham and eggs, and a litre of local Prälatenwein, but he wasn't going to drink all the wine himself, because several glasses were brought. Then the men talked in very loud voices. One of them was the Foreign Minister and was called Gruber.[69] They were telling him he ought to put pressure on the occupying powers, who liked it so much in Austria that they wanted to stay. Then another litre of wine was brought, and you and Mother had only half finished your soup. When Mother asked the waiter for the bill they were already on the third litre; by the time she got her change they had finished that too. Then the Chancellor said, 'Well, here we go, we have the principle of the thing now!' and as you left Mother said those gentlemen had an important meeting soon with the Western occupying powers about the freedom of Austria.

You yourself, however, were taken by bus to Hellbrunn. A Prince Archbishop[70] had built it as a summer residence for himself and his mistress, and they liked splashing about in the water. It was wet everywhere, and people got wet too and squealed. Though they only had to look and see where all the little jets of water were, but they wanted to squeal because it was hot. So the boy ran through the water once too, when no one was looking, but he didn't squeal because he wasn't a child any more. There were a great many toys in the park as well, all water-driven, because the Prince Archbishop and his mistress must have had very childish tastes. But they didn't even have a gramophone, water-driven or otherwise, just dolls, and no lavatory either. The Archbishop probably peed in the little streams, and there were a lot of fish still waiting for him. Since fish are stupid, they didn't know that the Archbishop was dead.

There were a lot of Philharmonic musicians' children in Mattsee, whom you knew from the previous year. They had all grown, and the Philharmonic mothers said the coffee in the Water-Lily Café had improved, but they didn't have to drink too much of it, because the weather was still fine. Only when the Festival opened did the bad weather come, as usual.

Mother was not in a good temper, because she wasn't to come and sing again next year, and she had thought she would earn money again then and do something with it. Sometimes she was cross with the boy's grandparents, who had delivered her up to the working classes, but there weren't any of those in Mattsee, and you didn't see many in Salzburg either. Then she told the boy that once he was in the boarding school she would have an easier time of it, which was exactly what the boy was thinking himself. Of course he didn't like the idea of living there with a lot of boys, because he knew about boys, and how horrible they are, and how one of them always plays the part of Führer and then they find themselves a Jew. He mustn't be a strong boy, of course, or it would have been no fun. The boy's grandparents had said it didn't just happen in the village, but everywhere where there was black soot about the place, and the Fathers at the boarding school were black too. Grandmother said they were black through and through, because the colour of their habits ran all the way inside them, except for their hearts, which were brown,[71] but so were all hearts in Austria. However, the boy thought it would be easier for him there than with Mother. Grandmother said she was going through the change of life, but she hadn't changed in a way that anyone would have noticed.

When you had this conversation your time at Mattsee was over. Mother was still there, because she had to sing for two more weeks, but the boy was back and enjoying the rest of the holidays, because the inn was on holiday too, and you had to go there only in the evening, since Grandmother said she wanted to see something of the boy. It wasn't so good that she wanted the boy to go and see Frau Wittmann, who had cancer and already looked very pale. There was nothing you could do about that, and Grandmother gave the boy a dark red tie of Grandfather's to persuade him to go, and he had to take a bunch of flowers from the nursery garden. At first there was almost nothing to see, since the light from outside was too bright for Frau Wittmann, and Herr Wittmann had had to draw the curtains. Frau Wittmann was sitting in the armchair by the window, looking pale, just as Grandmother had said, and people always did as Grandmother told them. The boy was reminded of a slice of cheese in the larder of the inn. A slice that had been cut long ago and then forgotten, all thin and dried up. Frau Wittmann had dark brown spots on her skin in many places, and a kind of mould on some of them, and she spoke very slowly and quietly. The boy thanked her for everything, as Grandmother had told him to do, and Frau Wittmann said she had always done her best for the boy. Yet she always used to say one should never tell fibs. You had never liked

Frau Wittmann, but there was nothing you could do about it, because she had been Mother's governess and was soon going to die, but you didn't want to say so to her now. Then she reached into an old jar of sweets beside her chair and gave the boy a chocolate. It was very old too, and all grey, and when you had to put it in your mouth it tasted musty. You didn't want to eat it, and pushed it into your cheek. Then you said you needed to pee, and Herr Wittmann said he'd show you where, and you had better say goodbye now. So you kissed Frau Wittmann's hand and went with Herr Wittmann, who showed you the lavatory and said now you could spit the chocolate out. When all that was done, you asked Herr Wittmann when Frau Wittmann was going to die, and he looked very sad and said he didn't know. Then he told the boy a lot of things, because he had been married to her for fifty years. The denazification tribunal had ruined them both, he said, yet they had been entirely innocent. Under the Emperor the teachers' union of southern Austria had made sure that the Germans in Transylvania got German school books – manuals, he called them – because the Hungarians would give them only Hungarian books, and Grandfather didn't approve of that, although he was really a Hungarian himself. Then the Romanians had come after the war, and then the Germans had really needed books, but Grandfather wouldn't pay for them any more, and Herr Rosenberg had taken to paying the bills. And then Herr Himmler had helped to pay too, because he had a great many very rich friends, but Grandfather wasn't to know anything about that because he didn't like Herr Himmler. But the Russians had found out, and were angry with Herr and Frau Wittmann. So Grandmother had forgiven him too, but now Herr Wittmann didn't know how he was going to live without his wife. Then he took a silver watch out of his pocket. It was called Omega and was very battered. He gave it to the boy, trembling, and his eyes were all wet. In fact it was some time yet before

Frau Wittmann died, but Herr Wittmann was much nicer than he used to be.

When you told your grandparents that, Grandfather said that at the end many people became what they always should have been, but it was too late for that to be any use.

RE-EDUCATION

There was a lot to be done in preparation for boarding school, and the boy had to chase around a great deal. The monastery had only sea-grass mattresses from the time when there was a Napola there, and they were worn out and stank so much that you took your own. Grandmother looked out two old horsehair mattresses which dated from your great-grandparents' time, made of horsehair from Lipizzaners. You pushed them up to the village on your bike and took them to the upholsterer's, where they were cut open, and the horsehair was rolled up in the workshop yard. It was done on a machine with a hand-turned crank, and made a great deal of dust. But there was still some horsehair left, and it was stretched over sacks with wire in them to make interior spring mattresses. Next day the finished mattresses were brought back, and Mother said Herr Wrskovic hadn't stretched the springs properly, because the mattresses weren't smooth but bumpy. Herr Wrskovic took twenty per cent off his bill, but the mattresses were still uneven and got even knobblier with time. However, they were clearly marked with the boy's number, 89.

A long ribbon with red 89s all over it came from town too, and Grandmother's seamstresses cut it up and sewed the numbers to all the boy's bed linen, shirts, undershirts, trousers, underpants, pyjamas, even handkerchiefs, and then they embroidered red dots beside all the numbers, because they said monastery washerwomen were very stupid and could easily mix 89 up with 68. Everything else the boy was to take was marked 89, from his butter dish to his cutlery and his penknife. 89 was scratched, engraved or carved into everything, yet it wasn't your name at all. But Grandmother said it had been like that in the war, people became just numbers, and it was never too soon to get used to the next war. She talked to the boy a lot these days, because she said she didn't know if she would ever see him again. But the boy said if he was to be a number, this was a good one, because it wasn't easy to divide, at most you could make it into $5 \times 10 + 3 \times 13$, and he got used to thinking he must like being 89. It wasn't easy to say, though.

On the first Saturday in September all his things were put on a small truck, a new one belonging to the factory. Or rather, it wasn't really new, but an old Wehrmacht vehicle that had been rebuilt with wood at the back and painted brown, and now it was loaded up with the mattresses, a suitcase full of bed linen, and another with the boy's number on it containing his other things. Herr Mandi was driving, and as there were only two seats you perched on a board between him and Mother, with the gear change between your knees. There was a blanket on the board, but it jolted a lot, since sometimes Mother's seat and sometimes Herr Mandi's seat wobbled, and once, going over a pothole, you fell against fourth gear, which hurt a lot. Then the boarding school came in sight, but Herr Mandi didn't stop but drove on and then up the hill, through the little courtyard, through the big courtyard with a fountain in it, and right into another yard which wasn't small either, and had a little fountain in it. This was called the Inn Yard, and the school was built around it on the first floor, with the boarding house on the floor above. Herr Mandi carried the things in, and Mother took the boy to see Father Coelestin, who took some money and looked at a list to see where he was going to put the boy. He was in Dormitory 4, where most of the new boys went, and outside it was a very dark corridor, with cupboards. One of them was his. It had his number on the door, and it was so dirty inside that he had to wash it out first. There were a few boards to take the bed linen and a locker for food; his clothes hung on the right and his shoes stood there too, and up above, beyond his reach, the case wouldn't fit in because the cupboard was too small. There were other mothers and fathers there too, all of them cross about the cupboards, and in the dormitories all the parents who hadn't seen the mattresses already were cross too. Some of the Fathers were walking up and down, but they weren't enjoying having to talk to the parents. You could tell from their faces. Father Coelestin's was very red, and he was baring his teeth in an effort to smile in a natural way. There was a fat man with a moustache, who had a very red face too, and was talking to him in a loud voice. Father Coelestin called him Departmental Head, which must have been something very special in Austria, because Father Coelestin invited him into his room, and after a while a manservant came and put different mattresses on his son's bed. But a father who was a butcher saw that, and when Father Coelestin and the Departmental Head came back he got so worked up that the Departmental Head went straight off, and Father Coelestin said he didn't have time to discuss it now because he had to pray.

Then all the Fathers went off to pray together for an hour, and the parents were left alone with their sons. There were twenty-six boys, all in Class One, because the higher classes weren't coming until Sunday. They knew the boarding school already and didn't need to spend a night getting used to it. There were in fact a few older new boys for the higher classes who had been at other schools before. The parents talked to each other, saying who they were, and how important they were, and how important this school was, and the boys stood around looking warily at each other. Then Mother and Herr Mandi went to the Monastery Cellar restaurant with the boy. Mother had a small plate of sliced meats and cheese; Herr Mandi had a large one and two quarter-litres of wine, because he needed something inside him for the drive home, and the boy had a ham sandwich and apple juice with soda water. Mother said they obviously didn't drink apple juice here much, because there was a piece of mould floating on top of the glass, and the waiter had to bring a new one, which he did very reluctantly. The boy saw him at the bar pouring the contents of the glass with mould on it through a tea strainer into another glass, and then bringing it back. Mother said the boys' parents were very high class: lawyers, medical superintendents, high-ranking ministerial civil servants. Although a third of them were butchers from around Vienna, because butchers had got very rich after the war.

When you left the cellar and returned to the boarding house the Fathers were back, and the parents said goodbye to their children. The boy was glad he didn't have to give Mother a kiss, and she drove home with Herr Mandi. Then Father Coelestin took the boys into the Museum. It wasn't a museum, but quite a large room with five rows of desks, and the boy was to study there when there was no school going on. The desks had pigeon-holes on top, you couldn't see over them, and drawers down below to take your school things. They were made of wood and painted in wood colours, brown and yellow, but they were very uneven because so many pupils had carved their names on them, and other things too. Someone had carved a cunt inside the drawer of the desk given to the boy, fitting it round a knothole in the wood, and he put a piece of paper over it. Then you were all shown where the wash-rooms were, and there was only cold water. But you were told you could shower once a month on the ground floor, where there would be hot water too. Then you went down the spiral staircase to the playground, which you had seen already at the entrance examination. It was uneven, with a wall and trees round the edge. There was a handball pitch in the middle, and everything was very dusty. A wooden gate led to the park, but it was locked, because you couldn't go in there, it was only for the Fathers. Then you were taken back to the Museum, and after a while the big old bell that you had already seen rang, and then you had to go to the refectory.

The refectory was two floors down, round several corners, large and vaulted, and there were plaster decorations like chicken giblets on the ceiling, like the ones in the Baroque Wing at Grandfather and Grandmother's. It was a handsome ceiling really, but there were ugly tables under it smelling of soft soap, and boxes with nasty tin cutlery in them. The boy didn't mind that, because Grandmother had given him his own cutlery, which he was always to wash himself. The boys had to sit at the lower end of the table, because the upper end belonged to the bigger boys who hadn't arrived yet. Some of the bigger boys who were there all the same were seated where they belonged, but all the gaps looked funny, like the old cook's false teeth. Then Father Coelestin gave a long talk about how you were with monks now, where food was intended only to fortify you for prayer, for it had been said since the time of Augustine that a full stomach was a lazy one, and one day you would think yourselves lucky to have studied in this famous boarding school. Then he taught the boys another prayer: 'All eyes are turned upon you, O Lord. You give food at the right time, and fill all that you give with blessing.' Then you all had to say an Our Father and a Hail Mary, and then came supper. It was a special supper, said Father Coelestin, because you were new to the monastery, and generous hospitality was the duty of all monks, and there were fried smoked sausages in lard with potatoes cooked to a mush. It was all cold because Father Coelestin had talked for such a long time, and there was a butcher's son sitting next to you who whispered that he'd never seen such tiny sausages before. Then Father Coelestin said you weren't to talk while you ate. He didn't eat any of the sausages himself, but walked up and down between the tables. Then he saw the boy's cutlery and took it away, because it was much too valuable for him, and no one was to have special favours. As it had already been used he wrapped it in the boy's napkin, because such a thing didn't belong in a monastery either. Sure enough, there weren't any napkins, and some of the boys didn't even know what they were for, but you were annoyed because your number was embroidered on the napkins and engraved on the cutlery. Father Coelestin added in a very loud voice that you were not among the nobs here, and some of the boys giggled. But the tin cutlery that the boy had to fetch was so smeared and slimy that he didn't want to eat the sausages with it, they were cold anyway, and the fat they had been fried in had solidified on the plate and turned grey. Some of the other boys were disgusted by it too, but Father Coelestin said they'd be glad one day to get anything to eat at all, and then he taught them all a prayer to be said after meals because the Lord had been so kind.

After supper you were sent back to the Museum, but there was nothing to learn, and the boy was worried about his cutlery. So he went down to the refectory again. Father Coelestin wasn't there. The boy found him in a room next to the kitchen, eating roast chicken with two other Fathers. Father Coelestin's face went red above the napkin tucked into his throat, and said that at the very most the boy's parents would get the cutlery back, and when the boy said he only had a mother Father Coelestin said, 'Ah yes, the war criminal! Prussian riff-raff!' and the other Fathers laughed, because Father Coelestin was their superior. Later you were all sent to the chapel for evening prayers, only it wasn't a real chapel, but a big room with a few pieces of sacred furniture in front and a harmonium at the back, and then you had to go to bed. There was only a chair in the dormitory for your things, and when you were in bed a Father came to inspect you and put out the light. He didn't put it right out, but switched on a blue lamp, called a nightlight, which kept you from sleeping. It took a long time to get used to it. One of the butchers' sons snored terribly, and a boy from Vienna was crying because he was homesick. It was horrible.

On Sunday you were all woken at seven. First you heard the big bell in the corridor, then a Father came along calling, 'Get up!' and went straight off again. This time you were first in the wash-room, and the water came out rusty for a while before it ran clean. The boy thought of the lead pipes at his grandparents' house and the inn. They were supposed to be in bad condition too, so he'd heard, but at least the water ran clean at once, and the monastery water disgusted the boy when he was cleaning his teeth. But there wasn't any other, and you even had to drink it. As there were only battered aluminium mugs for that, the boy was glad to have his own with him. It had once belonged to Father, and was a present from the Buchholz anti-aircraft artillery training centre, and the silversmith in town had filed the swastika off and engraved the boy's number in its place. The gilding had worn off it now, but you could drink from it only secretly, because your cutlery had gone, and you had to hide the mug under your shirts.

Your shirts immediately gave trouble anyway. Mother had altered several of Father's pastel-coloured shirts for you. She still had a great many because before the war she and Father had often gone to Italy and brought a few dozen new shirts home with them. You had put on Grandfather's dark red tie too, the one that Grandmother had taken from his wardrobe, but when you went into the Museum dressed like that Father

Coelestin, who was standing at the door, said, 'Oho, a silk shirt! Aren't we stuck-up!' and when you tried to explain that you weren't, Father Coelestin said, 'Snobs like you are riff-raff. You're a stuck-up snob and a stuttering splutterer too.' Some of the boys who had just come in too heard that and laughed. And you had been trying to say very little, so that no one would notice your speech impediment.

Then a Father came along who wasn't really a Father but a Brother, and wore a leather belt instead of a fabric one. His name was Ansgar, he rang the bell, and then you all had to line up in pairs. Since the boy was feeling upset because of Father Coelestin, he stood right at the back. But you weren't going to breakfast, you were going to a staircase you hadn't seen before, one floor lower and then along a corridor to the hall that you remembered from your earlier visit to the monastery. But this time you were a floor higher, and when you tapped the breastwork that looked like stone it was really wood. A little further on you came to a very long corridor. Pictures of the rulers of Austria hung between the windows, lots and lots of them. Most had been painted in the Baroque period, so that each looked like his neighbour, and their names and what they had done had to be written underneath them. The Habsburgs all had Habsburg lips, but even those painted after the Baroque period looked very foolish, as if someone had been trying to paint pictures of saints. Without his beard, Emperor Franz Joseph still looked very young, and you would have liked to read what all the others did, but Brother Ansgar swept the boys along too fast. Sometimes there were emperors hanging on both walls, and the windows opposite had doors with spittoons fitted in front of them. Your grandparents had some of those too, specially for when they had colds, but you never saw them. Perhaps habit-wearing pissers were proud of being able to spit like working-class children. But then you all went down a spiral staircase to the right, and you were at the back of a church. It was very colourful and Baroque, and when you had to sit on the pews your legs dangled. A few more people came through a side door, and then came the Fathers, a great many of them, who sat in the decorated pews at the front of the church, and when the organ began to boom the service was in full swing. It was all like the village church at home, but much louder and more colourful.

When it was all over Brother Ansgar asked the boy why he hadn't come up to take communion, and you could hardly tell him you didn't like what they put into your mouth, so you said it was a long time since you had confessed. Then you had better do it this evening, said Brother Ansgar, and after that you could all get your breakfast things from the lockers and go to the refectory for breakfast.

Breakfast was horrible. Sliced rye and wheat bread lay there all cheap and sticky, and it had been cut so long before that it was beginning to curl up. There was red jam of some kind with it, and very thin ersatz coffee with milk, and a slice of sausage because it was Sunday, as Father Coelestin said. He was walking up and down between the tables again. The butchers' sons all had thick sausages and bacon from home with them. The boy had butter too, and a salami from Grandmother, but he didn't want to cut into it yet, so he showed the butcher's son next to him how to make a slice of sausage go a long way, as he had learnt to do when the war was still on. You put a slice of sausage on a large piece of bread, pushing it ahead of you with your teeth, and biting off only a small piece of sausage every time, until at the end of the slice you had a proper piece of bread entirely covered with sausage to eat. The butcher's son hadn't known how to do that, and he was really surprised.

After that you had time off to go into the playground. But the boy had noticed the way to the church and he wanted to look at the emperors. He knew most of them from books, but he wanted to read what it said about them under their pictures. They were all Emperors by the Grace of God, and very devout, but the spelling was funny. They were all renowned too, and the last emperor of all, whose widow was still living in Switzerland, had died 'of a broken heart', but you knew from Grandmother that it was really flu. You were just reading about Frederick the Fair[72] when you suddenly found yourself facing a little man with a big beard. He was called Herr Hirthentaler; he had long white hair, and his beard was yellow around his mouth. He was the librarian. After you had talked a little, he was kind enough to show you the library. It was brightly coloured like the church, and much, much bigger than the boys' grandparents' library. Herr Hirthentaler also showed the boy some very valuable books dating from the Middle Ages, when people couldn't print yet but they painted very beautifully, and you had never seen anything like it before. His wife was sitting in a little study. She was very old too, and wasn't really allowed into the monastery because she was a woman, so she and her husband lived in town, but he never came home until the evening. Herr Hirthentaler said that he had once wanted to be a monk himself, but then he thought better of it, so he became a librarian, and now the boy must go back to the boarding house because it was lunch-time.

When you got into the refectory the other boys had already said grace, and no one else was being served. You didn't mind that when you saw the food. But it was unpleasant that Father Coelestin told the boy off in a very loud voice about order and discipline, and when you told him what you had been doing he said a library was no place for a stuttering splutterer, and the other boys laughed, because Father Coelestin was the housemaster. When the lunch you didn't eat was over, you still had to give thanks to God for his gifts.

Then you all had to get into a crocodile, two abreast, and go for a walk with Father Thomas. He was very friendly, a Bohemian and the natural history teacher, and he kept looking back to make sure all the boys were there. You were walking quite near the back yourself, with the butcher's son who sat next to you in the refectory, and he told you a lot about how rich his parents had grown since the war, and how they had Persian carpets everywhere now, and his mother had a great many diamond rings. He said 'didamand rings', and you didn't say anything, because the boys had laughed at you when Father Coelestin called you a stuttering splutterer. The walk was very boring, since it went first through the town, and then along the roads and the embankment to a little village, where you turned and walked back again. On the way back through town you found twenty groschen in your pocket, and you could have bought yourself an ice lolly, but Father Thomas wouldn't allow it because you would have had to step out of your place in the crocodile. Then he said that many boys didn't even have twenty groschen, and one had to think of them, and most of the boys laughed because they had far more money than that in their own pockets.

It was very busy back at the boarding house, because the bigger pupils had arrived. Some of the really big boys even came on their own without their parents, and were proud of it, bringing only one suitcase because their parents would arrive in a few days' time with the rest of their things. Those parents knew about the cupboards already, and many had brought their own mattresses for the boys, so they didn't have to get so cross, and Father Coelestin walked up and down among them in a very important way. Other Fathers turned up too, because they already knew the parents, but there was a certain amount of bad feeling over places in the dormitories all the same, and if the parents were influential their sons were moved somewhere else.

The older boy who told him this was called Dingo and came from the Waldviertel district, where his father was a doctor. He was in Class Three himself, and knew his way around the boarding school, and he told the boy that the

Fathers didn't like to see older and younger boys talking together because it was God's will for everyone to stick to his own age group. But Dingo added that they said so only to keep people from finding out what really went on in the monastery too quickly, because if they did no one would take any of it seriously.

Over the following days the boy learned a great deal about the boarding school and the monastery where he had ended up, because he wanted to know why this had been done to him. He thought that if he knew all about it then he would know the reason why too, but it wasn't simple. The Fathers talked a lot, but most of it was boring and much of it you didn't want to believe. The older schoolboys talked a good deal too, and told a lot of stories. You weren't really supposed to talk to them, because a first-year boy was inferior to a second-year boy, let alone a sixth-year boy, and the seventh-year boys even shared a smoking-room with the eighth-year boys, and they were the biggest of all. Consequently they were very arrogant too, and would call a boy 'First-year King' as an insult. The Fathers told the younger boys that everyone should stay with his own class and not mix with the others, and for that very reason they did talk to each other now and then. But it was seldom interesting, because the boys were all very keen to say how marvellous they were, and it was just the same as with the Fathers. You had a great many questions to ask Herr Hirthentaler, and he would say almost nothing for a long time, but when he did tell you anything it meant a great deal.

The yellow flagstones in all the corridors were Kelheim stone, and very valuable because they had been brought here from Bavaria centuries ago, but that wasn't why there had been war with the Bavarians, and though the other new boys gaped, you were used to them from your grandparents' house, where they hadn't been as badly worn as these before the

Russians came. You were familiar with the smell of oil on the floors and soft soap in the dormitories from the inn, and you couldn't make out why the Fathers talked so much about those valuable flagstones and how clean they were; Dingo said it was because they didn't have carpets to sweep things under, but they had carpets in their own rooms, and they weren't clean either.

Some of the Fathers liked each other and some didn't, and only Herr Hirthentaler could say why. Some had been with the Cock's Tail-Feathers, others had been Nazis, and then there were some who were just Fathers. It wasn't easy to find out who had been what, since the Fathers were all given different names when they joined the monastery. But they had kept their surnames, and if those were Bohemian or Czech, Croat or Serbian, they were Cock's Tail-Feathers. That organization had been modern in Austria when the Führer began to be leader in Germany, but they modelled themselves on the Duce,[73] who had been leading Italy longer. So they also called themselves Austro-Fascists, and the churchmen among them were well off because the Duce was friendly with the Pope too. Their own version of the Sturmabteilung[74] or SA was the Heimwehr,[75] and they wore cockerel's tail feathers in their hatbands, and after they had beaten the Socialists they all sang, 'Red, white and red, until our deathbed.' But they didn't have to die when the Führer came, because other Fathers had been Nazis although it was really forbidden at the time. Most of them had German names, and they had become Nazis because although the Führer might not be very religious he was very severe with the Jews. And as a Catholic of course you had to be against the Jews, because they had a lot of money and had killed the Lord Jesus, and even if they didn't have any money there was still the Lord Jesus to think of, and they didn't want to be Christians. It said even in the Bible that they had called for his blood to be upon their heads and their children's, so a good Christian had to make the Jews bleed, or shed their blood, which wasn't so easy now because Jews didn't have to wear identifying marks any more, and they were crafty and disguised themselves. None of this was easy to understand, and once Father Coelestin said that Hitler had not been a Christian at all because he had gassed the Jews, which meant that not enough blood had flowed, and he ought to have butchered them, as Christians who were well-versed in the Bible did. But Father Christoph said that was a Cock's Tail-Feather saying, because they hadn't liked the Jews either but they soft-soaped them to get at their money. Hitler had been more honest because he didn't beat about the bush so much. Father Christoph taught geography, because he had been in France and had lost a leg there. But you heard similar remarks from Father Romuald, who taught Latin and gave comfort to war widows in the town, and Father Bonaventura taught Religious Studies and said none of that meant anything, because we were living in Austria, and Austria had not existed at the time. That wasn't easy to understand either, but this was how the Fathers explained it: Austria was the greatest and best country in the world, and it had stayed that way even when it suddenly shrank and was very small. When it was great it had the Emperors, who had been very devout up to Emperor Joseph, and then along came the priest Seipel[76] and Dr Dollfuss,[77] who had been very religious God-fearing men too, and had opposed the godless Jewish socialists. And when the Führer came along there was no more Austria, so there couldn't be any Nazis in Austria. Of course there were a few, but as Austria didn't exist they were of the Prussian type, and those weren't Austrians, as anyone could see, because the *Magna Mater Austriae*, the Great Mother of Austria, was the Virgin Mary, whereas the Prussians prayed to Germania who had no son of her own. Before Hitler came along, however, there had been a very few Nazis in Austria, but after they murdered Dr Dollfuss they had either been executed or run off to Hitler, which made them Prussians. The only imaginable Nazi in Austria, then, said Father Bonaventura, was probably the boy, because he had been a Prussian born in Austria while it still existed, and that made the other boys laugh, but the boy was upset about Father Bonaventura.

But Dingo said Father Bonaventura was telling a few fibs there, because his own parents had been in the Party too, although they weren't Prussians. And such was the case with many of the boys' parents, as you could tell from many little details. Some boys at the school were cousins because their fathers were brothers, but they had quite different names. One was called Czerny and the other Schwarz, which both meant the same, but one said it in Bohemian and the other in the teaching language, and then there were Sedlacek and Sedelmaier, which showed you who had been deeply involved with the Party and who had kept more of a distance. And you could also tell from noticing which Father liked which pupils better, Bohemians or those who spoke the teaching language; but the Fathers had to tolerate each other even if it didn't come easily, and when they met in a crowd they would embrace each other very stiffly, calling it the fraternal kiss. It looked like the Commies on the weekly newsreel that you couldn't watch any more, but you remembered it from the village. However, they were all Austrians and conservative now.

Of course you learned other things too. In Latin with Father Romuald you had to decline *rosa rosam rosae*, and as the boy found the letter R difficult to pronounce Father Romuald said some funny things that made the whole class laugh except for you. There were more boys in the school itself than in the boarding house, because some came from the seminary for priests, a hill further away, and there were day boys from the town. The boys from the seminary were mostly farmers' children gathered in from all over Lower Austria, because they either had too many siblings for them to be able to inherit anything themselves, or their parents had once been ill or in difficulties and had promised the Virgin Mary to give their boy to God if she helped them. Many of them didn't want to be priests later, and only said so now because the bishop was paying for their education for the priesthood, and then they were going to change their minds. But when they said something like that it mustn't be within the hearing of any Father, because there were also boys in the monastery who would have to be Fathers later, and they ought not to hear such things in case it put bad ideas into their minds. You saw these boys only in school, because they lived in their hostel, and had to go straight back to it, and there weren't many of them. They got the same food as the Fathers to make them want to be Fathers themselves some day, so they looked down on the boys in the boarding house who had horrible meals. If one of those boys changed his mind the Fathers were very angry, and the boy was thrown out of the hostel and the school. The bishop wasn't so stern, because he lived a long way off and couldn't hear what the boys were talking about. There weren't many day boys, and their parents, like those of the boys in the boarding house, were 'the better class of people', and there weren't many of those down in town at all, but they were far better off than the boarders because they could live with their parents and ate different food. They didn't have to go for walks either and laughed at the boarders for it. The parents of one of these boys had a butcher's shop, and he often brought sausage to school and sold it in secret to boarders whose parents had sent them some money, but he was mean about it and sold it only on Fridays when you weren't allowed to eat meat. That was the kind of reason why it was better not to talk to the day boys, even in the playground at break. They always kept together then, and Dingo said the Fathers liked it that way, because then we wouldn't find out that they were better off.

When the boys talked it was better not to call things by their right names anyway. The younger pupils had learned that from the older boys, and you called Father Bonaventura the Whiner, and Brother Ansgar was Ganef, a word for a rascal. None of you obeyed him the way you obeyed the Fathers, because he was only a Brother, and very often, at least once a morning, he lost his temper and hit anyone within reach with anything he could lay hands on. Then his weapon was broken, because books and rulers aren't meant for hitting people, and sometimes he pulled out hair until he had enough of a handful. Then he would gasp for air and say things you didn't understand, and afterwards he panted and was all right again. Father Thomas was nicknamed Duck, because he taught biology and on walks always took good care that the boys were walking along properly after him, because he liked to walk with the younger boys, but only on boring, level roads. He wasn't fast, and it was fun to watch him waddling along. In addition you only had to sing a few bars before he went very red in the face, but he never hit out, and it was funny to hear him talking crossly. There were some songs he didn't like at all, and with some you could usually sing only two lines before he shut you up. One song was set in the Wild West and began very sadly:

It was a rainy night in the prairie
And the cowboys sat close together
Farting to keep themselves warm.

You would have liked to know how that song went on, but you never found out. Sometimes other boys said they'd tell you, but then they forgot, and you didn't dare ask them because talking wasn't easy for you, and they might make fun of you the way they'd learnt from the Fathers. But Father Thomas never made fun of you, because he was kind, and his one pleasure was entering pupils' names in the class register. It always lay locked in the teacher's desk, and the Fathers wrote in it that they had been there, and what they had taught, but sometimes they wrote other things too, and that was not so good, because then there would be punishments and it affected your marks. But Father Thomas wrote so much that it made no difference, and once, when a boy farted, he wrote that in the book too.

It was bad, however, when Father Richard wrote in the register, because he did that only very seldom, and it was horrible. He was mocked because he couldn't say the letter S well, perhaps because his surname was Cucinac. He taught maths, physics and chemistry, and the Fathers said he had once been a very famous scholar and would surely have won the Nobel Prize if Hitler hadn't come along. It was very difficult to understand him when he talked about maths, physics or chemistry, and he would say that was because the boys didn't want to be scholars. He was all right otherwise, though.

You had been in the boarding school for six weeks, and it was an art lesson when a boy came back to the art room from the lavatory and said there was this weird car standing in the Inn Yard, he'd never seen one like it before. All the boys ran to the window, but it was difficult to see through the trees, so many of them had to go to the lavatory, but not the boy, since he wasn't very interested in cars any more. When you went back into the boarding house Brother Ansgar said you were to go down to the yard, and there was Grandfather's Maybach with Herr Buchlar. He was not in a very good temper, and had a chamois leather in his hand because the boys kept touching the car and trying to look through the windows, and your grandparents were in the Monastery Cellar.

Grandfather said he hadn't really wanted to come, it was Grandmother's idea, although she usually only drove to funerals and then went in the Zeugerl, and the wine could be better than it was. If they drank this kind of stuff at Mass, all the Fathers ought to turn atheist. Grandmother was eating a plate of sliced meat and cheese and was pleased because her cheese was much better than what they served here, and she had brought a large parcel for the boy. Frau Wittmann was still dying, but it wouldn't be long now, and then Herr Wittmann would go into an old people's home, because he was good for nothing any more. She herself might sometimes feel she'd been dragged through a thorn bush backwards, but she was a woman, and women are tougher than men who don't have to bear children. Then she ordered a small plate of sliced meat and cheese for the boy, and a raspberry water, while Grandfather made his way through the wines, tasting them. Then he asked the boy if the Fathers were at least good teachers, useless as they were at making wine, and the boy told him what he had found out by now about the monastery.

Suddenly Father Coelestin came along. The boy saw him just in time, but Grandfather didn't, and Father Coelestin tried to kiss Grandfather's hand and called him Serene Highness. Grandfather said he hadn't been that since 1918, and he wondered what period Father Coelestin was living in. Father Coelestin said it was the fitting way to behave in a monastery, and went red in the face. Then he said he'd be happy to show Grandmother and Grandfather round the place. Grandfather said it would probably come too expensive, and anyway it was his philosophy of life to look at mountains from underneath, churches from the outside and taverns from the inside, and he had lived by that principle to such an age that he wasn't going to make exceptions now.

Father Coelestin's face was dark red, and he was looking very odd, and then Grandfather asked him if he'd like to sit down and drink a little wine. He couldn't recommend it very highly, but Father Coelestin probably knew what it was like, and one was used to better, even without being a stuck-up snob. Father Coelestin looked at the boy very crossly and said bringing up young people was very difficult, and Grandfather said he didn't know anything about educational theory, but he'd like to have the boy's silver cutlery back. Father Coelestin said something else about having to maintain discipline among his charges, and then he went off. The boy was feeling rather uneasy. Perhaps he shouldn't have told Grandfather what had happened to him.

After that Grandfather and Grandmother quarrelled a little, because Grandmother said Grandfather hadn't been very diplomatic, and he could have seen that the habit-wearing pisser was a dog with a nasty bite, and Grandfather said he couldn't stand being approached in that manner, and he would always react to bootlicking in the same way, she should know that by now. Then Grandmother said she knew it in her very bones, but Grandfather didn't have to live in the monastery, and the habit-wearing pisser would probably avenge himself on the first person who came to hand, and then Herr Buchlar came along with the boy's cutlery, which Brother Ansgar had given him. Grandfather looked at his pocket watch and said it was time to go, and they said good-bye to the boy. Grandmother gave the boy the parcel of food, and after Grandfather had paid the bill he said he couldn't help his temper; he gave the boy twenty schillings, and then they went into the Inn Yard, where he also tipped the boarding-house manservant, and the boy's grandparents drove off with, thank goodness, only brief farewells.

When you had put the parcel of food away in your locker and gone back to the Museum the atmosphere there was rather funny. The other boys asked quietly about the car, as if it were something special, but it was only an old 1927 Maybach, and the family had never bought another car because it still went well. And Brother Ansgar said the boy should have said who his grandparents were, but no one had asked. When it was supper time down in the refectory Father Coelestin gave a very long address. He spoke about the rich glutton and the poor man Lazarus, and how we were all equal before Christ, and birth gave no one any precedence now, for the aristocracy might be the will of God, but were a different case and shouldn't feel superior any more, and as he talked he kept looking at the boy as if he meant him. Then he talked about the hunger and poverty in the world, and how it was a Christian virtue to share everything, because it wasn't good for some to have everything and others nothing. You had heard just the same from the Commies, although they didn't quote from the Bible so much, and you realized what Father Coelestin was going on about only when he said your food parcel would be shared out among the poor boys. You had to take it to Father Coelestin directly after grace at the end of supper, and he opened it. It contained two pieces of smoked meat and four home-made salamis, butter that tasted quite different from the monastery margarine, paprika-flavoured bacon, three jars of the jam you liked because it wasn't too sweet, and twenty schillings from Grandmother. Father Coelestin took those and said he would put them in the charity box for the Mission, and the other things would be shared out to the poor boys. You were allowed to keep only half a home-made salami and a jar of jam for yourself. For the next few days the boy looked round at breakfast and supper to see who was eating Grandmother's things, but he saw nothing. There weren't any poor boys in the boarding house. Three days later Father Romuald said in the Latin lesson that he wondered if the stuttering splutterer knew as much about the ablative as his grandparents knew about making salami, but you didn't, because some words were very difficult to pronounce, and everyone laughed.

Talking was difficult anyway, particularly when you had to do it in front of the teachers, and once Father Thomas was very angry because you should have said 'leguminous plants' and he entered in the class register that you had given a quotation from Goethe instead. The boy was sorry, because he hadn't done it on purpose, but Father Thomas wrote so much in the register that no one else ever read it.

Herr Hirthentaler told the boy about Demosthenes, who had filled his mouth with pebbles to help himself speak more clearly. There was a heap of pebbles in the garden of the monastery, where you weren't really supposed to go, and you got a bag full and washed them. But they didn't work and just fell out of your mouth, because you had no difficulty with your speech when you were reading aloud. Herr Hirthentaler said the trick worked only when you were extemporizing, and you went to see him with a mouthful of pebbles, but they did make talking difficult, and it wasn't easy to pick all the little stones up again afterwards. You felt ashamed, and didn't go to see him for a week, but not because it was really forbidden. It was because of the way Herr Hirthentaler had looked when the pebbles dropped out of your mouth, and because he had said it was only a joke about Demosthenes. The others made jokes too.

But you could hardly tell Mother that when she turned up entirely unexpectedly a good week later. She was on her way back from Vienna, where she had been doing something at Aunt Anny's, and had time to spare between two trains. You were just sitting in the little Museum where the three bottom classes had to study, playing nine men's morris, because Father Thomas was supervising, when she was there all of a sudden. She went to see Father Coelestin first. He was rather sleepy because it was his siesta time. He adjusted his voice to the way he always spoke to parents, and said he was having a difficult time with the boy, because with the best will in the world he couldn't be cured of stammering, and he was always so unforthcoming and pigheaded. He wasn't at all interested in sport, and in gymnastics he was so clumsy that he really might have been sabotaging the lesson. His work in school subjects wasn't so bad, apart from maths, but he always appeared inattentive and sly, and the reason was that the boy had been dreadfully spoilt, if not by her then by his grandparents, but he would take great pains and do his best, and he went on talking for a lot longer, until Mother was very upset and shed tears. Then Father Coelestin mentioned the location of the charity box for the Mission to the poor heathen, for which the Holy Father needed so much money, and said that for the sake of Jesus Christ he would keep the boy in the school for the time being, and then he went off.

Mother wept a little longer, because of being afflicted with such a boy. His father had always feared the boy might not be normal, because his own father had gone crazy, but Mother's heredity was perfectly sound, and she didn't know what she had done to be so burdened, when his brother and sister had been perfectly normal and now they were dead. Then she went to the chapel where the Mission collecting box stood, a figure of a negro, and put ten schillings in it, but the Negro nodded only when you put in coins, not notes. You thought of telling Mother so, but she was in no mood to talk to you. All she said was that Frau Wittmann had finally died and been buried, and you could come home over the All Saints' holiday. She asked if you thought you could travel by train on your own, since she didn't have time to fetch you, and you nodded. Then Mother gave you a ticket that she had already bought, looked at the time and went back to catch her train.

Of course travelling home wasn't all that easy, and the boy was at the station half an hour before the train left. He had his cardboard suitcase with his number on it, containing the things that Mother had said weren't to be washed at school, two brightly coloured pullovers that she had knitted from remains of wool, and his good trousers which had a large greasy mark on them because one Sunday he hadn't changed them after church and before lunch. He had a guilty conscience about that, since Mother had said he should always change, but he hadn't because Father Coelestin once said that changing your clothes was vain, and vanity was a sin. So the boy kept only one silk shirt with him and wore pullovers instead, since they were not vanity, but now they smelled.

In the train he was afraid he might go past the right station,

although he had only to count up to three, and when he
changed in the town he was afraid he might miss the other
train, but there were still twenty minutes to go, and he found
something new: chewing gum for sale in packets of five pieces,
and three real film shots from real Hollywood movies with
them, fifty groschen for the whole thing. You bought three
packets, although you didn't particularly like chewing gum,
but you wanted to see the film shots and thought that then
you would resell the chewing gum. But when you looked at
the pictures at home they were disappointing, because they
didn't show much, just an open door once, and once a woman
from behind, but only the back of her head. Then you carefully stuck the packets up again, hoping you could sell them
for a schilling each back in the boarding house.

Frau Wittmann was lying in the graveyard next to the old
manservant; you found a nickel button from his waistcoat
right beside the wreath of withered daisies left by Herr
Wittmann, who was in Vienna now in the old folk's home
he'd been paying for in advance over the years. He had left
several books for the boy with his grandparents, but they
weren't very interesting, because all they said was how good
the German race was and what a blessing to the whole world,
and you knew about that already. Only one of the books was
interesting. It dated from the time of the monarchy, and said
that Bach, whom you were learning to sing now, was really a
Hungarian, and so was Haydn, with whose violin music you
were struggling, and of course Liszt was Hungarian (you
didn't like him so much), and Schubert, and Mozart, and so
on and so forth, and the book had been published in
Budapest. Grandmother said it was all nonsense, in Austria
every single person was a race unto himself, and then she
gave the boy twenty schillings, telling him not to tell
Grandfather. Grandfather too gave you some money that no
one was to know about, and Mother gave you ten schillings at
the station. You hadn't brought much to eat away from home

with you, because you were afraid Father Coelestin would just confiscate it.

However, he did confiscate the *Battle for Rome*,[78] because it was against the Church and was prohibited, but there was nothing you could do about that, because you had to show him everything you had brought from home when you came back to school. He didn't find the packets of chewing gum because they were in your coat pocket, and a couple of days later Dingo showed the boy a place just outside the monastery where you could put things when you came back and Father Coelestin wouldn't find them, because he seldom looked there. But you had to be careful about that hiding place, because there were dogs in the neighbourhood.

The boy soon realized just why an unpleasant person is called a dog, for at breakfast two older boys began fighting because one of them, a butcher's son, said a sausage was his but it seemed the dogs had eaten it, so now the other boy was a dog. Then Brother Ansgar pulled both boys' hair and forbade all the boys to eat sausage brought from home for a week, but there wasn't any other kind.

You had trouble in history too, because Austria was very hard to understand, and so was Father Columban, who was to be described as the headmaster of the grammar school and a historian. In fact you were very interested in history, but Father Columban had probably read different history books, and you had to answer his questions as if they were part of the Catechism. That was how you really had to answer teachers all the time, since the Catechism was the most important book in existence for all Catholics and Austrians, and there was the Greater Catechism and the Smaller Catechism, but you were still small yourself. Father Richard said that even maths was based on the Catechism, for it taught you about the numerical system and how to find out what x and y are. There were seven venial sins, seven grievous sins, seven deadly sins, and seven sins crying out to Heaven, and then there were

seven weekdays, just as there were twelve months and twelve
apostles, but there were only three virtues because of the
Trinity. It was a lot more difficult with Austria, which after all
was the oldest country in the world, as one could tell from the
fact that the Venus of Willendorf was found in the Wachau
area. The Egyptians and Babylonians learned from Austria,
and the Chinese learned from the Egyptians and Babylonians,
which was the primeval revelation, and Austria was very
important to the Romans because Marcus Aurelius[79] died
there, and then the miracle of the rain in the land of the Quadi
took place there too.[80] Then along came the villainous
Germanic tribes and the Slavs, and Charlemagne freed Austria
and made it great again. The Babenbergs[81] made it even
greater, and the Habsburgs made it so great that the sun could
not go down upon it any more, and then the socialists arrived
to spoil everything. So far, you had learned it all as you were
told, although it was not history the way you knew it, but you
had to say it their way. And then Hitler had brought Austria
under his rule because he had been thrown out of the country.
'And what were the Austrians then?' You hadn't prepared the
answer to that, and had to think about it. There were no
'Austrians', because you had been told that then there was no
Austria in the whole world, so you thought about it, until
Father Columban said, 'No stammering, please!' and many of
the boys laughed. So you said, 'They were Nazis,' and got a
bad mark, written down as Unsatisfactory, because the right
answer would have been that they were 'in the Resistance',
but you hadn't given that one because you hadn't thought of
it. A bad mark was very unfortunate, because one of the three
school terms ended just before Christmas and the first reports
were given out. All the pupils thought that was mean.

They were mean to each other too, beginning in class. The
desks where you had to sit, screwed to the seats so that you
could hardly move, were very old, and you could pull the lids
down a little way, and there was a hole for the inkwell and a

groove for your penholder. There were no inkwells now, for you had to write with indelible pencil or a fountain pen, and the groove didn't fit the boy's fountain pen, which was an old Waterman. It had what Grandmother called a 'sunken spring', which came out only when you unscrewed it, but then it was difficult to close up again, and when you had closed it you had to hold the pen upright to keep the ink from leaking. So you couldn't really use the desk, and before break one day there had been a Latin test. After break it was Religious Studies, and the lid of the desk was pushed slightly back. There was a small roll of paper wedged there, and when you unrolled it Father Bonaventura took it away. It was a crib to the Latin test, but you hadn't written it, and the ink was different too. But that did you no good, because Father Bonaventura gave the note to Father Romuald, who put an Unsatisfactory on your test although it was perfectly correct, and wrote that it was 'for cheating'. Some of the boys were still laughing a few days later, and that was how you found out that Petsch had written the note, and hadn't thrown it away but put it in your desk, but Father Romuald said that he was never wrong.

Petsch was always unpleasant to the boy, because he said he was against Nazis, and his father was head of a ministerial department, so none of the Fathers did anything to annoy him. When the Krampus came – St Nicholas, as he was called in the monastery – many of the boys wrote poems for St Nicholas to read out loud, so that other boys would get thumped by the Krampuses from the top forms. The boy didn't like it, because no one ought to denounce anyone else, but Petsch asked several boys how you spell *à propos*, and the boy told him.

St Nicholas was an eighth-year boy, who wore a real chasuble, because there were plenty of those in the monastery, and the Krampuses were sixth-year and seventh-year boys. There was plenty for them to wear in the monastery too, since

Krampuses are really devils, and the Fathers needed devils almost more than they needed God, for they were everywhere, but they only hit the smaller boys. You recognized them quickly because each had his own way of hitting, and the boys were called up by St Nicholas and read poems out while the Krampuses thumped the others and Father Coelestin laughed. Then the boys who wanted to please Father Coelestin laughed too, and it was all horrible. The boy himself was called into the circle, and a long poem about him was read out. Some of the rhymes were good, like 'Stammer-grammar' and 'monkey-shammer' – it meant the boy's untidy hair, which the Krampuses were supposed to pull – but then came the words *à propos*, so you knew Petsch had written the poem. You stopped listening, although the Krampuses hit out several times, and thought up a poem of your own, only four lines but they must rhyme, and when you had made it up you called out, 'Stop!' St Nicholas actually did stop, because he wasn't used to being interrupted, the six Krampuses were just standing around, and then you recited your poem. You hadn't found a rhyme for the name Petsch, but one of the Krampuses, who hadn't hit as hard as the others and was called Hinbecker, whispered to the boy that he'd done well. Father Coelestin said he'd had no idea that the stuttering splutterer was a poet in disguise, and could say a verse without stammering, but you had been furious, and then Petsch had to go into the circle and get thumped. He flailed about in such a funny way that he fell over and had to go and wash. He got his revenge on the boy when he came back and spat in his soup. It was potato soup, and now you didn't want it, although you usually liked it very much.

Soon after that the reports were given out, and yours wasn't good. You had Very Good for art and music, Reasonable for conduct, and Satisfactory for everything else, written right over the whole report. Dingo said it didn't mean much, all new boys got bad marks in their first term, so that in the summer the Fathers could say that a boy had improved, all thanks to their own efforts, but you didn't feel happy about it as you went home for the Christmas holidays.

Of course Mother was horrified by the report, and boxed the boy's ears a couple of times. Telling her what Dingo had told you didn't help, and you weren't allowed out of the house or to see your grandparents because of that bad mark for conduct. She talked about her own heredity which was quite all right, and her son's degeneration, which she couldn't explain to herself, although she did so quite often these days, and Director Sattler said the boy was lazy, that was all, and he came every day. Then you had to go to your room, but you had to stay there anyway if you didn't want to be pouring beer downstairs. It was very boring, because Mother had removed all your books except for the school books, and you couldn't paint either because your mark for art had been good.

Then you were allowed to go with Mother to see your grandparents on Christmas Eve, but it wasn't very comfortable there either. Mother made a meal of your report, and Grandmother said it was Grandfather's fault for not behaving to those habit-wearing pissers as they really deserved, and she'd had to throw all the liveries away because the moths had got at them. The mourning liveries were gone too, not that she minded having a middle-class funeral. Everything was over anyway, she couldn't do anything properly these days, she was worth nothing any more. Grandfather said this post-war period was much worse than the last one, but that could be because he was so much older, and there would never be peace again, you had only to look at Greece or China. He had nothing against it if the Commies took over the whole world, for the Russians had more culture than the Yanks, with the exception of the Russians quartered in this house, and he was so old anyway that he didn't mind anything any more. Then Grandmother said they couldn't all go on complaining in unison, and she felt sorry for the boy, having to listen. His grandparents gave him an envelope with money in it, his mother gave him some long, scratchy underpants, and socks, and that was Christmas. Oh yes, and a candle had been burning too close to the Angel Hallelujah and singed the hem of the angel's robe.

You didn't know which was better, home or the monastery, except for the food. You had to stay in your room and be bored at home because of your report, and at school the boys and their monstrous stories were boring, but at least there was more going on there. The older the boys grew the more they talked about what they called 'the meaning of life', and you never understood what they meant. It was called Philosophy, because from Class 3 onwards you learned Greek, and apparently the ancient Greeks had nothing better to do. It was always about two questions: why and for what purpose were we put into the world? The Fathers had begun with these questions, and they had an answer that you must know if you didn't want to get bad marks. The answer was that God had so willed it, and we must please him, which was why he had given us free will so that he could put us to the test. Somehow you could understand that, because as a child you had played with Fleischmann soldiers yourself, imagining them alive. Then you grew older, but as God is eternal he hadn't, so he needed the world. You could see that, but it didn't make God seem any nicer, and you knew not to say such things. Once you got a terrible bawling out and a bad mark from Father Bonaventura because when he asked you what God did, you said, 'He sits in Heaven playing games.' Well, he had sent his own son down to earth for the Jews to kill him, and he had sent him to earth as a Jew specifically so that they would do that, and then he had damned the Jews because, being omniscient, he'd known they would do it. So that was all right, and it was so horrible that the boy preferred not to think about God. You wouldn't want to be sent into the world for that sort of thing because Father and Mother had wanted it. And Mother was acting to the boy just like God, but as she wasn't omniscient it wasn't quite so bad. That half-answered the question why, although you didn't see any real sense in it. The question of the purpose was explained by the fact that the boy had grown up with domestic animals, and he knew about farm livestock too. So he knew that piglets would be sows one day, and calves would be cows or oxen, but the boys at school talked as if it would be quite different with them in the future. Only the sons of politicians and high officers of state wanted to be what their fathers were, and perhaps the sons of famous lawyers, but all the others imagined being really famous some day. How and by what means they didn't know, but they talked about it an amazing amount, particularly about space travel, which was coming soon and was in their books, although it was a long time yet before they would take their school leaving exams. The boy didn't know what he wanted to be one day, he wasn't interested, and Father Richard said the boy failed to take the long view.

In fact you had another model, though not one that you wanted to talk about, because you were afraid of being laughed at, and there was a lot more you had to learn. The man who was your model was rather stout, and in a way so were you, for you still had what Mother called your 'baby fat', although nothing like as much of it as the butchers' sons had, and the model lived in England where Grandfather had studied. You had met him long ago through Herr Brunner, when he was staying at the inn because he had come to buy paper for a publishing firm in Vienna that had once belonged to Jews, and now belonged to the State, and he sent the boy the first book in the series. At Christmas, the boy had asked everyone who wanted to give him a present for more books about the doctor in the story, and he got one too. The grown-ups would say the doctor had done nothing much in life, but that was the great thing about it: he could talk to the animals, not just the animals living in his house, and everything always ended well. Of course you knew it was all a silly fairy tale, and sometimes it fell flat – when a Negro sang Negro songs, whereas you could get real negro jazz over the Yank radio, or when Dr Dolittle was making fire for the Indians, which they could do much better for themselves – but the idea of understanding animals and being able to talk to them was so wonderful that you happily accepted the silly stories. You had taken one of the books to the monastery, and Father Coelestin allowed it because it looked harmless. It told the story of the Deluge. You more or less knew all the stories already, because the fire story was what Prometheus had done for the Europeans, and this time the good part of the story was that it depicted Noah being as unpleasant as the boy had always imagined him. But Father Thomas found you reading it in the Museum during the study hour, and first he mocked you for reading a children's book, but then he read it himself and was very cross about Noah. In the next Religious Studies lesson Father Bonaventura told the boy angrily that Dr Dolittle made a mockery of religion, and then he got all worked up about Charles Darwin who had been a heretic, and claimed that he was Dr Dolittle. You talked to Father Thomas about it, and you were annoyed because Father Bonaventura had been so angry, and Father Thomas said it wasn't that bad and gave you the book back. First, however, you had to tell him why you liked Dr Dolittle, and he said animals did have a language, but not a human one, and not like the animals in the book; it was called behavioural science and was very complicated. Of course you wanted to know about it, but Father Thomas said you'd get to the subject in the seventh year, maybe, and until then you would have to possess your soul in patience. But he was nicer to the boy after that.

Herr Leutschauer, who taught you the teaching language,

wasn't nice at all, though, because of a test in school. It was about Austria again, and you got a bad mark for writing, 'I am a German who was born in Austria, and I brought Hitler here.'

Easter was spoilt by another report. You had a One, the top mark, in art, music and natural history, and Three for everything else including conduct, which wasn't good, because anyone with a Four for conduct was expelled. So Mother was in a bad temper, but you expected that.

It was all very boring. Because you weren't being good you couldn't go home in between times, but you had to write a letter to Mother every week, and a letter to your grandparents. They sent a parcel every two weeks, and Father Coelestin always took some of the things away because they were too much for the boy, not that there was ever much in it, because your grandparents knew what went on too. Father Coelestin also read the letters that Grandmother put in because he could read the old style of handwriting, and once he asked nastily what 'K' stood for – it meant *Kurrentschrift*, the old angular Austrian script, but you weren't going to tell him although you knew, and when he asked more questions you said you supposed Grandmother meant the tom cat, the *Kater*, who was very ugly. On Shrove Tuesday there were pancakes, but they were very heavy because the yeast hadn't risen properly, and the fat they were fried in smelled very old. Most of the boys left them after eating one small piece, and you yourself, despite the disgust you felt, ate almost half yours because you didn't want to be a stuck-up snob, and because Lent was coming, and they observed Lent very strictly in the monastery. You couldn't spread butter on your bread, and of course no lard either, because those were animal substances like eggs and sausage, and all you had to eat was repulsive muck, but it was prayed over even more. Then, once, you had flu and were in the infirmary, where the nursing nun fried you an egg. That was really against the rules of fasting, because the egg was one of the ordinary eggs from

the time when hens were still laying, and they had been preserved in isinglass, so that you couldn't boil them but had to
fry them. And when the flu was over a Father came from
Vienna and gave instruction in spiritual exercises, with a lot
more praying.

Mother had to control herself a bit at Easter, because Aunt
Margarete had come from Sweden. She was Father's sister, so
she had a great many first names but she was called just Aunt
Grete, and now she wanted to come on holiday here, because
she'd sent us chocolate in the war. Mother had gone into
town by train to meet her, and you took the handcart to
meet their train in the village. Aunt Grete had a suitcase and
a big bag and talked all the time, but you didn't hear much of
it because you were pulling the luggage along. A room had
been nicely prepared for Aunt Grete at the inn, but she
didn't want to go up, she needed a double brandy first and
went on talking. The journey had been a great strain, so then
she needed another two brandies and two ham sandwiches
and a cheese sandwich before she could go to her room and
unpack. She had brought chocolate with her for the boy, and
he said thank you politely, while Mother looked at it greedily,
and Mother herself got a tablecloth with Swedish embroidery
on it.

Over the next few days, when she didn't have to drink
brandy on the ground floor, Aunt Grete kept going into
Mother's living-room. Then she said she had no memento of
Father, the brother she had loved so dearly, although Mother
had always said the two of them couldn't stand each other,
and she would pick up some Meissen plates that had belonged
to Father's great-grandfather, or the even older chocolate cups
with all the sights of Dresden painted on them, and Mother
could hardly say no, although she herself had nothing else left
to remember her husband by, and she had saved those things
from her own house. But Aunt Grete would never have

dropped the subject, and anyway she had asked mother and son to Sweden in the summer, a land of milk and honey because it had stayed neutral in the war, not fighting but just delivering supplies to other people. Aunt Grete was married to a big shot there, and her elder daughter to an even bigger shot, but he had crashed in a plane, and her younger daughter had hooked a big shot too. So you had to be polite to Aunt Grete, even when she'd drunk a lot of brandy because, she said, it was hardly obtainable at all in Sweden. She left on the same day as you had to go back to the monastery, and she had borrowed Mother's best suitcase because she was taking all Father's things away so that, as she said, they would stay in the family.

When you wanted a rest from Aunt Grete you had gone to see your grandparents. Herr Mandi had had another baby, which wasn't something he had planned, and now he would have to work even harder so that life would be better some day. Grandfather had given him a plot of land, and when he wasn't working for your grandparents he was toiling away there. Grandmother said that was right and proper for the domestic staff, and told the boy a great deal about such things.

All the domestic staff had their place, and had often had it for generations. A plain seamstress's daughter naturally became the next plain seamstress herself, having learnt her skills from her mother, and if she happened to escape this iron rule by marrying outside the estate then the next daughter would take her place – there were people in reserve. In view of the whole situation it was something of a privilege to be a member of the domestic staff, and there were plenty of comfortably situated farmers' wives in the area who wanted a daughter-in-law from the staff, because they knew a girl like that would be capable, at least if she came from the third or fourth generation of the staff. That gave them a sense of people's station in life. The smith, who was responsible in the sixth generation for horses and everything to do with machinery (so it was as if he'd been here longer than his masters) was a source of knowledge about the whole area; the gardener, Herr Mandi's father, had been responsible in the third generation for an ever-expanding nursery garden with more and more hotbeds and gardeners working under him, and he earned a nice little sum on the side with seeds and flowers; young cooks working for the present mistress were courted by all the farmers' boys.

Of course some people were relegated too. The staff felt they could afford to have many children, and if there was no place for a child in the house then he or she had to work in the factory. They still had certain privileges there, such as less strenuous jobs, or jobs where they could count on a bonus, but they didn't really belong to the house any more. Instead they were given a small plot of land where they could build a cottage of their own some day. Immigrants had to work for years for that kind of thing.

The domestic staff could afford cottages too, and as a bonus on the twenty-fifth anniversary of their starting work for the family they got twice as much land as people who had left the household earlier, admittedly poor land with so many stones that you had to bring in soil before you could work it, but that was something for their children to do some day, since the staff themselves had a rent-free home in one of the staff houses, which were graded by function, and later, if they had no one left to look after them, they got a room in the Pensioners' House, as the home for the very old was called. But they were proud of their own land, and in what free time they could find for themselves in summer and autumn they improved the soil. They got the farmers to let them have harvest refuse, easily obtained in return for a couple of bottles of wine as payment in kind; they spent a long time stacking compost heaps, and it made such valuable soil that sometimes – only by accident of course, and in the heat of the moment – they would encroach on a neighbour's compost heap. But that was done only by children, or because the beer had gone to their heads.

And at the weekend they made bricks. These were called slag bricks, because there was a lot of slag lying around the factory boiler-house, and it went into the bricks. The smith had made forty moulds for bricks, and they belonged to everyone who wanted to build a house, usually about ten people at a time, who drew lots for whose turn it was to use them and the hand-operated mixing machine. The slag was mixed with thick cement in this machine, and was put in the brick moulds, and if you had made them on Sunday morning instead of going to Mass, they were hard enough after the football game to be taken out of the mould and left to go on drying, and the moulds could be refilled again, ready for Monday evening. If the weather was good the men made bricks every evening, but there was no sense in moving the moulds and the mixing machine about the place. So the men would make enough bricks in one year to let them lay the foundations of their houses in autumn and begin building next spring, with everyone helping, of course, taking turns by lot.

Now Herr Mandi was busy making bricks, and as he was a very hard worker Grandfather had said the smith could make another forty moulds so that Herr Mandi could finish his building sooner, or build a bigger house. And although there was still some danger of frost, Herr Mandi and his family worked with a will. It was a pleasure to watch them, and even Grandmother came out once to see them, with the walking stick she had been using since last winter.

You had got used to her saying how bad and stupid she thought everything was these days, because in between these complaints she told you very interesting things. You found talking to Grandfather was even more difficult than before, although he had less to do, which annoyed him. Sitting behind his desk all day bored him, but he couldn't go riding or cycling any more, and that made him bad-tempered. He walked with his own grandfather's stick now, and he still went round the nursery garden and the outhouses every day, but he said it would all run without him now in any case, and it wouldn't pay anyway because of the present situation; he felt like a prisoner in his part of the house, not wanting to look at the other wings and the park, so as not to have to see the havoc wreaked by the Russians. Sometimes he said it was hard that none of his old friends were still alive, but that was the punishment he deserved for getting so old.

However, it was even more boring in the monastery, and not just because of the Fathers and their rules but because of the boys too. What interested them most was what the Fathers called 'unchastity' or 'unnatural practices', except when they were playing or scuffling, but even then they liked to grab each other's trousers and say 'Ow!' and giggle. You didn't have a little bunny any more now, you had a proper prick, and pricks seemed to fascinate everyone, because looking at them was strictly forbidden and you would be expelled from the school if a Father caught you at it. Worst of all was playing with your prick, or tossing yourself off, as it was known, because that made God so angry that if a boy did it he would wither the marrow in his spine, as Father Bonaventura always said, but the boys did it all the same; they did it more and more the older they grew. Long live wanking, they would say, it starches your shirt and makes you weak at the knees. Some of them had cut a notch in a doorpost so that they could measure and find out if tossing themselves off really did make them shrink, but no one was any shorter. The boy was growing too, as he noticed from the fit of his jackets and trousers. But it bothered him that all the boys thought of nothing but their pricks. For a start, when you had to piss there was always a boy standing beside you looking. They were always boys of your own age, and your prick was nothing to write home about. They didn't comment, but they looked, and sometimes you heard them whispering in the dormitory about other people's pricks. In time you got used to pissing in a lavatory with the door closed, but then they often looked under the door or through a hole in the wooden partition between cubicles.

The older boys behaved rather differently, and you didn't always realize at once what their idea was. Dingo, for instance, was two years older, and you liked him because he was seldom condescending and he knew his way very well around the monastery and all its secret routes. The monastery hadn't been built to such a neat plan as it looked from outside, but grew bit by bit, so there were staircases or corridors that sometimes led nowhere, sometimes up to the roof of the church, or down into forgotten vaults. Once Dingo said he was going to try getting down into the crypt some time. To do that you first had to get into the courtyard of the enclosure where the monks were really supposed to live, but hardly any of them did, for today's monks had moved into larger, more comfortable rooms in other parts of the monastery. From there you could get up to the loft, which wasn't very interesting because it had been cleared out in the war on account of the Allied incendiary bombs. After a while you came to a metal door on your left, leading to a smaller loft from which you saw the roof over the church, but on the right there was a small, dark spiral staircase, and that, thought Dingo, ought to lead down to the crypt. The staircase was very dark and dirty, but Dingo had some matches with him, and it was possible to feel your way along. But after a great many steps there was a wall half-way up the stairs, as you could see by the light of a match. Dingo was going to climb over the wall, but then he perched there for a moment and got off again. He said he had hit his balls on the wall and they hurt badly. He was whispering, though the boy told him there was no Father or any other boy to overhear them here anyway. After a while Dingo said he hurt all over because he had a terrible hard-on, and it was very painful. The boy said nothing, and stood there, but Dingo repeated what he had said. The boy waited, and then Dingo took his hand in the darkness. He had brought his hard-on out of his trousers, and he said the only thing that would help it and the pain he felt was being tossed off, and since the accident had happened on the boy's account maybe he would help him. The boy saw that, but he had to do all the work while Dingo leaned on him. When they went back through the dimly lit loft, however, he felt as if Dingo had been taking the mickey out of him, because he didn't entirely believe the story about the accident to his balls.

Then a few days later it was all clear, because Dingo showed the boy the cellar under the gym. The gym looked funny, since it was a Baroque, stucco-encrusted, gigantic vault where apparatus like the giant stride and the wall bars didn't really look right, and you didn't like it because of the smell. The cellar underneath smelled too, but different, like damp rooms that had never been aired. It wasn't easy to get down there, because the spiral staircase leading to it began behind a small door two floors higher, which looked locked but could be opened with a nail. The cellar consisted of three vaults, and was light, because it was built above the rock of the monastery, and all sorts of things that weren't needed any longer had been stored there, from school furniture to piles of papers that were rather smelly because of the damp. Dingo showed the boy a window that could be opened if you stood on a chair, and outside, a metre below, was the rock on which the monastery was built. Dingo climbed out, but it was too hot outside for you, and you had found a heap of old pay books in a corner. In only the second that you opened you read the name of the village, and the book had belonged to the carpenter's eldest son, who had fallen in the war. Or not really in the war but afterwards, when he was trying to cross the Enns and be taken prisoner by the Yanks, and they had shot him down with many of his comrades in the middle of the river. People had often told that story, and there were other pay books from his company too, though you had no idea how they had got here. You took the pay book from the village with you, and you were just deciding to take it to the man's parents some day soon as a memento of their son when Dingo came back in and closed the window. He said he had hit his balls again, but the pay books were far more interesting. Then Dingo started on about the pain, brought out his stiff prick and asked the boy to help him. You told him you didn't feel like it now, and Dingo was angry. He said he'd do anything for the boy, and it was all his doing that the other boys left him alone, so he could ask for a little something in return. The boy just pretended to be listening, and Dingo went on and on until his prick drooped again. Then the boy said that accidental hard-ons went away of their own accord, and Dingo did up his trousers and said he didn't feel like it now anyway. There was not a good atmosphere as they left the cellar, and that was the last time Dingo showed you a secret path.

You often heard a lot of whispering in the dormitory too, or saw a boy steal to another boy's bed, but it was boring. And once a boy who had been looking at you in a funny way during evening prayers came over to your bed at night. You woke up when he suddenly lay down beside you and began fingering his pyjama trousers, but you told him you were tired, and when he realized there was nothing doing he went away again. Later you heard him telling the others that you were boring, which was just as well because then you were left in peace.

You didn't like being unable to talk to anyone about these things, of course you couldn't talk to your grandparents or Mother, because they certainly wouldn't understand and would just think badly of you, and definitely not to the

Fathers, none of whom you trusted, nor to any of the boys, because they were all the same and would have thought you stupid or just a baby. After all, you'd played with your own prick when it was still a little bunny, and that was forbidden at the time too, but now you just didn't feel like it. But no one would have understood, and what with all the fuss the other boys made about such things you'd just have made yourself look ridiculous.

Much more important was studying for the next end of term report, because you were very keen to go to Sweden, not because of Aunt Grete, whom you didn't particularly like, but to see the luxuriant countryside she had described. It was annoying that in primary school all your marks had been Very Good, because now Mother kicked up a terrible fuss for a mere Good, and the Fathers were crafty and knew it. It is true that not all of them were spiteful to the boy, but there were enough who were.

Sometimes, too, it seemed as if you were inviting trouble. But that wasn't so: it was just that you were angry over things that weren't true. For instance, Father Bonaventura once talked about the cross for a very long time. A cross, he said, was not just a cross, and if someone claimed to have his mind on the cross he was more likely blaspheming. Most crosses were blasphemous, he added, or if not they were instruments of torture. A real cross, a Christian cross, pleasing in the sight of God, could be identified by the fact that the Lord Jesus was nailed to it, and all others were heathen, godless, false crosses. The boy didn't agree, because he had seen a great many crosses without the Lord Jesus – in graveyards, on war memorials, even set up to remind people of the Lay Mission – but when he told Father Bonaventura so, the Father said angrily that it wasn't true, and the boy had better keep his mouth shut, considering that his father had been hanged for praying to the swastika, which was a hooked cross. In fact, in a room that had once been the chapter-hall and was now full of lumber, you had found a large cross potent. This was the kind of swastika favoured by the Cock's Tail-Feathers militia, with extra hooks on each arm, since the Austro-Fascists wanted to go one better than the Nazis. There were coloured posters of the Lay Mission for 1937 lying beside it, showing Lord Jesus with outstretched arms blessing the whole world. You cut him out and fixed him to the cross potent with three drawing pins, and in break before the next Religious Studies lesson you put him up in front of the blackboard. Some of the boys giggled, others didn't get the idea, but Father Bonaventura was very angry. When he came into the classroom he went red in the face and said, 'This is . . .!' Then he went out of the room and closed the door behind him. After a good minute he came back, went red in the face again and asked, 'Very well, who did this?' He asked three times, but no one spoke up. Then he looked at Wildhölzel, who sat near the front and was always sucking up to him, and asked, 'Was it you?' Wildhölzel made a face, and Father Bonaventura followed the direction of his gaze. He stopped in front of the boy and looked at Wildhölzel again. When he asked the boy, 'It was you, wasn't it?' you stood up and said yes, because you knew that Wildhölzel had given you away. Father Bonaventura picked up the cross potent with Jesus on it and took it out of the room. After a while he came back empty-handed but with the caretaker, and then he made quite a long speech, although its content was simple enough, since the gist was that the boy was an enemy of God, and the Devil had afflicted him not just with stammering but with vice, and he was therefore going to be put in the detention room and taken before Council in the afternoon, for Lord Jesus himself had said if thine eye offend thee, pluck it out.

You had heard of the detention room but had never seen it yet. It was not at all as you had imagined it, but a long, narrow place on the way to the cloisters, and you had often passed its door. There were bars over the window, but all the windows in this wing were barred because it wasn't very far up to them from outside, and there was a small table and two chairs, all very old and decrepit. The walls were grey too and hadn't been painted for ages, and they had been much scribbled on. You put a chair by the window, though you had to dust it with your handkerchief first, and soon you were looking at birds nesting in a nearby tree. And so the time passed. You heard main break begin, because it was very loud in the play-ground, and the birds hid because some of the bigger boys went into the corner where the tree stood on the other side of the wall and smoked. At midday the caretaker, whose name was Herr Ludwig, brought you a plate of soup and said you were in for trouble. He always had a hip-flask with him, and often drank from it; it was never empty. But he seemed to like the boy, who always addressed him as 'Herr Ludwig', as he had learned to do from his grandparents, not just 'Ludwig' like the other boys. Herr Ludwig said all the Fathers were very angry with the boy, and then he offered him the hip-flask to strengthen himself for Council. The flask contained marc, known as Trebener in Austria, and tasted so strong that you had to have some of the soup after two sips, but Herr Ludwig said you should take another two. Then you finished the soup, and when he had gone out with the plate you felt pleas-antly woozy.

Then, a long time later, Herr Ludwig led you off to Council; it was held in the conference room next to the head-master's office, and you saw from the wall clock that it was just after three. The Father and the boy's lay teachers were all sitting there looking very portentous. Then Father Columban cleared his throat, thus declaring Council open. You liked Father Columban because he trembled a lot, and could hold so little in his hand that he once even spilled the wine at Mass, and he was one of the few Fathers who didn't call the boy a stuttering splutterer. Then Father Bonaventura told everyone what they knew already, and how the boy had committed a shocking act of blasphemy for which no punishment could be too harsh. After that Father Columban asked what the boy had been thinking of, and the boy told them that in the last lesson but one Father Bonaventura had said that any cross without the Lord Jesus on it was blasphemous – no one noticed that he had almost used Father Bonaventura's nickname, but quickly corrected himself. And he mentioned the Lay Mission cross by the parish church in town down below, which had no Lord Jesus on it, and the time when Father Bonaventura had said the swastika was the Devil's work but the cross potent was pleasing in the eyes of God because . . . Here Father Romuald and Father Christoph became rather uneasy, and Father Columban asked whether Father Bonaventura had really said that, and you said it was the only way you could understand what he said, so that was why you did it, and you weren't playing a trick, it was a real cross because Lord Jesus was on it. But by this time no one was listening any more, for Father Romuald and Father Christoph were arguing in very loud voices with Father Bonaventura and Father Coelestin, saying this was not a matter for children, and Father Richard said he wasn't going to listen to this stuff any more, and it was nothing to do with the boy, and the lay teachers and Father Thomas said nothing at all, and the boy was glad that no one was taking any more notice of him. When the hand on the wall clock had ticked six minutes further on the Fathers calmed down. All this time Father Columban had been trying to pick up the bell on the table in front of him, and when he finally managed to ring it he asked the boy where he had found the cross potent. The boy said it had been in the old chapter-hall, lying on one of the altars standing around there for the feast of Corpus Christi, which was not entirely true because it had been behind an altar. Father Columban said that room ought to be locked, and Father Romuald and Father Bonaventura began arguing again, but the boy was told he mustn't go into rooms that were out of bounds again, and such – Father Columban thought for some time and then said – such nonsense must not happen again, sheer nonsense, even though the Lord Jesus was on it, and now the boy was to go.

Herr Ludwig was waiting out in the corridor and asked how it had gone, and whether he was to take you back to the detention room, but you didn't know that yourself. Herr Ludwig knocked on the conference room door – it still wasn't quiet inside – and when he came out he told the boy it was all over, it looked as if he'd been in luck. You went and sat down at your place in the Museum, where an older boy was supervising because Father Thomas was still in Council. When he came back he said nothing to the boy, and then it was time for a walk.

The summer term report was better than its predecessors. You were given Good by Fathers Romuald, Columban and Christoph; you had Very Good in music and art; you were given a Three for maths and conduct, and Satisfactory for Religious Studies. You realized that this might not be very good but it was good enough for Sweden. When you thought about it, you didn't know whether you really wanted to go, but you'd be glad to get away from the monastery with its Fathers and the other boys, never mind where, the further away the better, and Sweden sounded a long way off.

Although Mother was not at all pleased with the report, she didn't scold the boy for long, because a bathroom was being installed at the inn, in one of the maids' rooms for which there was no maid any more, and it was on the first floor next to the lavatory and the water pipes. Herr Mandi had found two barrow loads of tiles at your grandparents' house and was fixing them to the walls, for there was nothing that he couldn't do, and then you couldn't go in for four days, because no quick-drying cement had been available since the war. Then your grandparents' old bathroom stove was put in, because they had got themselves a boiler just before the war, and an enamel bathtub, which was old too and knocked about at one corner, but that didn't matter, and Herr Mandi had got the fittings from the Russians. When it was all finished it looked beautifully bright, like an album illustrating all the bathrooms in your grandparents' house, because any left-over tiles from there were on the walls, and Mother was glad to have her first bathroom of her own since the war. The boy was glad too, because this was much better than the showers in the boarding house, where you always had to keep your underpants on because the Fathers said so, and all the boys were always looking to see how big their neighbours' pricks were.

Mother had got their passports after Easter, but the authorities took their time, because travel abroad was a luxury, and they didn't want to make out any papers in Austria unless you belonged to the right Party. Perhaps the authorities thought that if they did nothing for long enough Mother wouldn't go to Sweden after all, but she was persistent, and two days before the trip was to begin she got the passports. The tickets had arrived a long time ago, a lot of them, since you needed three for Germany and one each for Denmark and Sweden. And then you had to change trains a terrible lot of times. Often the train stood for a long time on the open line, because it was very hot and so the rails were always cracking, so the journey lasted much longer than expected, almost two and a half days. Another reason was that the train had to go a long way round quite often, because Germany was several countries now, and the people in the Western-occupied zones had just got a new currency, which annoyed the Russians, so now the Russians were annoying travellers and wouldn't let them go through their part of Germany. Mother said the new money was a good thing, and on the way back she would call at the Deutsche Bank and find out what had happened to hers. In between times, however, it was very boring, because there was no dining car, and only in the bigger stations did a man go along the platform selling hot sausages off a cart. There was nothing else, and not even that in Hanover, because the train was starting just as the man and his cart reached your window. Instead, you saw a good deal of the Lüneburger Heide, because the train stood there for four hours when there was a broken rail, and you could get out because it was so hot, but there was hardly any shade there either. You saw nothing of Lübeck, but soon afterwards the sea appeared on your right. You had never seen it before, and were very excited, and then it emerged between the landscape and the villages, a strip of dark blue, but only sometimes, because often it was out of sight for a long time. However, it was there in Grossenbrode, and as you had missed the ferry and the next didn't come for two hours you would have liked to look at it, but you were behind iron bars which were called Customs Clearance, and to make up for it you were given a lemonade.

Then the biggest ship you had ever seen came in, and it was called the *Kongen Frederik*. You saw it coming a long way off, and it was very exciting when it made fast to the bank, which was not a bank but a quay. There was a gangplank at the side of the ship, and a great many people came over it to the other side of the bars, where German Customs Clearance was, but much more exciting was the back part of the ship, spewing out a whole train and several cars on the quay. Some seagulls of the kind you knew from Hamburg were flying around, and you had made your way to the very front by the bars, wanting to see the sea at last. You saw only a very small part of it, and it was dirty, with a lot of jellyfish, which you knew about from books, and looked clean only in the distance. Almost everyone had gone into the German customs hut, and by the gangplank two sailors were restraining a fat woman who was talking in a loud voice. She was going back again with the ship so that she could drink even more, and a woman told the boy that the drunk was Swedish. She was holding a cigar in her hand and talking a lot, and the sailors laughed, because she was a day tripper. Alcohol cost much less on the ship than in Sweden. A train was being pushed into the back of the ship, the woman raised her voice, and you'd seen your first Swedish woman. When the bars were swung back and people could go aboard the ship, she was dragged away, because she was abusing the passengers, but first she threw up into the sea and over a sailor. That stopped the sailors laughing, but not the other people.

Finally you boarded the ship, and Mother said the sea voyage would last over two hours. So you could see all round the ship, but first she advised you to stand by the rail and watch the vessel cast off. You had to stand very still there, because Mother wanted to go down into the ship and see to the luggage. So you stood there, watching the vessel get under way, and then the ship blew its horn, high above, and the quay gradually retreated. The gulls flew along with the ship, since some people were throwing them biscuits which they caught in flight. Right behind you was the drunk Swedish woman lying in a deckchair and looking as if she were asleep. Now and then a sailor who was called the steward came to look at her. Once she woke up and vomited again. The steward swore in Danish, the Swedish woman dropped back in the deckchair, and another man came with a bucket and wiped it all up. Suddenly Mother was back. She had a linen bag with her, and now you could see round the ship. First Mother went into a big room where you could buy duty-free things. There were a great many people in there, and even more alcohol, brands which Mother said hadn't been available even before the war, and weren't now in the Russian-occupied zones. You'd have thought all the passengers must be coming away from those zones, because they bought like mad, but Mother said those must be Danes or Swedes, who had money and were willing to spend it, because everything here was cheaper than on the mainland. She bought two bottles of real brandy for Aunt Grete, who had ordered them, and a large pack of cigarettes for herself because now that she wasn't a singer any more she smoked now and then, because it was ladylike. Then you went into a very large room which was also full of people, and there you had to pay at the door as if you were going to the movies. Mother paid five Danish kroner, and that was a whole twenty schillings, and said that the boy was under ten so that he could get in free, and there was a buffet such as he had never seen before inside. The platters were even more lavish than at the magnificent wedding party given by the butcher at the inn, and the sausage was redder than you had ever seen before too, but Mother said it was the dye. There were many piles of beefsteak tartare, with an onion ring on each and an egg yolk inside it, large dishes of mixed foods which they called salad, but it wasn't green salad out of the garden, it was made of fish with stuff wrapped around it. There were incredibly large amounts of butter in yet more little rolls, there was pale bread that tasted doughy, but must be bread, because all these things were called open sandwiches in Danish, and there were varieties of smoked fish with which you were entirely unfamiliar. And you could help yourself to as much of this as you wanted, after paying for entry. As you filled your plates Mother said very quietly that this just showed what it was like to have lost a war. After a while she got herself another plate, and you ate a great deal too, for the train journey had lasted a long time, with only little sausages to eat – post-war sausages, as Mother said. However, you had to pay a great deal for drinks, so you went to the lavatory outside near the cash desk, said you must have a quick pee and then go back, because Mother was still inside. You drank a great deal of the water from the mains, which tasted strongly of chlorine, and then you went back to the buffet.

Later you were so full that you didn't want to see much

more of the ship until it came into Gedser, and by then it was twilight. Mother said it got dark much later here, because in summer the north had more light, but you were glad you could get back into the train that the ship had spewed out again, and you saw nothing of Denmark. When you woke up they said you were in Copenhagen Central Station, and it was dark, and the last ferry to Sweden had left long ago. Apparently the next left at seven tomorrow morning, so you handed in the bags at Left Luggage to go and look at Copenhagen. There wasn't much going on there except in the street leading away from the Central Station, on the left, where there were lights and a cash desk, and Mother said the Tivoli[82] was very famous. But you couldn't go in because you were too young yourself, and it would soon be closing time. The street lighting was so faint that you could see very little, but a big building must be the City Hall, because some light was cast on it from a hotel in the square. Then you went back and tried to settle down on the green leather benches in the waiting room. There weren't many people there, and they had all missed the ferry, but when you tried to go to sleep the Tivoli closed, and a lot of drunk people came in making a loud noise. A Swiss student, a very slender, polite young man, was lying down on two benches near the door, but along came a huge man looking the way you imagined a polar bear, grunted, and swept the Swiss man off the bench with a movement of his hand. The student woke up, but couldn't defend himself against the polar bear, and someone was throwing up in another corner. After a while Danish police came along with a whistle, and more came later, and then they threw all the drunks out of the waiting room and talked a lot of Danish. A woman translated, telling us that anyone who needed to go to the lavatory should go now, because then the waiting room would be locked until five in the morning, so you also got to see the Copenhagen station lavatories.

So that was Denmark, which was a pity really, because

you'd read everything you could lay hands on in preparation for it, and you'd imagined it as quite different. Hamlet was much further to the north, and his castle was really called Kronenborg, and there were many castles in Denmark, all ending in —borg, there were even some in Copenhagen, and the king lived in one of them, but you didn't see any castles or even a picture of the king, or the Little Mermaid, whom you knew from pictures, only the Villeroy & Boch station urinal.

The ferry left punctually next day, but the trip was only fourteen minutes. There was no buffet with open sandwiches, and the alcoholic drinks were more expensive than between the British zone and Denmark, because we were close to Sweden now, but Aunt Grete had already written telling Mother that, and you saw her waving like mad from the jetty in Malmö. After Customs you reached her, and she talked a terrible lot. She talked all the way to the taxi and even more inside it, about Malmö; all kinds of things were said of Malmö, but it was left behind you, even though it was the most important city in Sweden, and then the car stopped in Borgmästaregatan, which meant Mayor Street. It was where she lived, and right opposite was a large building site which would be the City Theatre one day, and on the right a large red house called Sockerbolaget, which had once been a store for sugar and was now a store for art. There was a notice in front of it about a painter called Grünwald, but Aunt Grete said this was not the painter Grünewald[83] but a degenerate Jew who had painted Swedish girls with green hair. That would have been interesting, but Aunt Grete had no time to tell you more. Then you went through a brown gate into a grey-brown passage and up grey stairs to a brown door. There was a fat mermaid in white plaster above it, made by the master of the house, who was a real artist, and Aunt Grete lived behind that door.

She didn't live alone but with a bank manager, who wasn't

there. He was her second husband, but she couldn't actually marry him because her first husband had been a big shot and had said in his will that she mustn't get married again, and the bank manager had two unmarried sisters who were quite old and terribly pious, and considered it a scandalous relationship. We were to visit them in the afternoon, because they too had inherited shares in the bank, and you had to be polite to them so that their money would stay in the family. You had heard all this while you were still in the corridor and had only put the cases down. Then Aunt Grete showed you round the apartment.

It was very large, but you recognized a lot of things in the salon. The chocolate cups that Father had inherited were in a glass case, but Aunt Grete said they were worth nothing, and Mother said it was news to her that neo-classical Meissen china was worthless. The boy said in that case they could take them home again, and Aunt Grete quickly changed the subject, because Father's old plates with his coat of arms hung on the wall next to the glass case, and there were some others that had been her first husband's too. He had been very much older than Aunt Grete, and after a very, really very harmonious marriage that produced two daughters he had a stroke and died three days later without recovering consciousness. And their elder daughter had embroidered this tablecloth before she was married, with themes from Swedish folklore, and she had made the best match in all Scandinavia. Now she was a widow with five daughters and a little boy and lived in Stockholm, but she had a very, very good income, and the maid was preparing a snack in the kitchen at this minute. The tablecloth in the dining room had been embroidered by Aunt Grete's younger daughter before she married, also with themes from Swedish folklore, and she too had made an excellent match and now lived in an enchanting house just outside Malmö on the way to Lund and was coming to supper today, and Mother said she was tired because she'd hardly slept a wink all night. Then we ate fried eggs and bacon in the Swedish manner, served up with many comments from Aunt Grete, and then she showed us the guest rooms. After that Aunt Grete didn't talk quite so much, because Mother was unpacking, and Aunt Grete was pleased with the cognac and the Austrian farm-baked bread she had ordered, because there was no proper bread in Scandinavia, and she was pleased with the ham too, because such things were very expensive in Sweden; neutrality in the war had its price, as Mother would see when she looked round the town, but Mother was tired and wanted to lie down for an hour.

However, the boy had slept well overnight and thought he'd like to explore Malmö. Aunt Grete said he wasn't to stray too far from the house, he must keep a close eye on the time, because we had to visit the sisters punctually, and she would be happy to send someone with the boy to keep an eye on him if she had anyone, but she didn't, and the boy said yes to everything, including the front doorbell that Aunt Grete showed him, and then he was glad to be out and about on his own.

The City Theatre was a board fence through which you could look into an incredibly deep pit, and there was a picture of Herr Grünwald outside the Sockerbolaget, but he didn't have green hair. And if you went a little further along the road down from Aunt Grete's street, and crossed a bridge, you were in Malmö. First there was a square with nothing going on in it. It was called Gustav Adolfs Torg, but all the kings of Sweden were called Gustav Adolf, and you didn't know which one this was. Nor did the Swedes, for they learned German in school but hadn't wanted to visit Germany since the war, but then an old man sitting there told him it was market-day here until noon, but the better market was in another square to the south. The old man was very difficult to understand, and there were a great many shops in the street straight ahead. You'd never seen anything like it. There seemed to be no space left inside those shops, for everything was out in the street: clothes, shoes and many other things that you knew about in Austria but hadn't been able to get for a long time. And Sweden had such vast quantities of them that they could be put out in the street, yet no one stole them. People just walked past; sometimes they touched something and then went on – such a thing would have been unthinkable in Austria. You watched for a long time and then looked at the time. You didn't have to go back yet, so you went a little further and looked at the green hindquarters of a horse on a memorial, but then you had to turn round. The way back took much less time than you had expected, so you stood outside Aunt Grete's door for a while until it was five minutes before the appointed time and you could ring the bell. Once again Aunt Grete was terribly worked up and said the boy could have been late back, and then they would have been late in arriving, and Mother said he was well brought up – as she liked to tell other people, but never the boy himself – and Aunt Grete said it was very difficult to get decent flowers in Sweden, but she had found some, although they were very expensive, and she was holding a perfectly ordinary bunch of snapdragons, and then at last they went to see the bank manager's sisters.

They lived a few streets away, also on the first floor and opposite a park. You had to get used to the dark, because they had drawn their curtains for fear of being tanned by the sun. That would not have been fitting for them, and as the visit went on they mentioned many other things that weren't proper, and they got a chance to say so because Aunt Grete was talking very little. They thanked her for the flowers in a very old-fashioned German, the kind you had sometimes heard from acquaintances of Grandfather's who were all dead now, and who'd had more wrinkles than face. After a while a maid brought tea and petits fours. The tea tasted funny, but you thanked them for it, and were told it was coffee brewed in the traditional Swedish manner, and with it the ladies drank traditional Swedish-made bilberry liqueur, thick as syrup. And when the sisters talked about 'our little boy' they meant Aunt Grete's second husband, who was over sixty himself, but much younger than them, because their father had remarried long after the death of his first wife and the result had been Uncle Nils. Sweden had an awful lot of families who were the subject of constant gossip. But only during the week, for Sunday belonged to God, and you had nothing to say to him except in church, and you weren't allowed to do anything else on a Sunday. The maid had her day off then, and the sisters ate cold food. Aunt Grete told you all that on the way home, for now she was talking volubly again, and Mother asked how they could live such pious lives without sinning all the time to make up for it. Aunt Grete was puzzled by this remark, and said the sisters were tremendously rich and her younger daughter was the only heir. Then we were back at the door of Aunt Grete's house, and then Mother had to look at no end of photographs while the boy had to sit there being good. There was only one photo of Father, as a child.

In the evening Uncle Nils finally came home, and soon after that Aunt Grete's younger daughter arrived. Uncle Nils had very short grey hair, and couldn't get a word in because after greeting everyone Aunt Grete and her daughter talked the whole time, but during the meal he did say something. When Aunt Grete said that roast veal was shockingly expensive in Sweden, a true luxury, since they didn't have an estate like Mother's parents, he said, 'We can afford it.' Then he said no more for the rest of the evening, because Aunt Grete went on talking even when her daughter had left. Sweden was a great strain.

To Mother, Sweden was downright incomprehensible, and Aunt Grete kept saying it was a land where milk and honey flowed. But you were not so fond of honey, and milk didn't flow. It was left outside the door in the morning in bottles, and nobody took it away, however late you brought it in, and then there was a thick plug of cream on top, and you had to shake the bottle to make the milk flow. At Mother's inn the rolls were delivered at the back door in a linen bag in the morning, so that the workers couldn't see them on their way to the factory, but milk was unthinkable, let alone butter, and here they stood around everywhere in the open. And things lay in the street outside shops without being stolen! Sweden had not had a war, it had just delivered supplies, which had certainly paid off. It was amazing to see all the different fish in the market too, some of them ugly, some of them funny, some of them just stupid, because they had eyes on the top of their heads and a mouth the wrong way round. If you fried them they were delicious, and Aunt Grete said the Sund was the richest fish-bearing stretch of water in the world, and was called the Öresund[84] for that reason, for the North Sea and Baltic fish came together there to be caught. What the boy liked best were the little herrings taken from stinking barrels and called Krütsillar. But the mainland too had interesting things, particularly a large stretch of land called the Folketspark where there was a great deal going on in the evening as long as the sky had a Nordic green glow to it. There were stalls with freshly baked waffles, very rich, because their dough was made with cream, called Fraswafler. Beside them were large, open wooden halls where young people could dance. The Swedish way of asking someone to dance was very peculiar: the man dug his elbow into the woman's ribs, then they went up the wooden steps, and while he paid at the cash desk – three dances for fifty öre – she threw her handbag into a corner. As all the women did that there was a whole pile of women's handbags in the corner, but after the three dances everyone found her own again, and they danced to American music. In the other parks, and Malmö had many parks, there were bronze statues of naked women standing about. The prettiest was called Solrosen, meaning sunflower, but she looked as if she were under the shower, and had large breasts, perhaps as an advertisement for Swedish milk. A large stone Pegasus was handsome too. He looked as if he had been lying in the water for a long time, he stood on an angular column, and was just throwing his rider off his back.

After a week Aunt Grete had enough of Malmö, and we went to Höllviknäs to enjoy the fresh summer weather. When a day had been spent in packing, with much talking by Aunt Grete, her son-in-law who was still alive came in his car and loaded everything into it. The car was a large one called a Volvo, which meant the same as Volkswagen in Swedish, but it looked very different from the car for which the Führer had been given a lot of money to build a Wolf's Lair in Wolfsburg.[85] Höllviknäs lay at the south-west tip of Sweden, which was so narrow that you could choose whether to bathe in the Sund or the Baltic, for it was only a ten-minute walk to both, but the Baltic was cleaner. In between there was sand, with pine trees and holiday houses, for the place had five inhabitants in winter and six thousand in summer. A light-house stood on a point beside the Sund, the only attraction in the district, and the holiday houses all looked the same, for they had been built from the pines in the thirties. The pines had grown again since, and their needles pricked you between the toes as you walked to the beach. Sea-grass grew there, and that was the sum of the local vegetation, so that only the holiday houses and two grocers who grew rich in summer were based here. All you could do in Höllviknäs was bathe, and not even that if it rained for a few days, when you had to read *The Saint and her Fool*,[86] the only book that Aunt Grete had in her summer house, which was so trashy and boring that you were glad to see the sun come out again after two hundred pages, just when someone was miscarrying in the bay window of a castle. Aunt Grete was rude about Swedish

cooking and cooked in the Saxon manner, but it tasted horrible. Mother cooked every other day, and that was edible.
Once the women quarrelled because Aunt Grete had over-
salted and overcooked the vegetables again, which is how the
Saxons do it, and as you and Mother were going down to the
beach she said she admired Uncle Nils for his patience, but
you'd noticed that already, and then you had to drink a lot of
lemonade at the grocer's on the way because the salt made
you very thirsty.

At the farthest tip of the promontory was Falsterbo, and
you walked there once. It didn't look any different there from
Höllviknäs, and there was a very famous bar with a complicated name and an owner called something-son, but everyone in Sweden had a name ending —son. The people who
owned the bar bred geese. The place was only made of wood,
but was very fine inside, which you saw only when you had to
go to the lavatory, because you had all been sitting out on the
terrace looking down at the sand between the thin boards
while Aunt Grete talked. Suddenly the ground shook, and Aunt
Grete fell silent. You thought of earth tremors, but when you
looked up a hugely fat woman was walking past followed by
a small man. Other people must have thought of an earth
tremor too, because all was still in the bar. First all the guests
looked at their plates to make sure they were still there, and
then they looked at the vast woman's back. She was wearing
a headscarf, a huge pair of sunglasses and a summer fur,
which was rather worn at the back, and when she was finally
far enough away, and people were looking at their plates
again, Aunt Grete repeated that this was a famous bar. And
Mother whispered to the boy, 'That's Zarah Leander,[87] but
it's not the end of the world.' Then she paid the bill, which
matched such a famous bar, and you all went back to
Höllviknäs.

One weekend, early in the morning, Aunt Grete's brother-
in-law visited, the father of the son-in-law who was still alive.

You had heard that he was a farmer with a very large farm, and his car was outside the grocer's, since it wouldn't fit into the narrow space in front of the holiday house, and now he had come to fetch both mother and son and show them something of Sweden. He was a grey-haired giant of a man, if not as voluminously fat as Frau Leander; he laughed a lot and spoke very good German because he had studied in Greifswald. He said he expected Mother needed a little rest from Aunt Grete, and Mother laughed. His car was really very large and full of leather inside, and we set off straight away. You were sitting in the back, looking out of the window, and the grown-ups were talking in the front. You were surprised at first to find that Swedish cars were different from normal ones and the steering wheel was on the right, but the gentleman said that Sweden drove on the left, like England, so he had bought an English car, and suddenly you were driving past a row of palm trees. That surprised you, and Mother too, but the gentleman said well, this was the most southerly point of Sweden. Trelleborg had once been much more elegant, but now the ferry traffic with Germany and Poland was of hardly any importance, and the people were doing badly. Then there were some strange-looking stones on the left, dating from the Vikings, and afterwards you all had coffee in a town with brightly coloured houses, called Ystad. It wasn't far from there to his farm, he said, and of course we wanted to see it. We drove away from the sea through a green, hilly landscape, and the fields were large, for Skane was a rich place, and this farmer was evidence of the fact. A great many trees came next, and the farm was behind them. You saw a tower, and then another, and it was all built of brick, and then you saw a huge house. The arches over the gate and the windows were made of grey stone, but everything else was brick, and Mother swallowed and cried, 'Why, this is a castle!' 'It's been in the family a long time,' said the farmer. Then he drove round the house into a large yard, and the outbuildings were on the other side of the road. His wife and his younger son, who would inherit the farm one day, were standing at the entrance, and while the grown-ups went into the house you could look at the car. It was called a Bentley. You all went through the house into a park with a pavilion where a table was laid, and you couldn't see why Aunt Grete was so rude about Swedish cooking. When dessert came, the farmer's wife brought out an old theatrical programme, and Mother exclaimed, 'Oh!' Then the farmer's wife said they had been to Vienna on their honeymoon, when Mother had been singing Pamina.[88] Now they wanted her autograph, all these years later.

Later you saw something of the house too. It was like your grandparents' house but different, since the old furniture was Swedish and so were the family's ancestors, and the younger son showed the boy their hundred and fifty cows and all the horses. Then he asked the boy if he'd like to ride, and while the grown-ups talked you saw some more of Sweden on the back of a patient horse. There were a great many fields that would soon be ready for harvest, and huge meadows that had already been mown once, with rows of trees and bushes between them, and as all this lay on gently rolling hills it was like being in a park. A pavilion surrounded by six tall linden trees stood on one little hill, and was the family mausoleum. Inside was a classical white marble woman with one breast hanging out of her robe as a sign of mourning, and a finger to her lips to show you mustn't laugh at it, for there were small stone slabs round the pavilion with the family's ancestors lying under them. The woman was not by Thorvaldsen[89] but by one of his colleagues. When you got back the grown-ups had finished coffee and had reached the liqueurs, and they were smoking. The farmer said his sister-in-law had not had an easy time after the war, although her elder daughter had married very well, and the younger was married to his son, but people had called her Nazissienta because she couldn't keep her mouth shut. And when the boy said this was the best day he'd had in Sweden, there was another meal, and the grown-ups drank old red wine that had to be decanted first. You weren't driven back until late in the evening, with the domestic staff lining the path as you left, and then it was soon back to Malmö. Once you were on the ferry again you decided Sweden was very nice, but you were glad not to have to listen to Aunt Grete any more. Mother said she talked in bursts of gunfire, and the boy had heard of the barrage at Verdun, but you had to understand that she couldn't speak German much in Sweden, and she was Father's sister even if the two of them had never got on well. And the boy should be glad that at least he had now been in a country which had seen no war for a hundred years, and had just provided supplies for other countries. What impressed the boy most, however, was that apart from Aunt Grete no one had said, 'That boy stammers,' and the Swedes didn't make jokes about him. Against that it hardly mattered that yet again you saw no more of Denmark than was visible from the train.

Hamburg, where you arrived in the afternoon, had certainly seen war, and looked quite different not just from Sweden but from the way you remembered it. Even as the train came through the city Mother had exclaimed 'Oh God!' several times, which you hadn't heard her say in years, and then the train came into a huge, black hall full of steam and stinking of soot. There was a gentleman waiting for Mother at the barrier. He wore a pale grey suit which fitted him, although you realized that only later, for all the other men's clothes were loose-fitting and nothing like as elegant, and the people here were much thinner than in Austria. The gentleman was called Sauerland, and Mother said Willy to him, and he claimed to know you although you couldn't remember him at all. When you went to the tram there were small stalls everywhere like the ones at the fair in the village at home, and Uncle Willy said those were the new shops, for since the introduction of the new currency Germany was booming again because everyone wanted money. He talked to Mother about money a lot too, and then you got out in a district that the boy thought he did know. However, you went down unknown streets, past small houses with little vegetable gardens in front of them, and stopped outside one. A little woman came out of it and, after she had hugged Mother, she said she was Aunt Else. She was Uncle Willy's wife, and they didn't have the whole house any more, they'd had to take in two bombed-out families after the war, so they now lived in the upper ground floor. There were beds made up for their guests in the salon, hidden behind a screen, and the Sauerlands were sleeping in the smoking-room with their beds in front of the writing desk. Then Mother talked to Uncle Willy about money, and seemed very pleased, while Aunt Else made matjes herrings with boiled potatoes. But you weren't hungry because you had eaten so much on the ship from Gedser to Grossenbrode.

At table the grown-ups talked about mutual acquaintances. Herr Hagenbeck, Uncle Heinrich, had died immediately after the war, and Frau Meyen in the winter of '45, when there had been nothing to eat, for with the collapse everything else had collapsed too, and supplies were even scarcer than in the war. Uncle Willy himself had got off fairly lightly, since as a businessman he had had excellent relations with the English before the war, and he had inherited some of them from his father; he had enough put away in Switzerland too to take care of number one, and now, fortunately, Hamburg was in the British zone of occupation, which had been a small blessing to him, given the proverbial reliability of the British upper class, and Mother said it was a great blessing for her. Before the war, she had invested money with Uncle Willy, and in the war she had invested more than ever, for Uncle Willy knew all the tricks of an honourable businessman's trade, so Mother had money again even though she had been expropriated, or rather not she herself but Father, so she could almost have it, but only almost, and she would have to invest it again quickly, for Uncle Willy said he was beginning to feel very old and wanted to retire from business, but he had discussed all these matters with a friend from Deutsche Bank, and they would go and see him tomorrow. Then you felt tired.

The centre of Hamburg, which now called itself the City, was very colourful. There were only the ruins of many buildings left, and there were small caverns in these which called themselves shops. They had wooden stalls in front of them, and these were shops too, and there were little wooden villages made of Nissen huts. Many buildings were being restored, some had been repaired already, and the City Hall Square, which had once been Adolf Hitler Square, was almost intact. The trams ran in an oval there and the overhead lines were new, like those in Vienna. The Deutsche Bank was at the back, and it too had been restored. Mother said you were to wait half an hour for her, so you had time to look round Hamburg. Not that there was much of it. The streets looked like Grandfather's mouth when he had taken his false teeth out – a few buildings were standing, others were in ruins, and there were holes in between. There was a particularly good hole at the Neuer Wall, which it took you only three minutes to reach, and through it you saw the Michel[90] and, a little further off, the Bismarck memorial. But people working on the hole said it would soon be gone. You had been waiting another ten minutes outside the bank when Mother came out with Uncle Willy and was in a very cheerful mood. Then you went into a cellar in an almost ruined building, but the cellar wasn't ruined and was called Cölln's Oyster Cellar, although there were no oysters because you don't eat them in months without an R. It wasn't a bar, but little oak-panelled rooms, and you had to ring for a waiter to come. He was very polite, and Uncle Willy said with the new currency there would be many things around now that hadn't been available for a long time.

People might think that equality had broken out, since everyone was given sixty marks, and they might even expect democracy to break out soon, but it wouldn't, and equality wasn't as advanced as all that, since most people had made sure number one was all right and would now do well lending out their secret savings. Most of the old civil servants were still around, and they would ensure that order prevailed, and the coming man was Herr Erhard,[91] who had recorded the real war damage done to German industry by the Nazis and knew how much or little it would take to put it all right. People might say everything had to start from scratch, but ultimately that applied only to works that had been dismantled by the British, which would now become the most modern industrial plants of all, and England wouldn't be able to compete. The word 'reconstruction' was just right, said Uncle Willy, for everything that wasn't still there would be back, except for the Party, but no one needed that, for all decent Germans would agree with him anyway, although they'd have to be cautious now. The one disadvantage of the new currency was that soon there would be two Germanies, for Stalin wasn't going to let the Allied zones put him in the shade. 'The red will divide off from the red, white and blue,' he said, and when you asked what he meant he told you to look at the colours of the occupying powers' flags, and you'd have more chances where there were more colours.

You didn't quite understand that, and you had enough to do anyway eating your princess pasty with ragout neatly, which isn't easy, because puff pastry splits when you stick your fork into it. You tried hard, because Mother had said such things wouldn't be available in Austria, not yet, or not at all because the war had been lost. That wasn't quite correct, because Mother could make excellent puff pastry, and a ragout that tasted very good, but she said a ragout was like a party, it all depended on the ingredients available. You wouldn't be able to get proper prawns in Austria any more, and Worcester sauce, the real sauce from Thingummy & Whatsit, she still had a little left from before the war, which showed that Austria had lost even more in the war than Germany. Herr Sauerland said the east of Germany had lost considerably more than the west, and the boy thought of the crayfish that he caught at home and Mother put in the ragout. You did it by taking the broken remains of the inside of a sprung mattress, you tied some very old meat to it and put it in the brook where the water was clean, half an hour's bicycle ride away. The crayfish came because they liked bad meat, and if you pulled the skeleton of the mattress out quickly they couldn't get out of the spirals in time. Then the meal was over, and in Hamburg the sun was so hot that Uncle Willy needed a nap.

As Mother had plenty of money again, she said, you could ask for something, and of course you wanted to visit Hagenbeck's Zoo. You recognized the big gate at the end of the tramline, although the rocks looked like papier mâché now. But Roma wasn't there, and nor was August. Only when Mother had asked one of the keepers, a man she knew, did they find August with the gnus, which were standing about behind the fence of their enclosure looking bored. He was very surprised, and said how much the boy had grown, but August himself had changed a lot too. He had almost no hair left on his head, and his face was very thin, with big red swellings, but he said it didn't matter, it was cancer. When you told him he might die of that he laughed and said everyone was going to die of something. Roma had died immediately after the war, and many of the animals had had to be slaughtered, because they couldn't be fed. So they talked for a while, and the boy looked at the dappled sunlight coming through the trees so as not to have to see August, who was so different, but then you and August went into a hut where some new crates were about to be unpacked. He rummaged around in the hay inside one crate for a minute, and took out a round thing that he said was a Javanese musk turtle. He gave it to the boy, who called it August, and it got very lively later in the night. When they parted August took a large gulp from his hip-flask. Then he coughed, wiped his eyes, and said it was only because of the schnapps.

SNAGS

To her great delight, Mother had found some genuine DDT in Hamburg. She bought ten of the round, brown cardboard cylinders, saying that she had got through the whole war with six. You made a small hole and then dusted the powder out. It had a sweetish but uninteresting taste, and was good for just about everything.

Uncle Nils had given the boy a book as a goodbye present, although he didn't have many books, and it was in German although it had been written by a Dane, and since the war Danes didn't know German any more. But this book[92] was much older than the war and very difficult to read; it took you a long time to understand a single sentence. The author seemed to be in the same situation as the boy, finding it difficult to say what he meant, so you took trouble with it, because the Dane was very kind and was trying to comfort you for everything that made life so very tedious.

'*Repetition*', it said at the very beginning,

is a determining expression for what the Greeks called 'memory'. As the Greeks also taught that all recognition is remembering, so more recent philosophy teaches that all life is repetition ... Consequently repetition, if it is

possible, makes a man happy, while memory makes him
unhappy, always presupposing that he takes the time to
live and does not, at the hour of his birth, immediately
find an excuse to steal away from life again, saying, perhaps, that he has forgotten something . . .

It is a part of youth to hope, it is a part of youth to
remember, but courage is required to desire repetition.
He who would do nothing but hope is cowardly; he
who would do nothing but remember is sensual; but he
who desires repetition is a man, and the more thoroughly
he has understood how to make repetition clear to
himself, the more profound a human being he is. But he
who does not understand that life is repetition, and that
this is the beauty of life, has condemned himself and
deserves no better than to perish, as he certainly will;
for hope is a tempting fruit that does not satisfy, memory
is wretched provision for our journey, and does not
satisfy; but repetition is the daily bread that satisfies
and blesses us.

You therefore made up your mind not to see the boarding
school in its true bad light, difficult as you knew that would
be. Herr Hirthentaler, when you once showed him the book,
said Kierkegaard was much too difficult for the boy, and he
himself hadn't read him because the Dane was a Protestant,
but you found that intriguing, for you didn't like the Catholics
any more now that you had met the Fathers. They lived in a
state of constant repetition themselves, their whole day was
repetition, with the prayers for the different canonical hours
and the offices, yet they thought that made them superior
and would take them straight to heaven – well, you supposed
that Kierkegaard had meant that too even though, apparently, he was a Protestant – but Father Christoph had once
told the story of how the Chinese kill a man by letting a drop
of water splash on his head once a minute, just a single drop,

and after a few years it drives him mad and then it kills him, and Father Christoph hadn't been able to say whether he died of the drops of water or the madness. He just said it was all the same, and the drops of water would teach us to be better, not to be Chinese. That was true humility before the Lord, yet there were plenty of Chinese about – it was an Austrian term for idiots.

This time you didn't have to go back to the boarding school until the Sunday, because you weren't a new boy any more, but otherwise it was the same as usual, and one of the class wasn't there. He had been blown up collecting scrap metal. You had to pray for him in the evening, and Father Columban, whom you saw next day, was trembling even more than last year. Otherwise it was the same except that you were one class higher, which wasn't much. Grandmother had said that if the repetition got too much for someone he just had to kill himself, and you thought about it. There were many places in the monastery from which you could have jumped, and what made it specially tempting was that the whole monastery would have to be reconsecrated afterwards, so Father Bona-ventura had said, but it wasn't really worth it, and you secretly hoped that everything would change some time. But you happened to be thinking that just when Father Romuald, who was your form master this year, asked where you had been in the holidays. You were going to say, 'In Sweden,' but you didn't get beyond 'S – S – S' before he was saying, 'Ah, so our stuttering splutterer has been in S-S-Silly-Billy Land,' and everyone laughed. You had hoped the name would be forgotten at the monastery over the holidays, but they'd remembered it.

One thing different was that now you were in a new dor-mitory, in a bed right by the door, and Father Bonaventura kept talking about a very special event for the monastery: there was to be a new Father. You had learned that the monastery had been in existence for three-quarters of a millennium, and there had always been Fathers here, more of them or less of them but never none at all, but Father Bonaventura was making a great fuss about this, calling it a 'solemn profession of vows' and 'ordination to the priesthood'. However, that just meant that someone would be making a solemn promise to be a Father, and then he would be ordained. The Father, whose name was Anselm and whom we didn't know yet, had already said he wanted to be a Father, and then he had studied to be a Father, and he hadn't changed his mind about it. So that was what was being celebrated.

There was a lot of work for you, because as you didn't stammer when you sang you had been recruited into the church choir, so you were in the dormitory where the sopranos and altos slept, and on four afternoons a week you had to rehearse the Mass to be sung at the celebrations, Haydn's Mariazeller Mass with the squeaky soprano solo in the Kyrie, but another boy was singing that. You had a new suit too, made of a lighter fabric than Grandfather's altered suits, and the village tailor had gone to a lot of trouble, because Mother had brought a good deal of money back from Germany, hidden in her corset because of currency controls. The boy had been told he could have something he wanted because he had been 'relatively good' in Sweden, and he had only had a very sweaty suit with him. However, when Father Coelestin first saw the new suit he had said, 'Stuck-up snob!' again, and looked in the boy's locker. But he found only half a home-made salami, and he had to leave the boy that. You knew he was mean, but it was still annoying.

The rehearsals for the Mariazeller Mass were nerve-racking in another way. You liked Orgi really, the music teacher who called himself general musical director of the monastery. He was not a Father, but had a wife in town, and the monastery's violin teacher was his girlfriend. Everyone knew that, for his wife was fat and grey, while Fräulein Lunzer had red hair and was well endowed, and every time she saw Orgi the look in her eyes changed, only the Fathers mustn't notice, so Orgi was very often nervous. It seemed that he didn't hear quite so well since the summer, and he often struck wrong notes on the piano. So you sometimes had to sing him a C and then a D because he had gone wrong, but he didn't know it, and when he did notice his mistake it was a C again, but it was often the same with F and G, and when Orgi got impatient you never knew if he was impatient with you or with himself. When he noticed his mistake he was angry, really with himself but pretending it was with other people who couldn't read music. Sometimes he corrected himself at once, and as he then quickly struck the right note there were interesting variations of key that had not been foreseen. On the other hand, you could talk to each other during rehearsals with Orgi, because he didn't hear you and noticed only when he saw your mouth movements.

And Father Bonaventura was going on so much about the solemn profession of vows and the ordination that you were sick of it. On the Saturday before the ordination, however, the Little Museum had its autumn outing, and four sixth-year boys from the Large Museum had come to supervise us, so that Father Thomas could enjoy looking back over fifty years here. First the boys went down to the Danube and crossed it by ferry. The ferry had no engine, but was attached to a rope, and the current made it drift back and forth. Father Richard had explained how that happened in the last physics lesson, and now you could see it, but it wasn't exciting, because there were ferries like that everywhere on the Danube and you were familiar with them. Then you all went to the Oberhaus ruins, which were interesting because you could still see the kitchen and some of the rooms, but their plaster was gone, and the ladies' apartments were now the farmer's goat-shed. He lived in a house called the Vorburg. Then you went back up the hill above the Danube, where there was a country inn. The boys had to sit outside in the garden, where there were tables and benches. Father Thomas sat in the wooden arbour by the house door where it was shady and had a plate of cold cuts and some wine, and the sixth-year boys walked up and down keeping an eye on us. Soon word got around that on the way to the lavatory you passed a room where there was another bar, and the landlady was selling things there. Most of them were home-made liqueurs whose essences you could buy and make into liqueur with boiled sugar and spirits of wine, and they were called Emperor Pear, Glow-Worm (green), Midnight Secret (red) and Parfait d'Amour (mauve). They were very cheap, and so sweet that they tasted good only if you poured them into the beer that the landlady was selling too. There was a sixth-year boy in this room all the time, making sure that Father Thomas didn't get wind of this, but he was sitting in the arbour dozing, tired out by the excursion, the cold cuts and the wine, and the boys could stay in the room only for quarter of an hour each, so that the others could have a turn too. But since Father Thomas was dozing everyone got in three or four times. The sixth-year boys drank a lot of beer, and they didn't have to pay for the last bottles because the landlady said she had done excellent business, and she gave them a home-made brandy too. It was six by the time they woke Father Thomas, and time to go back to the monastery for supper. But the way home took much longer than expected. Even in the village some of the boys were staggering about and falling over, but things really got out of hand only when they were crossing the fields, where there was a light wind blowing but it was very hot. Father Thomas went ahead, fanning himself with his prayer book, because he had drunk three glasses of wine and was sweating heavily. The boys were having trouble too, since many of them were very tipsy and fooling around, and one rolled down the hill almost as far as the road below. Two sixth-year boys had to catch up with him, but they weren't too steady on their own legs, and then the first began throwing up. Father Thomas was well ahead by this time and hadn't noticed anything, but now he came back, saw the unfortunate situation and was angry, but that did no good because the sixth-year boys were drunk too. The whole party arrived at the monastery three-quarters of an hour late, and Father Thomas was very red in the face. Father Coelestin was very angry, and the boys got only a piece of bread for supper because of their sin. That was not very good, for the boy knew that you ought to drink a lot of soup if you're tipsy, but Father Coelestin didn't take that into consideration, and some of the boys were really ill.

Next day was the great event, but many boys were still unwell from the day before, particularly the one who was to sing the solo, and whose face was all green. That was how his solo sounded too, and Orgi was not happy. From the gallery where the organ, choir and orchestra were you couldn't see much of the ceremony at the other end of the church, all about Brother Anselm, who was now going to be a Father and a priest, and for whose sake the Bishop himself had come. He was lying on his stomach in front of the Bishop, with the other Fathers standing around and looking very solemn. The new Father had a chasuble on too, but it was rolled up at the back and was unwrapped only after much singing and prayer. For lunch there was fried pork schnitzel in honour of the event, but many boys were still so unwell that they couldn't eat any, and all the Fathers said this had been a very great day.

Next Sunday was Father Anselm's solemn First Mass, meaning the first time he would read Mass as a priest, and all his family had come, and other people too, because Father Bonaventura had said that the blessing given by a priest at his First Mass was worth wearing out a pair of shoes for. Father Anselm blessed and blessed, and put his hands on everyone's heads, but it was meant in a solemn way, and the organ played preludes. In the afternoon the Little Museum went on another excursion, again with Father Thomas, but there were other sixth-year boys with them this time, and Father Thomas made sure they didn't pass any inns. He needn't have bothered, because most of the boys had no money left anyway.

Father Anselm had a room near the choirboys and was to supervise the three dormitories to make sure that no sins were committed there, because he hadn't studied anything except how to be a Father and a priest. He took over supervision duties in the Museum from Brother Ansgar, and that was good because he wasn't so short-tempered, and Brother Ansgar had to go to hospital. Later you heard it was a psychiatric hospital, a loony bin, but he had been there quite often before and was in the boarding house only now and then, which was why he was still a Brother and had never become a Father. There was talk about him, but it made no difference to the boy, who was just pleased not to have to see any more of him.

Directly after Father Anselm the Egyptian came. He was smaller than the boys in the top form, although he was in his mid-twenties, had dark skin and curly hair like a Negro, and he was not really an Egyptian but a Copt from Egypt. Copts were good Christians, Father Coelestin said, and they didn't have an easy time, because they were surrounded by heathens there on the Nile and couldn't convert them, the heathens being in the majority. Father Anselm had met him praying in Vienna during his studies, but the Egyptian didn't want to be a Father, he wanted to be a doctor, so he was studying medicine and preparing for a state examination. He was given a small room near the spiral staircase where a monastery servant had once lived, and Father Coelestin said it was Christian generosity and monastic hospitality, but the Egyptian got the same food as the pupils. His name was Talat Amer.

You hardly noticed him, because he spent a lot of time with Father Anselm, and when he wasn't praying with him he was studying his books. Otherwise, he liked talking to boys, but they had to have dark hair like his. He was afraid of blonds, he once told the boy. It was in the playground that he spoke to you; you were sitting on a bench by the wall and he sat down with you. He had a funny accent, but you could understand him, and he said he felt very lonely here, and homesick, and it was always so cold that he was freezing all the time. You told him it was really hot today, that was why you were sitting in the shade, and if he felt cold he had only to move into the sun, but he said the freezing came from inside, because he was so lonely outside Egypt. Then he told you about a fat king who owned the whole land, and was good to the Copts, but he was a heathen and had many wives, though most people couldn't afford that in Egypt, but it was nice and warm there, and so cold here, and he talked so much and so long that you promised to lend him your scarf after supper.

You had always had a big scarf, for a scarf was something wonderful and could work miracles when it had been your father's. If you had a stomach pain you just had to wrap it round your stomach, and if you had a cold you put it round your head. Your best scarf was the Red Fruit Pudding, very long, striped red and yellow, and dating from before the First World War. It was called Red Fruit Pudding because it had once looked like a red fruit pudding with vanilla sauce, but it had been washed so often that it no longer looked like red fruit pudding but like something that had been thrown up, and it had been a help to you so often that it was all ragged and had to stay at home. So you had got the tartan scarf, which looked like its name, was made of very thick silk, came from Hamburg, and was shabby only on one side. If you wore it with the inside showing the tartan scarf still looked good, and it was almost as helpful as the Red Fruit Pudding. You lent it to the Egyptian, and he wrapped it round his neck so that he wouldn't feel so lonely. Then he wanted to show you his medical books, but you didn't feel like it.

Other boys were interested in them, because sometimes you saw one come out of the little room, looking right and left to make sure no one could see them. Now and then he came into the Museum with a few sheets of paper and showed them to a boy, although the boy couldn't know if the Egyptian was studying properly. Once you saw one of those sheets. It showed the sexual organs of a man and a woman, very badly drawn, nothing like as good as the anatomy book at your grandparents' house. You said so, and the Egyptian was disappointed. Then he went over to another boy sitting close enough to hear everything. He showed the same to him, and added that he could show him the coloured originals in his books. Father Anselm had supervision duty in the Museum, but he didn't seem to see or hear anything. A little while after the Egyptian had gone the boy said he had to go to the lavatory, and stayed there a long time. Father Anselm spoke to him about it, and he blushed.

In the evening, when you were really supposed to sleep, the Egyptian was always going into Father Anselm's room to pray with him for about an hour, and you could tell from hearing the door of Father Anselm's room open, because you slept beside a door right next to it yourself, and you could hear when it opened and closed unless you were asleep yourself. This time they were talking in very loud voices. You could hear them even through the wall, but when you got up you couldn't understand a word they were saying in Father Anselm's room the other side of the double door, you just knew that they were quarrelling, and then you heard firm footsteps and several angry words that you didn't understand and were probably Egyptian. Next morning the Egyptian was at Mass as usual, and then at breakfast, but he was looking very grave, and Father Coelestin didn't say a word to him, although he usually liked talking to him. And at lunch time he was gone. You saw Herr Ludwig clearing out his room, but there was no sign of the Egyptian, and what hurt most was that he had taken your tartan scarf with him. Now you were left defenceless.

On All Saints' Day the sky was almost blue, but a terrible stormy wind was blowing, putting out almost all the candles in the graveyard and pulling the flowers on the graves about. You met Herta, a girl you'd known for ever, just as she was tidying up her great-grandparents' grave, and were glad, because you hadn't seen her for a long time. She was three years older than you, and had played with you a great deal when you were still a child, and now she was going to commercial college in town because she wanted to be a secretary one day. You could talk to her about everything, and on the way back to the lower village you told her all the things you hated at the monastery. Herta said you'd better not tell Mother because she wouldn't understand. She probably thought she had done the best for her boy, and wouldn't be able to understand that it was no such thing. There was nothing to be done about it, for the opposite of 'good' was 'well-meant', and life often turned out much worse than people expected. For instance, said Herta, she herself couldn't understand why most girls wanted to get married some day. She for one never would, because she'd seen what it was like for her parents, and she didn't want children either, having had to look after her three brothers when she was a child herself. It was always like that once parents had a daughter – then they could go ahead and have boys without another thought. For a while she had thought of becoming a nun, but then she realized that there is no God. At least, all the clergy talk about God a lot but act as if he doesn't exist, and since they ought to know about God there can't be much to him. It wasn't easy to accept that you were all alone in the world without any higher being, for you couldn't talk about such things to parents, they'd never understand, said Herta.

Then you had reached your grandparents' apartment,

where the boy was to have tea, and Herta was going home, but Grandmother had seen her through the window and sent her maid down to invite Herta in with you. She didn't say much, although Grandmother asked her a lot of questions, and when Grandfather came in she said nothing at all, although he said she used not to be so shy. When Herta had gone, and Grandfather was back in his study, you told Grandmother what Herta had said. Grandmother sighed and said parents and children would never understand each other, and the fault was on both sides. She had once known a girl who wouldn't listen to her parents and had paid a heavy price. But she didn't know if that was quite right, for she had also known another woman who didn't listen to her parents, and that had turned out well. It was a fact, however, that children never understand why their parents think as they do, and parents never understand why their children always want to be different, because they'd thought they were setting a good example, and didn't realize how many good examples there are, being sure that they themselves are the best. But you had better not tell Mother you were so unhappy with the habit-wearing pissers, because she knew her daughter and that would really make her obstinate. However, she told the boy that if he could stick it out in the monastery he would get twenty schillings a month, and she gave him the first twenty at once.

So you had a good reason to go back to the monastery, and you didn't upset Mother. A few days later, however, you were sorry. You were in your pyjamas, and were just putting your toilet things away in the cupboard, when Father Anselm came along and told the boy to come with him. Then you were in his room, with plenty of time to look around, since he said he had to go round checking. It was a real Father's room with old brown furniture. There was a large tiled stove on the left, and a desk beside the bookshelf near the window, with a big copperplate engraving of a Raphael Madonna hanging over it.

On the right beside the window was a set of Biedermeier chairs, and over them hung Jesus on the cross. There was a door to the bedroom beside it, and a glass case containing holy things – tapers, candles – and stuff his family had given him for his First Mass. The one attractive thing was a fat Baby Jesus made of wax with tow for hair, but it was old and must have belonged to his great-grandparents, and then Father Anselm came back into the room. He wanted to talk to the boy, he said, and you had to sit on the sofa beside him. He asked questions and said a few things, laughing, and he began to tickle the boy. You were very ticklish and laughed too, and suddenly Father Anselm was tickling you in the pyjama trousers. He asked the boy if he liked that, but he couldn't reply, he was confused, and afraid of stammering, and he also knew he had to obey the Fathers, but Father Anselm had picked him up and carried him into the bedroom. He put him down there on an armchair, which was very uncomfortable. Then the Father pushed the front flap of his habit aside, and his soutane was open under it. He took out his prick.

'Put it in your mouth,' he said, breathing heavily.

You didn't want to, but you couldn't say no. He slapped the boy's face, and then slapped it again, and pushed his prick into his mouth. It was disgusting and hurt, because he was pushing back and forth, making you retch and cry. Now and then he kept slapping you, and the Father moved the boy's head back and forth, gasping, 'Do something,' or, 'Do it properly,' and you were hit for not doing anything, but there was nothing you *could* do.

It went on and on for ages, and the boy was still crying when the Father buttoned up his soutane again. Then the Father stood there, looked at the weeping boy as if he didn't know what to do next, until there was a knock at the double door outside. The Father whispered to you to keep quiet, went out of the room, closed the bedroom door and opened the other one. Then you heard the voice of a seventh-year boy you

knew, and Father Anselm saying, 'Not now,' or 'Not today.'
Then he closed the door and came back. He told the boy not
to cry. He had only wanted to find out if he had been doing
anything wrong with the Egyptian, and now he knew he
hadn't, and the boy was not as bad as he had thought. The boy
felt the tears streaming out of his eyes, and his chin hurt in a
strange way and couldn't be moved. He turned aside and tried
to put it right with his hands. After a while it worked, and he
felt ashamed. Then the Father said he had been obliged to discover the truth, and it had been painful for him too, and you
were not to talk to anyone about it because it was a secret of
the confessional, and he forgave the boy, who was to go now.

But you didn't go to the dormitory, you went to the wash-
room first, because your face was all tearstained and your jaw
still hurt, and you needed a great deal of water. Then you stole
into the dormitory and pulled the blanket over your head,
which you didn't like doing, because you got hardly any air,
but you wanted to be left in peace. However, you didn't get
peace, because after a little while a boy whom you didn't particularly like crept up to your bed. He whispered, 'Did he
want to know if you'd been doing anything wrong with the
Egyptian?' But you told him to leave you alone, because you
didn't want anyone to find out that you were still crying. And
you also thought you didn't think that what Father Anselm
had done to you was right, but you didn't know how to say
so, and anyway it was a secret of the confessional, and talking
about such secrets was a great sin.

Next morning you went to see Father Coelestin before
Mass. He was standing at the chapel door making sure that
all the boys arrived punctually, but there were still almost
none of them there, and Father Anselm was standing nearby
too. Then you told Father Coelestin that Father Anselm had
hurt you, but you realized you were having difficulty getting
the words out. Father Coelestin narrowed his eyes. 'Why are
you stammering?' You said, 'Father Anselm hurt me in the

mouth.' 'What is he talking about?' Father Coelestin asked
Father Anselm, who had come up and was looking sharply at
the boy. 'I've no idea what he's talking about,' said Father
Anselm. You repeated what you had said, and Father
Coelestin asked, 'Did he slap you?' It was true that he had, so
you nodded and said, 'And he hurt me in my mouth.' 'He's
lying,' said Father Anselm very quickly. 'That's a wicked lie.'
Father Coelestin looked angrily at the boy. 'You are a slanderer! A stammerer and a slanderer!' And he said you were
unworthy of the monastery, you were nothing but a little
criminal, and you were to beg Father Anselm to forgive you
on your knees, this minute, and as this was Saturday you
would get detention after school for the weekend, and the
next two weekends as well. There were quite a lot of boys
standing around now, some of them grinning. So you had to
kneel down in front of Father Anselm and ask him to forgive
you, but you tried to give him a nasty look at the same time.
Father Anselm's face wore a smug smile, and he said he forgave the boy, and then he went into the chapel to robe himself
for Mass. The other boys went into the chapel too and sat
down, but you had to stand at the back by the harmonium
yourself, because you were a sinner.

You had thought a great deal about God, not just because
you were in a monastery, and now it occurred to you that you
could find out whether he existed or not. You had heard
many stories to the effect that God was very angry if a priest
read Mass in a state of sin, and you were sure that Father
Anselm had committed a sin last night, and as it was very
early he couldn't have confessed it yet. So you were expecting
God to send a thunderbolt into the chapel to punish Father
Anselm. But when he came in with the servers it was all the
same as usual.

Alas, where shall I turn
When grief and pain oppress me . . .

Then, at the Confiteor, the servers had to count quietly up to twenty, to give time for everyone to say *mea culpa, mea culpa, mea maxima culpa*, but still nothing happened. However, that was right really, you'd have to wait for the consecration, when God would enter into the wafers and could send proper lightning. You held your breath when the service reached that point, but still there was nothing. It was an ordinary Mass in green,[93] that's to say with the priests wearing green chasubles, and at the end of Mass all the boys went up to swallow wafers, which was called taking communion, but you yourself weren't allowed to because you were sinful. You were to confess next day, before the Great Mass in church. But you were no longer afraid of going to Hell if you died before that, because now you knew that there was no God.

Before lunch you had to go into detention, but it was the school detention room, and Herr Ludwig brought you a plate of soup. He told the boy he had been very stupid to complain of Father Anselm, because they said one crow would never peck another's eye out, and the Fathers were black like crows, but you couldn't tell him why you had complained because you felt so ashamed of the whole thing. Then Herr Ludwig gave you a sip from his bottle of schnapps, which did you good, and you heard the playground outside getting noisy and then quietening down because the other boys had to go for a walk. You had time to think about the God who didn't exist. So he was a lie himself, and in a way it was funny that there had been people who believed in him for so long, and still were. That was because the Fathers had studied, so people believed in them the way people in the village believed in the doctor. He had a little bag with a stethoscope and a few other little things that looked as if they were very precise. It all seemed scientific, and people believed in it. The clergy had far more things, beginning with the magnificent chasubles and going on to all those golden and gilded vessels, and they made such a fuss about it all with incense, singing and music that people were impressed and believed there really was a God. Well, some people didn't, and the clergy called them 'luke-warm Christians', because of the Biblical saying that you should spit out what is neither hot nor cold. But that wasn't right either, because you yourself had often burnt your mouth on hot food, and if something too cold got into your mouth that hurt too. However, people believed in God the way they had believed in the Führer, although now they all said they'd never believed in the Führer at all. So they must have been luke-warm Nazis, although the Austrians had always had the reputation of being one hundred and fifty per cent Nazi, but perhaps that was luke-warm too because it was so much. Perhaps they had cooled off over the years, like soup that you didn't like any more, but you'd eat a few spoonfuls if you were thirsty. Still, your grandparents, Mother, and many of the people you knew were luke-warm Christians too. Perhaps they'd been luke-warm all through the years, but anyway they were better than the Fathers. You were feeling angry with God, but then it struck you that you couldn't be angry with something that didn't exist. You looked for the right word, and came up with 'disappointed'. But here you had the same problem, because if you were disappointed then you'd shown yourself up as a fool for expecting an ox to be more than just a piece of beef, as Grandmother used to say. So you had believed in God too, if not so much, but very firmly on this occasion. Now you didn't have to believe any more, and nor did the Fathers, for Father Anselm had shown that he himself didn't believe in God by lying when he said you were lying, and then reading Mass. But it was very difficult not to believe at all. Believing was easier, as you'd noticed yourself with other stories which you had believed, and then you found you'd been taken in, for believing was easier up to the moment of disappointment. So you had to force yourself not to believe, and you thought for a long time, and then Herr Ludwig brought your evening soup. You were let out of the detention room for evening prayers, but you didn't talk to anyone. Some of the boys mocked you, and then you pretended to be asleep, but you still went on thinking.

On Sunday morning you had to go to confession before Mass. You saw Father Thomas slip into the confessional, and went to him because he was kind. He knew what had happened already, and said you must tell him all about it, it would be a secret of the confessional and only God would know. So you began telling him, but soon Father Thomas was saying this was all terrible, and he couldn't forgive you your sins if you did not repent of them. What the boy was talking about was unchastity, even if only passive unchastity, and he must admit to it if God was to forgive him. That was the sensible thing to do, as the boy realized, so he confessed to passive unchastity and was absolved. After Mass he had to go back to the detention room, but this time he was thinking about getting away from the monastery.

That wasn't easy either. Mother certainly wouldn't understand, and Grandmother would say he must obey Mother. So he was on his own and didn't know where to turn. There was only one thing to do: find a quiet place for it and then die. But he didn't want to die.

On Monday life was back to normal again. When the other boys went to the playground you visited Herr Hirthentaler. After the business with the pebbles you had avoided him for some time, but he was the only person you could really talk to, so with time you had become friendly with him again. Perhaps Herr Hirthentaler would know how you could survive, because he had once called himself an artist in survival. But even Herr Hirthentaler had to go along with the system. He said at eleven and a half no one could survive alone in this world. However, he had heard of someone who was accepted by the Academy of Art at fourteen. A Jewish boy, of course, surprising as it was that any of them were still around. But the

Jews were good at survival too. So the state would pay for this Jewish boy now, and he was only fourteen, but it was hoped that he would be an artist some day.

As the boy went along the long white corridors paved with Kelheim flagstones, past the doors behind which Fathers were supposed to live but didn't, he went over everything that had happened these last few days. He thought they had been the worst time of his life, and he hated everyone who had delivered him up to the monastery. He hated himself too, for having no chance of surviving on his own. And he decided to be an artist.

After that everything seemed much easier. He just had to wait for his fourteenth birthday. He took a blank arithmetic exercise book and drew up a precise calendar in it, one square for every day until his freedom, to be crossed out in the evenings, and he asked Father Thomas, who was supervising in the Museum, about the leap years to make sure he didn't miscalculate. His decision was rock solid, and it made him see the monastery and his situation quite differently. Herr Hirthentaler said that kind of thing was called getting it into perspective. But the boy hadn't told him exactly what he was planning.

The annoying thing was that Mother suddenly turned up on Wednesday in a state of great agitation. Father Coelestin had written to tell her that the boy had slandered Father Anselm, and would probably be expelled from school for it. It took the letter two days to travel the sixty kilometres, and the very next day she closed the inn and set off. She had been to see Father Coelestin before she saw the boy; she had to give a great deal of money for the Mission, and she was so angry that she slapped the boy's face first thing. The Fathers had a right to chastise boys, just as the teachers and their parents did, she said, and quite right too, and she didn't know what she had done to be afflicted with such a child, and she went on at the boy like this for a long time, slapping now and then, but he avoided the slaps, and didn't stop until a lot of other boys had gathered around to watch. Then she took the boy to the large staircase leading to the school and the refectory, where there was no one around at the moment, and asked why he had done something so bad. You tried to tell her all about it, not the things you were ashamed of, of course, but Mother interrupted, because you were stammering worse than ever, and then she said what she always said when she was angry: her own heredity was fine, and she was in despair, she wanted only the best for the child, and so on. You didn't doubt that, but you couldn't talk to her about it all, since she didn't understand it, or she misunderstood it, and before you could say anything she was gone again, because she had to open the inn, it cost a lot of money to close it and that was the boy's fault too, for otherwise Father Coelestin wouldn't have had to write to Mother. When you went back to the Museum Father Anselm was on supervision duty there, and you thought how mean he was.

You were looking forward to detention next weekend, because you knew you'd be left in peace and could think. But this time Herr Ludwig had something else to do, so a seventh-year boy escorted you to the detention room. He was very friendly and said everyone in the monastery knew that Father Anselm was a queer who fancied little boys, except for the Fathers, who just didn't want to know, and it had been stupid of you to try complaining to Father Coelestin. Then he locked the detention room door on the inside and told you to give him a blow job. The boy was frightened, thought of Father Anselm, felt ashamed and began to cry. The seventh-year boy was embarrassed, and said he hadn't meant it that way. He'd just thought you were experienced anyway, so you wouldn't mind, and he hadn't thought you'd be so squeamish. He was feeling really randy at the moment, he felt like that the whole time in the monastery, he didn't fancy tossing himself off and it was perfectly safe here, no one would barge in. It would be very quick too, because he was feeling so randy, but the boy just went on crying. Then you might at least watch him, said the seventh-year boy, undoing his trousers. You didn't want to cry any more, and looked out of the window with your head turned away while the seventh-year boy tossed himself off, spurting liquid over the boy in the process. He really was very quick. Then he did his trousers up again, said you mustn't mind, it had been really urgent, he had to get rid of it somehow, and you weren't to tell anyone. When he had finally gone you cried for a while longer, because you were ashamed. It was cold in the detention room. You should have put a pullover on. There were no leaves left on the trees, and you couldn't see any birds either. Soon you needed the light on, and there was a bulb, but the switch was outside the detention room. You didn't say anything when the seventh-year boy brought your evening soup, but he didn't say anything either, and that was good. He said nothing on Sunday either, but he left the light on all day, and you had a pullover and had hidden something to read under it. When the detention was over you avoided the seventh-year boy as much as you could, and it worked. A little while after Christmas you heard a strong seventh-year boy and an eighth-year boy saying they would have to beat him up because he wasn't willing to make himself useful, and you felt almost sorry for him.

Christmas was the same as usual. Your report was middling – the only Threes were for maths, Latin and conduct – and everything was the same at your grandparents' house. Grandmother had even more wrinkles now, and looked like a pug dog. She said she had difficulty breathing, and the doctor had diagnosed a weak heart. Grandfather didn't say much, except, 'Trautmannsdorf will be coming the day after tomorrow.' The boy thought of rice pudding,[94] but an old man of that name came to see his grandparents on St Stephen's Day.

Old as he was, he was actually the son of a friend of theirs.
The boy was allowed to serve refreshments, because the staff
had the day off, and the old people talked about their trouble
with the Russians, because their guest had some billeted on
him too. Then Grandmother said the boy could go downstairs, but he was to stay within hearing of the bell in the
kitchen in case they needed him again.

Herr Mandi was working in the stables. He never needed
time off in winter, because he couldn't make bricks then. Herr
Buchlar should really have been helping him, but he was old
now, and was always ill or drunk when there was work to be
done. In between the horses and cattle the boy made Herr
Mandi a Krupnik. You heated two spoonfuls of honey with
water, pepper and cloves, and added plenty of vodka, which
mustn't be too hot. Herr Mandi told you to go easy on the
water, and later said that he noticed, from his work, how old
the master was getting now. Once everyone in the house had
his own job and had learned a trade, and Herr Mandi's father
had said crossly that his son did all sorts of things and didn't
specialize, didn't become a gardener as family tradition
demanded, so now he was well out of that and did just about
everything. His own grandfather had lived to be almost as old
as the master, and indeed had served him when he first
became master. It had been the same with his father, and the
master had been the master, usually keeping out of sight, and
the principle was that his will be done, except that you were
more likely to pray not to meet him, because he had a way of
turning up unexpectedly and seeing at once what had been
done wrong and what was still undone. And in the past he
had usually been right too, so he was thought almost omniscient. And the mistress had ruled the kitchen just as the master
ruled the rest of the place, and everything had turned to gold,
just like it did in a butcher's shop. Well, times were different
now, and the master and mistress were old; the mistress
seemed even older than the master although she was said to

be younger, but women age faster because of having husbands and children, and they had no heir left now that their son was gone. This made you curious, but Herr Mandi said it was a long time ago, he hadn't even been born, only his father really knew about it, and he mustn't talk about it or the master would throw him out at once.

Now you were feeling really curious, but Mother was very funny about it too when you asked her. She said she'd had to promise your grandparents never to tell anyone about it, so she wouldn't. Before you had to go back to the monastery you talked to Herr Mandi until he promised to ask his father, and said he'd tell the boy what he had found out at Easter.

Everything was the same as usual in the monastery, although sometimes there was some entertainment by way of a change, because a great many people were going around trying to earn money. The monastery had a large hall, the largest in the town, and as the pupils had to attend any performances in classes and pay privately, there was always money to be made at the school even if hardly anyone from the town itself came. Sometimes no one needed to come because the whole show took place in the morning. For instance, there was a man who bent iron bars. He bought them from the metal workshop and bent them out of shape until they were useless, he showed his muscles, he had the third-year boys put him in chains and then broke free. Or there were Resistance fighters whom no one in Austria wanted to listen to, so they had to talk to the schools, since they were of some slight educational value and showed that you didn't get as far by resisting as by compromising. Then there were writers who had always set an example, so they had proclaimed themselves 'illegal' members of the Nazi party with a slight delay when the Nazis came to power, and then it had taken them a little while to become secret members of the Resistance too. Now they wrote about sunbeams, babbling brooks, mountains and inherited snuffboxes, politically innocuous subjects, since there was no call at the moment for blood but the soil was always in demand.[95] If they were very famous, like Max Mell[96] and Karl Heinrich Waggerl,[97] they could read to us in the evening. Waggerl described how the Negro king was ashamed when he came to Bethlehem in case baby Jesus might be afraid of his black skin. So the palms of his hands turned pale, and since then all Negroes have tried to be white, for they are really human beings too. That was something for the evening, of course, and clapped-out chamber singers came and gave song recitals too, much in the same way as Mother had tried it, and sometimes there was a real chorus. You would have liked to hear the Don Cossacks under Sergei Jaroff,[98] but they couldn't perform in the Russian zone because Stalin hated them, so you always heard them over American radio, because the Yanks liked annoying Stalin. That was why Stalin was hanging on to Austria, said one Resistance fighter, but another said the Yanks would pester him for not letting Austria go, and it was difficult to understand why the pair of them, Stalin and the Yanks, needed Austria to annoy each other, for Austria was a small place even if, as we learned, it was the most important country in the world. It said so in the national anthem,[99] which had been written by the mother of a Resistance fighter and mentioned mountains, fields, domes, hammers and great sons who, 'hotly disputed, fiercely opposed' had come to occupy 'the centre of the globe', and as a result the country was 'much tried and tested Austria'. You were much tested yourself, and you didn't pass all your tests, but that was normal, and you couldn't see why the Yanks were quarrelling or feuding with Stalin about it. Every Austrian said, ten times a day, that he wanted to be left in peace, and so did you, but on account of the great sons and the 'nation blessed by its sense of beauty' the world would not leave you alone, and you couldn't defend yourself. So in the afternoon there were theatrical shows with glove puppets and marionettes, and sometime even real actors. These shows took place not in the Great Hall but in the boarding house, in a room known as the Theatre Hall because a stage had been built there. The ceilings on that floor were not high anyway, and as the stage was mounted on a podium, and the lights above had small curtains round them, the ceiling there seemed particularly low. You noticed that one day at a performance of *Madame Kobold*,[100] given by one of the many companies travelling about with their scenery from school to school to earn money. The backdrops fitted, being very small: two chipboard triangles that could be put together and showed all kinds of Spanish themes, and behind them hung the permanent backcloth, a view of the monastery painted by the art master, and was attractive by virtue of showing the monastery from a long way off. So now the backcloth was meant to be Spain, and the monastery was meant to be Spanish, and the actors put on a fencing scene. One of them waved his sword so high that a piece of board with a couple of light bulbs on it came down. The bulbs broke with a loud crack, whereupon the other actor jumped back and shredded the monastery backcloth with his own sword. He didn't do it on purpose, for he had been holding the sword behind him, and when he tried pulling it out of the backcloth again he ripped the monastery worse than ever. All the boys laughed, and the actors said they were very sorry. Then Father Coelestin announced in a loud voice from down in the audience that he would deduct the damage from their fee, and they had better get on with the play, because it would be time for prayers in half an hour. The actors went on, but you could see they were sad about the deduction from their fee. But there was fun of this kind only once or twice a month.

At Easter you hadn't forgotten what you'd asked Herr Mandi, but he had, so you had to spend half of Holy Week asking all over again. Then he said that Mother had had an elder brother, called Stefan like your own brother. He had quarrelled with his father frequently, particularly in the summer of 1914, because he had said he wanted the war, but Grandfather didn't, and then he died on the very first day of the war, although he was in Transylvania where there wasn't any front line, and he had been buried there. Well, everyone knew that the master could put up with anything but contradiction, and a quick temper had always been the family's besetting sin, and there were some situations when all you could do was pick up a pistol, so before the master's son set off for Transylvania a notary had signed and sealed a document disinheriting him. The boy did not entirely understand this, and when he asked his grandparents about it in the evening Grandfather was furious. First he asked who had told the boy this story, but as he had promised Herr Mandi not to give him away he said he didn't know. That made Grandfather even angrier, he said it was stupid gossip and he would have no more of it, and he slammed the door with a very loud bang. Grandmother had said nothing all this time, but now she took the boy into the conservatory part of her boudoir. There was a very dusty dressing table there, with ancient beauty aids and skin lotions that Grandmother hadn't used for ages. It had a secret drawer in it that was new to you. There were photographs in the drawer, and after some searching she showed you the photo of a young man, wearing a grand uniform that you had seen before, because it was the uniform of a nationalist German student association, and the Christian student association in the monastery wore something similar. 'That's him,' said Grandmother, and added, 'That was him.' If you loved her, she said, you must never say another word about it. This made you really curious, but you did love Grandmother very much, and she was so sad that you didn't want to hurt her any more.

At the beginning of May she wrote to the boy and to Father Coelestin saying she would like to see the boy on his birthday, and she enclosed a train ticket. When you got home there was a brand new wooden summerhouse in the garden outside your grandparents' apartment. At least, it wasn't really new, but was made from two summerhouses that had once stood in the park and had been damaged by the Russians. Herr Mandl and a few workmen had taken them down and rebuilt them to make a new summerhouse, which worked because they were very like each other, and he had painted them, because there was still some green oil-based paint left and white paint was available again. Now the summerhouse stood in various shades of green in the green garden, instead of its wrecked copper roof it had a new one made of bituminous felt, and it looked more attractive than you remembered it. Grandmother said it wasn't much, but people ought to enjoy themselves, and she had needed it. Your birthday had been a few days earlier, but this was the weekend, and the summerhouse was inaugurated with a wonderful birthday tea party. All the family were invited, though that just meant Grandmother's youngest sister with her husband, who had been manager here for ever, not that there was anything much left to manage, and whom you disliked because he was always so self-important. Then Grandmother made a little speech, saying she was glad that the boy was a year older and she had lived to see the day. She was old now, she said, good for nothing any more, and Grandfather hadn't noticed it only because he wasn't in any better state himself. But she needed someone to look after her, and she had decided on Mother, because after all she knew Mother best, and she needed her as soon as possible. Grandfather seemed surprised, and mumbled a little. Mother was surprised too, and said she would happily look after her Mama, but she couldn't do that and run the inn as well. Grandmother said that of course she had thought of that, and the inn would have to be closed, because she wanted to have a real family around her at least in her last days. Mother was radiant, but Grandfather didn't look very happy, and just said, 'Oh well,' adding later that Grandmother had taken him for a ride, and had done it very cleverly too. To which Grandmother said he surely must be used to that by now, and everyone laughed.

As the weather was fine on Sunday, lunch was in the summerhouse too, and then Grandmother invited everyone to tea again in the old summerhouse that was now new, because she said she wanted to get some more enjoyment out of it. Before the boy went back to the inn she took him aside and gave him a little package which neither Mother nor Grandfather was to know about. When you were back at the inn the place looked quite different. You had become used to it; it had been one of your many homes. You calculated the number and made it three, because Berlin and Hamburg didn't count. The monastery for which you were packing your suitcase certainly wasn't a real home, and Mother's house had burned down, so that just left your grandparents' village, and the place there where you had lived longest was the inn. Now that was to go too, but you didn't mind. It had meant a lot of work for you, but there had always been a good deal going on there.

At tea you saw Russians driving through the entrance in a truck again. Grandmother said she hardly noticed them any more; they were always there, like weeds in a garden run wild, one didn't see them because one was fully occupied looking for any vegetables that might be left. And Grandfather said he had stopped looking out of the windows at the Baroque Wing, which wasn't what it used to be. He had been through the end of the world twice, he said, and a third time would make no difference. Then he went into his study with Mother to discuss business matters, and Grandmother told you a little about herself. She came from a very old Viennese family which owned a lot of land in the Ottakring district, she said. Her father had been the fattest man in Vienna, and he could afford to be, because fields fetched very high prices as building sites when the city expanded, and he had built on some plots of land himself, but then he died prematurely, and her mother had managed the entire property right through the First World War with the aid of war loans, and then died of influenza. There had been some money left for her four siblings, who had all been capable people except for her youngest sister, but she'd always been the baby of the family, and Grandmother herself had more luck than anyone because she had been married to Grandfather for . . . she worked out how long, and said, 'To think I've put up with him for fifty-nine years! High time I died.' You told Grandmother you still needed her, and so you talked until Mother came and said it was time to go to the station. Then Grandmother said you'd have to wait half an hour in town for the next train, and Herr Mandi had better drive you in the car. So he did, and you had to sit at the back, because Herr Mandi wanted to be left in peace and was rather grumpy about being asked to work on a Sunday when he would rather have been making bricks. At the railway station in town people gaped at Grandfather's car, and whispered when it was only the boy who got out with his cardboard suitcase. In the train you opened Grandmother's little package. There was a small gold signet ring inside, which even fitted you, but the letter on it was an S.

Summer soon came, which was good, because at the boarding school Father Anselm was getting more and more horrible. The reason was canned sardines. They were available again, and it was UNRA's fault, something to do with the Yanks wanting to make themselves popular in Austria and sending a great many cans of sardines. They were supposed to be for the poor, but the poor didn't like them, so they were for sale in almost all the shops, even in the Russian zone, and were so cheap that even the butchers' sons in the monastery were given them. Sometimes the heads were still in the cans, but that didn't matter, because you could cut them off, and if you put salt and pepper on the rest of the fish they tasted good – excellent if you had lemons too. Many of the boys ate a can every evening, but you yourself made one last two days, and the sardines annoyed Father Anselm. He said that a can was a complete supper for a family of six, and he told Father Coelestin so. Father Coelestin agreed, saying *Plenus venter non studet libenter*, and he banned the sardines. And a sixth-year boy was expelled from the monastery without notice for calling Father Anselm a 'child-fucker', and when Father Anselm was going to hit him for it the boy hit back. Father Coelestin thundered on about that half the evening, but Father Anselm had a black eye that was soon all the colours of the rainbow.

Unfortunately you yourself had some trouble you'd never asked for. Early one morning you had to go for a pee, and there was a large black heap lying outside Father Romuald's door. It was Father Romuald himself with a puddle around him, smelling strongly of schnapps. He was snoring aloud and holding his bunch of keys in his hand. It took you a long time to wake him, and then he gave a start and tried to stand up. It wasn't easy, and now and then he said, 'Ouch,' because he was lying on a linen bag with something broken inside it. At last he struggled to his feet, put his key in the keyhole, and disappeared. When morning had really come for everyone, Father Romuald looked so ill that you asked him how he was feeling. He gave you a venomous glance and later, in Latin, he asked you questions until you got an answer wrong. Then he kept calling you a stuttering splutterer until the whole class laughed, and you felt so angry that you were almost in tears. At break another boy told you everyone in the top classes knew that Father Romuald sometimes got drunk, and usually had a drink with him. It was something people accepted, like the fact that the baker's wife in town was his girlfriend, and those who knew about it were not popular.

Then you heard Father Coelestin talking to Father Bonaventura once in the school corridor just as Father Columban had walked past. It was a long time since he had really walked, he just shuffled very slowly along, and he spoke even more slowly these days when he was teaching history. It sounded as if he were deciphering prehistoric languages, but he told you about the magnanimity of the Babenbergers, and one would never have thought it would take so long. Now and then he lost the thread too, and just sat there trembling and looking at the class. But he was kind, and looked at you kindly, even when the saliva was dribbling from his mouth and he was trying to wipe it away with a handkerchief in his shaking hand. No one laughed at him, although it was tempting to do so, because you were all sorry for him, and he was never as unpleasant as the other Fathers. Now you heard Father Coelestin saying that this couldn't go on, not with 'him' still there, it was high time he took over as head of the grammar school himself, and would Father Bonaventura vote for him? It was important, because the lay teachers who were not monks had no vote anyway, and Father Richard must be prevented from getting the post. Then he noticed the boy and told him to make off, which you couldn't do for another five hundred days and more, and it was not a pleasant prospect, for if Father Coelestin was going to be head of the grammar school it would be the same there as in the boarding house. But you had a report that Mother didn't comment on much: two Satisfactories, in the teaching language and in maths, and the usual Three for conduct.

Then there was a great deal to be done closing the inn and moving house again. August the turtle moved first. You had made him a home in a small old hotbed in the vegetable garden behind the inn, with a bath made out of an old steel helmet, and August seemed to like it, because he was very lazy. He went for walks by night, as you could see next morning, and he ate during the day, green lettuce along with the snails sticking to it. He had hibernated in the cellar, in a crate of hay next to the carrots that spent the winter buried in sand, and now he moved into a large hotbed in the nursery garden, where only half the beds were under cultivation. His steel helmet came with him, to help him to settle in, and his new home was more than twice the size of the old one.

However, your grandparents' house had been smaller since the arrival of the Russians, how much smaller you noticed only now. Mother's room and your own were still there, and so were the music room and the library, but the double doorway to the large staircase had been blocked up, and there was extra furniture retrieved from the Russian wing everywhere, so that the place was rather cramped. You remembered the library as much larger too, and thought that was because of the library in the monastery, but Grandmother said it was just that you'd grown. On the floor below, a wall had been built between the kitchen and the staircase too, and there was another at the entrance to the farmyard and park, but you knew that already, because ever since it went up you'd had to go the long way round in the nursery garden. Herr Mandi's father said he was glad there wasn't much work to do, since not much could be sold to Vienna these days, but Grandfather didn't agree. Sometimes he said times were sure to change again, and then Grandmother said he'd go gaga in his optimism. Sometimes the walls inside the house were a nuisance, but Grandfather said at least the Russians could be kept at arm's length in this way, and a wash-stand was put in the boy's room so that he wouldn't have to keep using his grandparents' bathroom. Mother could use it every day, but the boy only twice a week.

All the glasses were polished again at the inn, and then put away in cupboards. Mother washed all the tablecloths and the household linen too, and then she packed up the things that were left from her old house. There wasn't much. When it was all done, Grandfather arrived with Herr Mandi and two workers. Grandfather went all round the house, looked at everything, and said that Mother had left it neat and tidy. Perhaps a tenant would come along some time or perhaps not, it was all the same to him, and then the windows on the ground floor were boarded up. A few windows were left ajar behind the boards, so that dry rot wouldn't get a hold, and then the house was abandoned. You really liked it although you had not had a very nice time there, but Grandmother always said one should pay close attention to the past, because only fools believed that the future would be any improvement. As she was clearing up Mother found the ring that Grandmother had given you, and when you told her about it she just said that the worst thing of all for a mother was having to look back at her child, but you didn't entirely understand what she meant by that.

Then Grandmother gave Mother a week off so that she could go to Vienna. The boy went too, and they stayed in an apartment belonging to some friends of Mother's who were still away on their summer holiday. You were glad to see Aunt Anny again, and she had her hands full, because there were a great many Yanks in Vienna just now making a movie. The city looked very romantic, since the houses had been given only emergency repairs, and no one knew what to do with the ruins that were still standing everywhere. There was barbed wire around the opera house, since it was going to be rebuilt, and no one was to steal anything. Operatic performances were at the Naschmarkt now, and many thought that was a much better place for the Opera. But Mother and Aunt Anny wanted to have it back where it was before, and Aunt Anny said it would be ready when the Opera Café too was rebuilt. It was to be entirely demolished and then reconstructed, and Aunt Anny must earn money now if she was to afford her new café. There were still a good number of customers, and many of the Burgtheater actors. These days they were performing in the Ronacher, which was a music hall, and they came because it wasn't far. They earned their money from the Yanks, who paid in dollars, and every dollar was a fortune. Once you saw the Yanks. The top Yank was called Welles,[101] he drank a great deal of schnapps, and he had brought his director and his scriptwriter with him, but there was an Englishman called Grün,[102] who was very famous and knew some German. An ancient lady was sitting with Aunt Anny, a genuine chamber actress called Bleibtreu who had appeared before the Emperor, who was already hard of hearing at the time, and she said now all the war profiteers were united, including those who had been in the Party, because now they were being paid by the Yanks. And there was a man called Willy Forst,[103] who said they'd soon be making good films in Austria again too, since people had nothing to laugh at, and the actors needed for the movies had all been magnanimously denazified. Even Werner Krauss would be able to perform again, but the boy didn't care about that either way.

Then, in the autumn, Father Coelestin became headmaster of the grammar school, and Father Columban also gave up teaching history. He was allowed to keep his rooms on the grammar school premises, since Father Coelestin lived in the boarding house, but he was hardly seen around any more. You had been moved to another dormitory yourself, since you were no longer in the church choir. Orgi had said your intonation was uncertain, and so indeed was his own. You did your best, but sometimes your voice tipped over and another sound entirely came out. It happened when you were talking too, and it wasn't to do with the stammer. When you asked Father Thomas, since he was a natural scientist, he said your voice was breaking, but there was nothing broken when you felt for it. Afterwards, said Father Thomas, you would be grown up, and you liked that idea, although you had a great many days still to cross off on your calendar. Another new thing was that there were now two Germanies, quarrelling over who had started the split. Father Christoph said it was Adenauer, because he couldn't abide the Prussians, and the Western powers kept him on a short leash, although it was a little longer than the one that Stalin allowed Ulbricht, and everyone knew what happened when two dogs held on leashes met in the street. As their masters were not keen for them to bite each other, they would have to negotiate for a very long time before letting them loose at the same moment, and meanwhile the dogs' barking would have made them so aggressive that they couldn't be let loose at all. The real question was whether the Yanks or Stalin were stronger, and the Germans would go along with them and play their game, because they had already fallen for the Austrian who wasn't really an Austrian, having deserted to the Reich before the First World War, and then leaving Braunau to be naturalized in Braunschweig. In fact all the elements in that story were very simple: you had Braunau, Braunschweig, Braunhemd, Eva,[104] and black, red and gold[105] mixed up made brown too. Then there was Wolf: Wolfsburg, Wolfsschanze, Wehrwolf,[106] and for the better understanding of future history we would now turn to Thucydides on the Peloponnesian War.

The boys in your class were odd, and began to act the way you had seen older boys behave. They scuffled at every opportunity, and there were always a few who were the strongest at that – not the best but the strongest, so they bossed the others around. It was horrible when you were just a stuttering splutterer. You were reading an old author who had done a lot of play-acting:

'I believe the worst of every man, even myself, and I have seldom been disappointed.'[107]

Father Bonaventura was carrying on again, because next year would be a Holy Year, when a bricked-up door was to be opened in St Peter's, and you thought of your grandparents' house, but St Peter's in Rome was even larger. All who went

there would have their sins forgiven them, and Father Bonaventura told us he was going himself. Perhaps he needed to.

'Man is the creature which occupies the first rank in the visible creation, which claims to be made in the likeness of God,
and God should not feel flattered. Man is a mammal and
sucks at the breast, taking many fluids into himself . . . man is
also a worm, for he often crawls in the dust, and so makes his
way forward . . .[108]

It was boring, and now and then you played with your
prick again. When you were at home for All Saints' you soiled
the sheet by accident. Next day Mother had placed an open
book in your room. 'Soiling oneself,' it said, 'is in the realm of
carnal sin . . . leading to intellectual and physical weakness,
degeneration and complete breakdown . . . Associated dis-
eases such as hysteria, hypochondria, profound mental
disturbance, etc., as well as male impotence . . . are caused
more particularly by too lavish a diet given to children.' So
now you knew why the food in the monastery was so bad, but
the book also listed the symptoms for identifying a sufferer:
'Pale, grey, sallow complexion, pale lips, bluish eyelids, rings
around the eyes, unsteady gaze, soiled linen. Then fatigue and
general wasting despite a good appetite, withered skin,
sweats, trembling, backache, dull pain in the thighs and
calves. Gradually the speech becomes a stammer, the voice is
weak, the hair has no lustre, splits at the ends and easily falls
out.' Of course you immediately looked in the mirror, but
you couldn't see anything, and you had been stammering for
a long time anyway. To be on the safe side, you took a little
face powder from Grandmother's old dressing-table, but
unfortunately it was very pale too, and could work only in
winter if at all. And you abstracted a little hair oil to make
dull hair gleam again. But that was not clever of you, for a
few days later Father Coelestin was checking the cupboards,
found these things and said you were a pervert. He thought
you were going to make yourself up to look like a woman,

and as he said it so very loud in the Museum there was horrible talk that you had to listen to, since you couldn't say why you had really wanted those items.

Prejudice is a wall, and all who run their heads against it have withdrawn with injuries.

Then word went around that the Chancellor had come to visit. The Fathers gave him a solemn reception, and Father Coelestin showed him round, but you saw none of that, since you had to stay in the Museum. Later, when the Fathers were all back, you and three other boys were looking at the Chancellor's car, a large, black American car with a low Viennese number, although Herr Figl[109] came from Lower Austria. The chauffeur was wiping the car with a chamois leather, and said the Chancellor was still in the Monastery Cellar, but then he came along. He was in a good mood, and talked to the boys. First he asked how they liked it in the monastery, and they said diplomatically well, they had to like it, they weren't allowed to do anything else, and Herr Figl laughed. Then he looked at his watch – he carried one like Grandfather's, only his was silver – and said he had a little time to spare, and he was thirsty, and then he invited the boys into the Monastery Cellar for some apple juice and soda. They told him they weren't allowed in the Monastery Cellar, but Herr Figl said he was sure Father Coelestin wouldn't be angry with him, so they went in. He ordered apple juice and soda and cheese sandwiches for the boys, and quarter of a litre of white wine for himself, and then he talked to them. He asked them about the monastery, and where they came from, and you told him you had seen him once before, and he was having such a good time that he drank three quarter-litres of wine. When you told him you were very impressed by that he laughed, and said he had a high alcohol threshold, and one day it would be said of him that he had sacrificed his liver on the altar of the Fatherland. Soon after that Father Coelestin arrived and looked at the boys with great venom. Herr Figl told him why they were here, and he was so cheerful that Father Coelestin soon went away. Then you told Herr Figl that you'd have to leave now, and he left too. Unfortunately he bumped into the cellar door, and his way to his car was not an easy one. The boys got no supper because they had been impertinent to the Chancellor of Austria.

In the Christmas holidays you met some boys you'd known in primary school. Now they were at secondary school, and they talked about their pricks and how good they were with women. Egon said that what the boy had read about masturbation in that medical book was total nonsense. Masturbation was more like podipilding[110] for the prick. Podipilding was a new word, very modern. It meant 'making something big and strong', which everyone wanted, but no one knew how to spell it, because it was an American word and you lived in the Russian zone, where Russian was the only foreign language. And Ernstl said there was a brothel in town where he went every week, but you didn't believe him, because he had an elder brother who had probably told him about it. Otherwise it was all the same as usual. Grandmother said she felt as if she'd been dragged through a thorn bush backwards, and Grandfather said he had half a century of the worst events in world history behind him. You didn't think it was so bad yourself, because you'd known nothing else. And you were pleased with the fur coat your grandparents had given you. It was made of little hamsters – Grandmother said it was an old fur lining of hers, and luckily the husband of one of her plain seamstresses had trained as a furrier – and on the outside it was made of a piece of absorbent felt from the paper factory, coloured to look like camelhair. It was very attractive, and you particularly liked to think of wearing it to the monastery church where you had to go on Sundays, and where it was so bitterly cold that there was a thin sheet of ice over the holy water in the stoup. It was a very severe winter. The Danube had several side arms near the monastery, and they had frozen hard. You could see dead fish in the ice that had simply frozen there. It was a strange sight.

The Holy Year was a year of Colorado beetles and boredom. In between was school as usual and praying as usual, even more of that now that Father Coelestin and Father Bonaventura had taken over the school. Father Romuald and Father Christoph didn't have much say in the conference room, since they had once done deals with the Nazis, or had been Nazis themselves, and Father Richard felt hard done by, because Father Columban had really wanted him to be his successor. He was very devout himself, but he was not comfortable with the way that Fathers Bonaventura and Coelestin carried on, because as he once said in class, you got to heaven not so much through praying as through good works, and excessive prayer could lead to hypocrisy and atheism. He knew that, even though maths and physics were the subjects he taught, but then he had been a Father for a long time.

Carnival was rather silly, because there was to be a large Carnival party in the boarding house, and everyone had to dress up. The boy couldn't think of anything special, so he dressed up as the kind of nomad Grandmother had told him about. It was not very comfortable, since he had only shoe cream instead of fig coffee, so he turned out a particularly dark-skinned nomad, but unfortunately made a mess on the sheet he was using and a good many other places too, because the shoe cream made his face itch. Most of the boys had dressed up as girls, even the big ones in the top forms, with clothes borrowed from their sisters, mothers or aunts, and suddenly there were more girls than boys in the boarding house. Many of them got Father Anselm to make them up with lipstick and rouge, and then they acted like girls who had fallen in love, and you thought that was very stupid. As breasts they had stuffed apples or pieces of cloth inside their dresses, and other boys felt them like the drunks at the inn – all that was behind you now – and the radio was turned on loud so that they could dance to music. No one wanted to dance with the boy because his colour came off, but he was glad of that.

There was a novena during Lent, when you had to pray for eight days, and then there were spiritual exercises. A Father came from Vienna specially to conduct those, but they were just more praying, even if, for a change, it was called a time for reflection. Your Easter report was good enough for you to go to Vienna with Mother at Whitsun, for by now she was used to the Three for conduct. This time Mother's friends were at home, so she and the boy stayed at the Golden Lamb, which called itself a hotel but was no better than the inn that was now closed. The Opera Café was still standing, and it had even had new bituminous roofing felt put on it in the winter. You met Mother's friends there, the ones in whose apartment you had stayed while they were away, and the father of the family was a very stout doctor who was a famous surgeon. So he had come through everything with ease, including his denazification, and the Yanks thought highly of him, so he said he always fell on his feet. He was so round that he could hardly have seen where they were. He drove a very big American car, but as the whole family was very fat he complained that its springs were gone already. Mother said she wished she had his worries, although she usually watched her figure very carefully.

Another movie was being made in Austria, and this one was a matter of state, for it was to promote the freedom of Austria and oppose the occupying powers without hurting their feelings. Because of the great coalition, there were two scriptwriters, one Black and one Red, and all the actors who had been in *The Third Man* were engaged unless they had died in the mean time, and many more too. There wasn't so much money as the Yanks paid, because it was a patriotic duty for everyone to be in this film so as to do their careers political good in future. Black and Red were equal, or at least cast in proportion, and the leading lady said we were getting back to Brown. She laughed at that, like all who frequently make such jokes, for her name was Hilde Krahl,[111] and her husband was the director. Another actor was called Curd Jürgens[112] and said the screenplay had to be written by two authors because no one could produce such rubbish on his own, but anyone who didn't go along with the movie would be written off as a Nazi, meaning Werner Krauss[113] and the Hörbiger family except for Paul.[114] Frau Jürgens was really called Judith Holzmeister.[115] She was a real actress and was to play a Spaniard or a South American, it didn't matter which, because it was all the same for the movie, in which she was to fall in love with Austrian dirndl dresses, since there were plenty of those around and they fitted better than anything Spanish that could be patched up. Her father was the most famous architect in Austria, and even greater than Prinz Eugen,[116] for he had given the Turks such a capital city that they would never again venture to attack Vienna, and he was very important because of his political connections, and everyone stopped to listen to him. So when everyone sang:

The sun on rich and poor may shine
Why not on Austria, country mine?

it was all about the freedom of Austria, which the film was supposed to achieve. And to illustrate the fact that we needed our place in the sun the movie showed everything that made Austria so great, such as new wine, the Habsburgs, the landscape, Lipizzaner horses, the Vienna Boys' Choir and a lot of operettas. All these things were mounted on floats, as characteristic Austrian scenes, and wheeled along the main avenue in the Prater.[117] You saw them the next day, and it really was a funny sight, because the avenues of the city had had all their trees cut down, and so had the Wurstlprater amusement park, so they had to go to the Pleasure Pavilion, and the floats looked as if they were part of a male voice choir's celebration. Mother said people were anything but simple in Austria, they were drunk on patriotism, but little countries were like that, the smaller the piece of dirt the worse it smelled. The evening, unfortunately, ended rather badly, because a fat young man playing one of the occupying soldiers came along and said the film was going to be a total mess, and then everyone who had been saying just the same united against him. Aunt Anny escorted him out because he was drunk, and said later that Herr Qualtinger[118] was not an attractive character. But it was all part of the trouble you had in the restaurant trade.

You also saw your first Existentialists. They were said to be even worse than the Schlurfs, and they were very smart. They wore their hair short, had Wehrmacht sunglasses on in all weathers, wore dark blue studded jeans that could be bought only in American shops, and black roll-neck sweaters coming down almost to their knees. Part of the uniform was a black knitted scarf, two purl, two plain, that had to be long enough to drag on the ground. Why they were called Existentialists no one knew, but they listened to French and not American music. Because the French had music too, by Piaf or Greco since Chevalier had done a deal with the Nazis, or they listened to Beethoven by candlelight, because Beethoven had no electricity either. They impressed the boy, because everyone was so indignant about them, but Mother wouldn't buy him any studded jeans.

However, he ordered the sweater for his thirteenth birthday. Grandmother had given him a whole hundred schillings, which was a lot of money, and then he went to Frau Marie Luftensteiner, one of the old seamstresses, and she said she would knit him one of those sweaters, and took fifty schillings for it. Soon after that the Colorado beetles arrived. They were black and yellow like the Habsburgs, but there were more of them, and there was no pesticide to spray them with. So every time the boys went on an outing it was to a potato field belonging to the monastery, and they had to take empty jam-jars to collect the beetles. They were crawling all over the field, but their caterpillars were even worse, big and dark red, and they lived on the undersides of the potato leaves. At first it was fun harvesting Colorado beetles, but soon it got boring because it was always the same. However, it had to be done, because Father Coelestin said otherwise there'd be nothing to eat, since those Habsburg beetles would eat till there was a famine, and that was the way Ireland had lost its population, who all emigrated to America. To prevent that the Colorado beetles had to be collected, although life was better in America.

At last the holidays came – your report was the same as usual – and then your grandparents had Colorado beetles too. Grandfather said they were as bad as the Russians, and Frau Marie Luftensteiner said she needed more money for the sweater, because it was so difficult to see the black wool. Grandmother showed the boy a jar. When it was full of Colorado beetles and caterpillars, he would get fifty schillings. Unfortunately it was a gherkin jar, and of course he went out collecting with a smaller one, and it took him more than two weeks to fill the big one. He was afraid there might not be enough Colorado beetles.

Luckily Mother went away for a few days, and then you didn't have to do anything except collect beetles. You stuck to the beetles, because the caterpillars soon became mush in the jar and were no good. Beetles were better, and you put a little earth in the middle of the jar, out of sight, but it improved the look of the whole thing. Mother had been invited to Salzburg by Herr Furtwängler to hear Bruckner's Eighth. You didn't know it, and would have liked to hear it too. When you did hear it on the radio it was loud and powerful, like a Baroque vault with a painted sky, and it went up in the air, loud and very slow, and when it reached the finale you thought of the village wind band when the players blew particularly loud tunes to the glory of God at Corpus Christi. They always had to drink a lot afterwards, and it seemed so funny that you didn't like to tell Mother, when she came back, that you'd heard the music she was so keen on. But perhaps it was Herr Furtwängler she was keen on, because he had a bald head like Father.

Then the sweater was finished, and Mother said it had been very expensive at a hundred schillings. But you thought it was great, and wore it every time you went collecting Colorado beetles. Of course you perspired terribly, but that was good, because it made the sweater look as greasy as the ones the Existentialists wore. You anticipated looking like a real Existentialist in the autumn, but then Mother spoiled it by washing the sweater with some Fewa detergent left from before the war – people still knew the hit from the People's Radio:

Take your scooter to Addis Ababa
And wash all the Negroes with Fewa
How amazed they will be
How they'll stare when they see
That wonderful powder from High Germany.

And she washed it at such a hot temperature that it lost its stretch. You got it baggy again later, but the sweater was never really greasy any more, because the weather wasn't hot enough for that, although you put it on for collecting Colorado beetles back at the monastery after the holidays. And you were looking forward to getting a scarf at All Saints', having given Frau Marie Luftensteiner the fifty schillings from Grandmother for more Colorado beetles.

*

Grandmother talked to the boy a good deal. In summer she liked best to sit in the new old summerhouse, where it was shady and airy, but it took her a long time to come down the steps from her boudoir, and even longer to go back. She was short of breath, panted a lot, and said there was no medicine for cardiac oedema, and at Christmas she'd be pushing up the daisies. She meant that she would die. You didn't like to hear that, and you didn't believe her either, for a great many people you knew had died, but you didn't believe Grandmother would.

She told you that Grandfather had studied in England, although France was the modern place to go at the time, and in England he had met people like the members of the Fabian Society and Mr Morris, who had impressed him greatly. He had even seen old Marx and Engels, who were to blame for Communism, but he had still been very young then and hadn't seen through their plans. Then he had founded a health insurance scheme on the estate, to prevent the Communism that wasn't there yet, and kindergartens and little hospitals so that people wouldn't skive off work because someone at home was a child or sick. That worked until the First World War, which he hadn't wanted, because he knew it would go wrong, and ever since they had been muddling on through life. The boy listened, because he knew that old people like talking about the past, and Grandmother was always very generous to him, saying you should give what you can while your hand is still warm. You didn't like to hear Grandmother say that either, for you loved her very much.

When you walked around the place you were surprised to see how small everything was now. You hadn't grown so much yourself, just a few centimetres, but when you rode your bike to the farmer's family where you had helped to make hay as a child, it had all shrunk. The old farmer had shrunk too, for he had suffered a stroke and now sat in an armchair. You cycled quickly on, and then pushed your bike up a large hill, for there, in the no man's land between Grandfather and the neighbour who had been his enemy, but was long dead now, there was a little church that you had often seen, although not from the inside. The first time you went into a church you could make a wish, but only the first time, and the boy had a wish. He also had August with him in a box. He had found August dead in his hotbed that morning, and Herr Mandi said he probably hadn't hibernated properly, and had given the boy a small shovel. The church was locked, but the farmer next to it had the key, and it was very dusty and brightly coloured. The altars were rustic Baroque, gold, blue and red, and painted like chests with bunches of flowers at the front, and on the back of the high altar was a chicken cage, for the church patron was head of the Small Livestock Association, and was happy to take votive gifts of poultry, which the priest in the next village would eat. But nobody believed in votive gifts any more, so they stopped bringing chickens, and the priest got his from the farmers, who of course had to sell them to him cheap. You grinned at that, and then you buried August beside the church. You were a little heavy at heart, for you knew that you would see none of this again until you were an artist, and that was still a long way off, you didn't even know how long, or if you would be an artist at all, and it all looked so dusty and old that it would surely have fallen into ruin by the time you next saw it. But perhaps you would be able to find August's shell again. You had read about reincarnation, and thought that a turtle was well placed for that, because of its shell and all the time at its disposal.

You discussed it with Herr Hirthentaler when the holidays were over. Of course you didn't tell him why; the occasion was that Father Columban had died at last. It had been a happy release for him, almost everyone said, for he hadn't left his room for a year, and he had been very upset when Father Coelestin took over because of his trembling. So you talked about time, and Herr Hirthentaler talked about a river in which huge rocks were ground into little pebbles and sand until they had disappeared. The boy liked that idea, although he would rather have been water, but then it occurred to him that the source of the river must be supposed to be God, and as God didn't exist it couldn't any of it be true. So you borrowed a small book about peas and someone who always had to eat them, as if he were in the boarding house, but a character who was a doctor said, 'Mankind is free; in mankind individuality is transfigured as freedom. Can't you contain your urine?'[119]

At All Saints' Frau Marie Luftensteiner had finished the scarf, and it was very black and long. You negotiated with her, because the pattern was really very simple, two plain, two purl, but she had miscounted so often that she had to deduct ten schillings. Grandmother said she had never seen any Existentialists, but she could imagine them, and the boy should be proud of the first things he had bought for himself. As you had been feeling cross with Father Bonaventura you began drawing a story in pictures about him, for you had read Busch's St Anthony,[120] and you filled a whole school exercise book. You thought your story was very good, and showed it to some of the other boys, who laughed a lot too. One afternoon Father Coelestin came into the Museum, made for the boy's desk, and when he had found the exercise book he boxed the boy's ears a couple of times. Then everything ran its usual course. You had two weekends of detention, you had to kneel and beg Father Bonaventura's pardon for the terrible insult – he unctuously forgave you – and Mother got another letter and had to come to the monastery. But it was rather different this time, for Father Coelestin showed Mother the book and used words like 'monstrous' and 'obscene'. Mother said she couldn't quite see the boy producing something obscene, so she read the book while Father Coelestin sat in his armchair smoking a Virginia cigarette, and the boy had to stand. After a while Mother said she didn't understand the whole thing, because she was not a member of the clergy, and she knew they had a morality of their own, but as far as she could see it was a perfectly normal schoolboy joke. The boy thought it was good that Mother was back with Grandmother now, and Father Coelestin said this kind of thing had to be nipped in the bud. Then the boy was sent out, and when Mother joined him after a while she boxed his ears for being so stupid as to forget that boys in general are sneaks and like to tell on each other. Beyond that she wasn't particularly angry, which rather surprised you. Of course you didn't say so, but she said she'd had so much trouble with her son that she must be getting used to it.

When you went home for the Christmas holidays, Grandmother was ill. She had been in bed for a week, said Mother, and the doctor said that ultimately there was no cure for cardiac oedema. Grandmother looked very yellow in the face, and had many pillows wedged behind her back, because she couldn't breathe if she lay flat. Her voice was all different, and very quiet. She told the boy to sit down beside her, but he didn't really want to, because the way Grandmother looked now was a little creepy. Her bedroom seemed quite different too. There was a commode beside the bed, and several of the little upholstered chairs had been brought in from the boudoir, because Grandmother was seldom alone. Usually Mother sat with her, or one of the old maidservants, and Grandfather sat in his study and mustn't be disturbed. It was very quiet in the house, for not even the maids in the kitchen were singing, but talked about what was to become of them when the mistress was gone. The oldest cook said 'the little one' would just carry on, and it took you a while to realize that she meant Mother, who was now fifty-three. Mother told the boy to sit with Grandmother when she wanted, and a chair was put in the window niche next to the dressing table, for it was already dark there on this December afternoon, and you could be seen by Grandmother but didn't have to see her unless you wanted too.

Grandmother asked if you were used to the habit-wearing pissers now. When you said no, she said there were many things she had never managed to get used to herself, all her life, and the boy didn't have to bother about getting used to the way she looked now, because it would all pass over. The comforting thing about life was that nothing is for ever, she said, which hurts with nice things but can be a comfort with the others, so long as you don't keep forgetting it. So you sat with Grandmother for two hours, until she said you could go now, and then Frau Philipp came in with a cup that had a spout and gave Grandmother a drink.

You sat with Grandmother on the 23rd too, for an hour in the morning and an hour in the afternoon when it was dark. In between you sat in the library. No one had dusted it for a long time, so not just the furniture and the globe but the books too were very dirty. You looked at some of them, the ones you had always liked, felt annoyed with yourself for colouring in Herr von Humboldt's Amazonian Indians so badly, and you couldn't imagine how everything would go on here without Grandmother. At six you went to sit beside her again. She was in a happier mood, so that you hoped everything would be all right, and she talked to the boy more. She said being young was terrible and being old even worse, and as for what lay in between, you could seldom say it had been worth while. You made her give her word of honour to keep it secret, and then you told her you were going to be an artist, and she said it was all the same to her; she would just ask the boy to make his future decisions in a way that didn't shame her. Then she told the boy to look in a cupboard, and there was a photo album there. She wanted to see it, and you put it on the bedspread. They were ancient, brown photographs stuck on card, and the first showed Grandmother as a girl.

Then came one with Grandfather, very young, playing with a huge mastiff. She told the boy that, and then she didn't want to look at the photos any more, for all that was behind her now, and you had to clear the album away again. After that Grandmother said nothing for a long time, and when Frau Philipp came with the cup that had a spout Grandmother said she could go again, because the boy was there. Later she said she wanted to sleep, and asked you to give her a sleeping tablet. They were in a little drawer in the dressing table, and you were to take the tablet out and give it to her. You found the glass tube, and Grandmother asked you to tip the pills out on the bedspread. Then she took some and drank from the cup with the spout, and the boy was told to go away and tell Mother not to be too late. The boy had to bend down to Grandmother and got a kiss on the forehead, which he didn't particularly like, and when he said, 'See you tomorrow,' Grandmother just murmured, 'Yes, yes.'

Mother was already standing outside the door, and she went in. She stayed for a long time, and when she came out she looked at the boy and began crying. Before you could say anything to her she said it was late, but she was sure there'd be something to eat in the kitchen, and then you had better go straight to bed because tomorrow was Christmas Eve – she sobbed very hard here – and everyone would be up late then, so it would be best to get some sleep now. There was an opera on the kitchen radio, because it was the second cook's birthday, and she liked hearing operas but not seeing them. She said she had been the victim of her parents, who didn't want to give her a present more than once a year, so they had brought her into the world at Christmas, but she'd got her own back by being a day earlier than the Lord Jesus, not that it had done her any good. The maids were sitting together, and some of their daughters had come – the daughters were very old too – and they were drinking glühwein, because the master had already had his supper in his study, so now they were celebrating. When the boy came in one of them got up and prepared Mother's supper, which was carried upstairs, and the elderly birthday girl lit a fire in the very small stove and cooked the boy some scrambled eggs. On the radio an old man was just fetching his son home, because the son's great love had tuberculosis and a dubious past,[121] and the cook sang along, for she had an impressive bass voice. At the end of the aria she grated cheese over the eggs, and the boy was allowed to sit with the maids, who all smelled the same. The Mahlwomen told the story of how they had come here from Transylvania, but you knew it already, and then one of the maids let you taste her glühwein. It was good, and as there was still a fire in the very small stove they made more glühwein. Later they made yet more on the electric ring, and then Mother came down with her empty plate and said it was getting late. The oldest cook said it was only ten, and they'd go on celebrating a little longer as they had always done when the mistress was still the mistress, but perhaps Mother couldn't remember that, she'd been singing on stage at the Opera then, and she said it in a way that made Mother blush. Then Mother said at least the boy had better go to bed, but he wanted to finish his glühwein first, and Mother waited. You followed her in silence, and on the landing of the stairs she said life wasn't easy. You knew that already, but the way she said it now was different, and she looked tired. When you went to bed you thought that perhaps life wasn't easy for Mother either.

In the morning, when the boy had had his breakfast and was coming out of the kitchen, he heard Grandfather and Mother talking in the boudoir. Grandfather was saying that something really wasn't fitting at her age, and she didn't have to do this to him, and Mother said she just couldn't stand it any more. Grandfather said she might at least tidy up neatly, for this was nothing to do with anyone else, and when the boy tapped at the half-open door the grown-ups fell silent.

Grandfather went into his study; Mother was carrying a small tray with Grandmother's medicines on it, and she took it downstairs. The boy went quietly into the dressing-room and saw Grandmother sleeping in her bedroom, snoring. When he stole away again Mother came back with the empty tray and told him to fetch Herr Mandi. Herr Mandi was at home drinking tea with rum, and Mother told him to go and fetch the priest to give Extreme Unction. Then she sat down again beside Grandmother, who was still asleep and snoring. The doctor came at ten, and said Grandmother was probably suffering from uraemia, and there was nothing that could be done now. Then you heard the car down below, and Herr Mandi arrived with the priest. He had no server with him, because it was Christmas Eve, but he told the boy that being at the monastery he was sure he knew how it was done, but he didn't, and the priest said he had better do it all the same, and he would prompt him. Mother fetched Grandfather, and then the priest went to Grandmother and gave her Extreme Unction. She didn't know anything about it, though, since she was asleep and snoring, and Grandfather went out before the sacrament was over. When the priest was packing up his things Grandfather came back and told Herr Mandi he would be needing him again, and then the priest was given some money and driven away. The boy was angry with him, because he knew that when people had had Extreme Unction they were bound to die.

Later Grandfather talked to Herr Mandi, who told the boy to go with him. He went to the old tool shed in the nursery garden, the one you knew well, and moved the stack of old covers for the hotbeds that were needed only when there might be hail. When he got down to the trodden earth floor, he fetched a spade and drove it in. There was a hard sound, but it was a stone, for when Herr Mandi drove the spade in again close to the first place, it met soil. Then there was another hard sound, and Herr Mandi dug up a small and rather rusty iron box. Grandfather had buried it in the war, he said, and he had known nothing about it himself, so he'd taken the boy along as a witness. When they got back to Grandfather's study with it the key that Grandfather had wouldn't fit, because the lock was very rusty, and the boy watched as Herr Mandi used all kinds of implements in the metalworking shop to get the box open. There was a leather bag inside, and Herr Mandi took it all to Grandfather, who said everything was in order. Then the doctor came back and told Mother he had already made out the death certificate, because it was Christmas Eve, and Mother would only have to enter the time. You sat down beside Grandmother, who was asleep and snoring. Sometimes her face showed that she seemed to be dreaming, but she didn't move and she didn't wake up. Frau Philipp was sitting in the other corner praying. After a while Grandfather came in and gestured to Frau Philipp to leave. Then he sat down on the other side of the dressing table. He looked at Grandmother for a while, and then put his hand in his jacket pocket and lit himself a cigar. 'It won't bother her now,' he murmured, seeing the boy's look of surprise. After a while he went out and came back with an ashtray and two glasses. He pushed one glass over to the boy. It contained slivovitz, which he liked but you didn't. You sipped from the glass, but the spirit was too strong. When Grandfather had half-smoked his cigar he went out again with the ashtray and the glasses.

Frau Philipp had been back for quite some time when Grandmother began snoring in a different way. So Frau Philipp went out and came back with Mother, who had brought a candle with her, put it on the dressing table and lit it. Then you heard more and more people coming into the dressing-room and praying quietly. Grandmother snored faster, and the servants were praying outside. You recognized the voices of Herr Mandi's father, and the kitchen maids, and still more people kept arriving. They were very quiet but you could hear them, many of them were crying quietly, and Grandmother was snoring very slowly. Suddenly she opened her eyes and her mouth, belched, and stopped breathing.

You had to get up when Mother and Frau Philipp opened the windows, and then Herr Mandi came in and stopped the pendulum of the clock. It was five-thirty, and Mother gestured to the boy to go away. That wasn't easy, because the dressing-room was full of people, and there were some in the boudoir too. You knew them all, since they worked for your grand-parents, but you'd had no idea just how many there were. Many of the women were crying, many others were pretend-ing to cry, and the old men had tears in their eyes too. Herr Mandi knocked at Grandfather's study door, but it was a long time before it was opened. Then Grandfather walked past the people, who made way for him, went into Grandmother's bedroom, closed the door and stayed inside for some time. The people were praying quietly, and after a while Grand-father opened the door, left it open and went quickly back to his study, and the people went in to see Grandmother. Her eyes and mouth were closed again, her hands were folded round a small golden cross, and there was a napkin tied round her head. The boy stayed in a corner while the people walked past Grandmother, and Herr Mandi's father put a beautiful bunch of flowers on her.

Then you went into the library and looked at books, until Mother said you had better go and have something to eat in the kitchen. People were sitting together there, not talking much, but there were fried schnitzels because it was Christmas Eve. Afterwards you went to bed of your own accord, taking care not to run into Mother and Grandfather, who were sit-ting in the study. The Christmas tree stood out in the corridor, but this year it wasn't decorated and had no candles burning on it. In fact you did not go straight to bed, but sat in the library for quite a long time.

*

Next day there was a great deal of activity, even though it was the first day of Christmas. Herr Mandi and the carpenter were in the workshops getting the coffin ready. They said the mistress had really spoilt their Christmas for them, and there wasn't any proper mourning paper to stick on the coffin. 'They thought of everything,' grumbled Herr Mandi, sorting out the stockpiled purchases of the Nazi period made in view of the certain prospect of war. 'Everything except dying.' Then he found some paper in the loft above the workshops, left over from the funeral of Grandfather's mother in 1918, but it had turned brown with age, and they had to piece it together a good deal. Palm branches came up from the nursery garden; Herr Mandi painted them with silver stove enamel, and they were nailed over the coffin so that you didn't see the patching. In the house Grandfather was saying crossly that there was no room anywhere now that the chapel belonged to the Russians, and the boudoir was cleared and hung with black fabric. The pall had got the moth in it, but candlesticks were placed over the holes so that you hardly saw them. Then, in the afternoon, the coffin was closed and Grandmother was placed on the bier, and the commandant came to offer his condolences. Grandfather asked him if he could use the forecourt of the Baroque Wing on the day of the funeral, and the commandant agreed. Mother was sitting by the telephone in Grandfather's study, telling all kinds of people that Grandmother was dead, and you didn't know what to do. Then Grandfather gave you a job, because people kept coming up from the village to see Grandmother's coffin, and you had to pour them all a schnapps.

In the evening Grandfather came into the kitchen feeling hungry. He had been drinking but hadn't eaten anything all day. A goose had been roasted at midday, as usual at Christmas, but as Grandfather was not there it had not been touched, and now it was warmed up. Then Grandfather disclosed the contents of Grandmother's will. She didn't want to be buried in the church and never had, nor in the mausoleum, because she didn't want to be quarrelling with the other occupants. She had chosen her own place for a grave, and she wanted to be buried there, without any long orations.

Over the next two days a great many people who had to have schnapps poured for them turned up, and it was very tedious. Grandmother lay under the patched-up mourning paper and the silver-painted palm fronds, and when you thought about it she was the best person in your life. You had always kept out of Grandfather's way, and he had kept out of yours, for he was too big for you and you were too small for him, just a child and then a little boy, 'unable to give any satisfaction', as he often said, and you always felt you were disturbing him. And now Mother belonged to him too. He had 'pounded her tender', as she had said to Aunt Anny, and she wanted to be always perfect and for you to be perfect too, but that was simply too much to ask. You tried as well as you could, but it was never enough for her, and she was always nervous. Another reason why she was nervous was that Director Sattler still called in the afternoons and mustn't be seen. There was nothing now to connect you with that inn and the village, where the villagers' greatest satisfaction had been in malice and backbiting. It was most clearly obvious when women who called themselves friends met in the café. As soon as one of them had to go to the lavatory she was the subject of conversation for all the others until she came back. Once Frau Haberfellner tried holding on so long that in the end she couldn't contain herself any longer. That must have been when the cinema still had no sound, but everyone in the village knew the story because it was told again and again, always beginning, 'Well, she's my best friend, but she once had this funny accident . . .' That was what the village was like, and the men were no better, except perhaps for Herr Mandi, who did everything for Mother and Grandfather and was always around, although other people said that he must be a fool or he would at least have put enough funds to one side. Now he was standing in the salon where you could hardly see him, but he could see the people arriving, and when some of them came he knocked on the study door and Grandfather came out. People expressed their condolences, and he said he had been married to Grandmother for over sixty years, and he was sorry there was not enough space in the house now.

Space was the subject of all conversations with the domestic staff, and when the funeral took place the boy understood why. Mother said she had phoned only the most important people, but word had got around, and it was even in the newspaper, although no one had told the paper, so a terrible lot of people arrived. Three wind bands came – Grandfather had always given them free beer for their rehearsals – and several fire brigades to show their gratitude for the uniforms and hosepipes they had been given, and the Bishop sent a high-up cleric who was a godson of your grandparents. And a great many people came with cars, which stood side by side in the forecourt where the Russians were, and a lot of them said they had last seen the boy at Grandfather's last round-number birthday, and he had grown a lot. That was probably in the war, when the Philharmonic musicians came, over six years ago, and you didn't remember them because they were older now. You did recognize the milk pudding man at once, the man whose name was Trautmannsdorf, and he came with his wife. Grandmother had been taken from the boudoir to the small stairway, because the big one was full of Russians, and the black draperies were moved there too. Over the last few days the cartwright had repaired the hearse, which had been standing at the very back of the carriage-house, since it hadn't been used since 1918, and the woodworm had liked it so much that parts were missing. They were patched up with putty and papier mâché, and what couldn't be replaced that way was covered with palm fronds from the nursery garden, and then it was all freshly painted with black oil-based paint and silver stove enamel. It was put in a small shed with a wood-shavings stove lit there to dry the paint, because it was cold. Then four teams of horses had to be found; they were carthorses, and to hide the fact large black blankets were thrown over them. Then the village priest came, and the priest of the next village, so that there were three priests, all wearing black robes with silver embroidery. They prayed a little while in front of Grandmother in the stairway, and meanwhile the men formed their procession: a wind band, a fire brigade, another wind band, and then the hearse drove out of the farmyard. Four grooms led the horses, wearing what was left of the mourning livery, but the coats didn't fit because people used to be fatter. Then Grandmother was put on the hearse; a server went ahead carrying the cross, and when the first wind band played the procession started off. The priests went ahead of the horses, and Grandfather walked on the right behind the coffin, with Mother on the left and the boy between them. Not much of Mother could be seen because she wore a black veil reaching down to the ground. The boy tried not to cry, and behind went friends of his grandparents, then the village men, finally the village women, and right at the end came Grandmother's little funeral carriage the Zeugerl, as if she wanted to see everything herself, but this time it was empty. The servants wept a lot, because they had to stay at home and get everything ready for the funeral meal, and the wind bands took turns playing funeral music. Grandfather said nothing and held tight to his stick, for he was very old now. After three funeral marches you couldn't help thinking of what Grandmother said at funerals, and you almost grinned. Grandfather saw you and asked quietly what it was, and when you told him he laughed very briefly and then said, seriously, that was how the dead live on in us. Going up the slope the bands had a break, but once at the top they went on with their funeral music, and Grandfather said Chopin was

unable to defend himself, but he was going to have different
music at his own funeral, the Schönfeld March or the
Radetzky March,[122] which didn't sound so much like someone chopping onions. Then we reached the graveyard.

After that there were a great many hands to be shaken, and
many thanks to be expressed, and you drove home with
Grandfather and Mother in the Zeugerl. Some of the guests'
drivers had brought their cars up, so they were down below
again much sooner than we were, but they still hadn't gone
into the house, they were standing outside drinking glühwein
served to them by the maids. The servants looked hot and
bothered, and when you went into the house you could see
why. The funeral draperies had been cleared away, and tables
had been laid in every room available and even in the carriage-
house. Downstairs tables were laid for the fire brigades, the
wind bands and people from the village, upstairs they were
for the other guests, even in Grandfather's study. Grandmother's boudoir looked as usual, but different, because
nothing was lying around in the normal way, and there were
two tables there for widowed ladies. Gradually all the guests
arrived, and the boy went round yet again with trays and
canapés. The maids served drinks and coffee, and then the
boy had to go downstairs and hand round large trays of rolls
with sausages in them. The people downstairs were talking
more than the guests upstairs, many of them reminiscing
about the mistress and the times they had known with her.
You would have liked to listen, but you had too much to
do. Once Grandfather himself came down with a large glass
pitcher – you knew it, it was Baroque – and Herr Mandi followed him with an even larger pewter pitcher from which he
refilled the glass one, but even the pewter pitcher had to be
changed over quite often, because Grandfather was pouring
everyone an extra glassful from the glass pitcher – they all
drank up the first one quickly before Grandfather came
round – and he talked to them. One fire captain wanted a new

pump, and Grandfather told him to go and see the cartwright who knew about such things; another man asked Grandfather if he would be honorary head of the shooting club which was going to start up again, but he said he didn't think the Russians would want any more shooting around the place, and he was too old for it. So he went from one guest to another, and after two hours people were very merry, and maids came with large trays of schnapps glasses. All the men took one and stood up. Herr Mandi sent the boy upstairs, where he found Grandfather standing at an open window, saying he had always wanted to go first; it would have been more comfortable that way. What is called grief is really just annoyance because you miss something. And you can't ask the pardon of the dead for what you did to them in this life, said Grandfather, but this century had not been anything he wanted either, and he thanked his wife for all she had done for him. Then he raised his glass, said, 'To the next,' drank its contents down at once and smashed it on the floor. All the other guests did the same, and so did the people in the farmyard who had gone out from downstairs to hear Grandfather at the window. Then they all said goodbye, picked their way over the broken glass and went home. When the upper floor was empty Grandfather drank another schnapps. You told him it was a pity about all those glasses, and he said they had been very cheap, and it was what you did at a funeral. Then the servants cleared up, and when the work was all done they went into Grandfather's study in turn. Those who had been in his employment for twenty-five years were given four gold ducats, anyone who had been there for a shorter time just got two, but that was only three women and a groom. Later you asked Grandfather where he got all that gold from, and he said you had dug it up your-self, with Herr Mandi. However, you didn't get any of it, because Grandfather said he would need the rest for his own funeral. But you were allowed to look at the coins, which had been minted in 1902. 'One was still someone at that time,' said Grandfather.

Mother had given you a very modern pen for Christmas. It looked like a propelling pencil, but it was called a ballpoint. There were no such things in the Russian zone, and she had brought it back from Munich where she had been in the autumn, and where the women wore things to shape their hips because of the economic miracle, for the Deutsche Bank was there now, and it was closer than Hamburg. She had given Grandfather a ballpoint too, a much better one, of course, and he said it was very useful although it smeared easily. It had a cartridge inside made of metal and full of very thick ink that ran out if you left the ballpoint lying on your desk too long, and the ink was sticky and difficult to wash off. Luckily Mother had brought several refills with her. But the Fathers didn't like the ballpoint, saying it was bad for the handwriting, so you could use it only in your free time.

Soon afterwards, unfortunately, your fountain pen got broken because you didn't want to keep polishing the stronger boys' shoes. It was always the weaker boys who had to do that – they called it making yourself useful, although the Fathers didn't agree about the principle. Father Richard once said in maths that it was a sin of pride; Father Thomas said it was the behaviour of wild beasts and not right for man, who had been made by God and should act as if he were worthy of his maker. Father Anselm had his shoes polished by third-year boys, and Father Coelestin said the Lord Jesus had actually washed people's feet, and so had the Pope and the Emperor themselves, although only on Maundy Thursday, so it was all right. But you didn't want to, because you couldn't do it right for the stronger boys anyway, and when another boy once stuck his shoes in front of you without a word you refused to polish them. Then he was angry, pulled at your jacket until it came off, and then jumped on it. Grandmother's fountain pen broke and there was ink everywhere. Then he hit you, but after that you were certainly not going to clean his shoes.

At Carnival the boys were to put on a play, but you didn't want to be in it because Father Anselm was the director. The boys who were acting made a great fuss about their parts; the smaller boys played the women characters. The art master and the sixth-year boys painted the scenery, and you helped them mix the paints. It meant boiling up glue made from bones, which smelled horrible, and when everything was ready a lot of the parents of the actors came to the first night, and you were to be at the dress rehearsal beforehand, but luckily you were ill. You had found out from another boy that you could run a temperature if you ate toothpaste, but as it didn't work with Lacalut tooth powder he showed you how to rub the thermometer until it was hot. So you were in the infirmary being spoilt by the nursing nuns, which was very nice.

During Lent there had to be far more praying than usual, since you were getting confirmed at Whitsun and would then be a real Christian. You couldn't refuse, but you just pretended to be praying, since there was no God anyway.

At Easter the radio was allowed to be on again in the kitchen at home. It should really have been switched off all year because of Grandmother, but Grandfather said he didn't mind, and there was no need for the domestic staff to be bored all through the time of mourning. The oldest cook had retired, because she didn't get on with Mother and wouldn't do as she said. Herr Buchlar had been retired too, for insubordination. It didn't matter because Grandfather had a pensions fund of his own, and Mother said there were too many servants anyway. Herr Mandi thought many of the old ones were getting out of hand because they had a new mistress now, and he showed the boy his building site, which was just a large grey set of foundations and a huge pile of grey, home-made bricks. Herr Mandi said that was his future, the shell of the house would be finished in autumn, and you made out you were enthusiastic about it because you liked him. Mother gave you a large beige leather bag, which she called a Wuchtel because it looked like the yeast pastry of that name, and you could stuff a lot in it. You were very glad to have it. And you went for a great many walks, looking at your native place – well, you had been steered here, you had no choice in the matter – and you decided it was a good thing. Grandfather had given you a hundred schillings, and you were glad of those too.

There were only a few empty squares left in your exercise book, and you began to feel impatient. You realized that, because you found you were becoming indifferent to the monastery. The habit-wearing pissers were the same as ever, but they couldn't help it, so you were not particularly angry with them. You just still wished Father Anselm would be struck by lightning, but you knew there was no higher justice. Up till now you had thought and believed things that weren't true, but you were sure everything would be different as soon as you were grown up, and you were making precise plans. Seventh-year boys could go out unsupervised in the afternoon, and you gave one of them, a boy you trusted to some extent, money to buy a bottle of lighter fluid. You said you needed it to clean some marks off your clothes, and he brought it, although it was twice as expensive as you knew it should have been. You had decided on the Wuchtel bag and packed the essentials into it carefully. Unfortunately you'd had to leave your fur coat at Mother's at Easter, but there was nothing to be done about that, and you left Kierkegaard in your desk too. You hid the bag in the cellar under the gym, and since other boys must certainly know about the cellar and its windows too you pushed it behind some old furniture and covered it with the old pay books. On your walks you had often seen people standing down on the road to Vienna, waving their arms about. Then cars stopped and picked them up. Father Thomas said it was called hitchhiking, and was a good idea, because the hitchhikers didn't own much, so they were friendlier to each other.

You had feared that Father Anselm would be on supervision duty on your fourteenth birthday, but this time it was Father Thomas's turn, and the weather was fine. Even lessons seemed less tedious than usual.

When it came to study time the boy said he needed to go to the lavatory. He quickly went off to his cupboard and the dormitory. There he arranged his mattresses the way he had learnt to put them to be aired, and poured the petrol over them. The boy had been hoarding the matches for a long time, and the jet of flame alarmed him because he hadn't expected it. But then it all began to smoke and stink, and he ran back to the Museum and said there was a fire. Father Thomas waddled off to see what was up, and a good many of the pupils went with him. Then Father Thomas called for a fire extinguisher, but the boy had run the other way, down the spiral staircase and through the school entrance hall. No one saw him, so he was soon in the cellar under the gym. His bag smelled slightly of old paper, but that didn't matter, nor did the fact that he hit his knee climbing out of the window. He had practised getting down the path to the road several times, but it was a little different now because the bag was very large, and he had to go carefully with it among the big rocks and the bushes. He looked back, but no one was following him. His knee didn't hurt too badly, and he thought of *The Thief of Baghdad*. In the film, the genie from the bottle rose out of the stony ravine and cried, in a voice of thunder, the words that the boy was now whispering as he stumbled down the slope. 'I'm free! FREE!' But he had no idea yet what the word really meant.

EPILOGUE

Austria obtained its State Treaty on 15 May 1955. Herr Figl had already been demoted by friends in his party to the post of Foreign Minister. He fell lower still, but remained Austria's most popular politician. He died an embittered man, and there was a joke going round, saying that his widow lived on the deposits from his bottles.

During that summer the occupying troops moved out, and 26 October, their last day in Austria, became a national holiday. It had originally been called Day of the Banners, but as that conjured up unfortunate associations in view of Austrian customs, it was renamed Day of National Celebration.

Grandfather's estate was devastated, and his agricultural methods were hopelessly old-fashioned. The home farm was closed down in 1956. One reason for the decision may have been that Herr Mandi died one hot summer day, whether of overwork or alcohol no one could be sure. He was only forty-one, and provision was made for his wife and four children. Grandfather bore him a grudge for dying, having expected him to be the prop and stay of his old age.

You occasionally heard from the monastery too. Father Coelestin caught Orgi and Fräulein Lunzer at it. They killed themselves, and so were not given Christian burial. When

Father Anselm made a pass at the Abbot's great-nephew there was a scandal. He made a full confession, and as a result many pupils and former pupils at the monastery school were prosecuted for sodomy under Paragraph 129 of the Criminal Code. However, the public prosecutors actually took to court only cases where those involved had been fourteen at the time when the sexual acts were committed, describing this as undeserved leniency. Father Anselm was handed over to monastic jurisdiction, and was transferred for disciplinary reasons to a convent of nuns. Paragraph 129 was rescinded many years later.

Grandfather died in 1960 at the age of ninety-six, having chosen the programme of music for his own funeral. Nothing that sounded like chopping onions, and the funeral went at a rapid pace. The men did try to walk solemnly to the lively march tunes, but the horses did not keep pace with them, and the hearse trundled briskly along to the graveyard in time to the Radetzky March. Almost all the mourners had tears of laughter in their eyes, but they were sad to see a long-gone epoch finally dead and buried.

Two and a half years later, during repairs to the roof, the house burned down except for the boy's grandparents' apartment. The paper factory bought the site to extend the works. In the year 2000 the apartment itself, already falling into ruin, stood in the way of progress. Today there is nothing left to remind anyone of the past.

Many of the boy's former fellow pupils became men of importance in Austrian politics, and even as schoolboys they had been particularly brutal and stupid.

The boy's mother reached the great old age of ninety-nine. She had seen two world wars and four devaluations of the currency, and was astonished to live through fifty years of peace after that.

NOTES

1 The Austro-Hungarian Monarchy, organized by compromise between the powers involved in 1867, remained in existence until the end of the First World War, when the last Emperor abdicated.

2 The German word *Kind*, child, is a neuter noun, and in grammatical terms takes the pronoun *es*, it.

3 Not just a submarine, as the baffled child understands it, but also a term for someone who had had to go underground in Nazi Germany, in this case clearly for reasons of non-Aryan descent.

4 Matthias Claudius, 1740–1815, a talented journalist, writer, poet, and author of many popular German hymns.

5 Hermann Göring, Reichsmarschall, second most prominent Nazi after Hitler. He was condemned to death at the Nuremberg trials, but had hidden a phial of cyanide on himself and committed suicide.

6 Albert Speer, Hitler's architect and armaments minister. He expressed remorse at Nuremberg and got off with a sentence of twenty years' imprisonment.

7 Josef Goebbels, the charismatic Nazi Minister of Propaganda, and a noted womanizer despite his deformed foot. He and his wife Magda killed themselves and their six children in Hitler's bunker.

8 Ernst Kaltenbrunner, 1903–46, head of SS Security and the Gestapo.

9 Hitler's birthplace just on the Austrian side of the country's border with Germany.

10 A poem of 1788 by Matthias Claudius, 'Kriegslied' (War Song), in which the first and last verses end: "s'ist leider Krieg, und ich begehre / nicht schuld daran zu sein' – 'Alas, 'tis war, and I desire to bear no blame for it.'

11 A reference to Göring's notorious prediction: 'If an enemy bomber reaches the Ruhr, my name's not Hermann Göring, and you can call me Meier.'

12 For propaganda purposes, the figure of a bogeyman called 'Kohlenklau', coal-stealer, was manufactured to symbolize the squandering of energy which would otherwise have gone to the war effort.

13 General Paul von Lettow-Vorbeck, 1870–1964, campaigned during the First World War in the German African colonies, and never suffered a defeat; he surrendered to the British only on hearing of the Armistice in 1918.

14 *Lustig*: merry, cheerful.

15 The aristocratic Esterhazy family.

16 In Austria, the traditional colour of the Social Democratic party.

17 *Eiswein*: made from grapes that have been exposed to the frost.

18 Special coins given at a child's christening.

19 Miklos Horthy, regent of Hungary during the war until 1944, when he was forced to step down. He had protected the Hungarian Jews, and although in some danger of prosecution himself at Nuremberg, he eventually acted as a prosecution witness.

20 In 1687 the Austrians and Hungarians defeated the Turks at the Battle of Mohacz.

21 The Providentia fountain of 1739, the work of Georg Raphael Donner, 1693–1749, Austrian sculptor of the Baroque period.

22 Features of the late Gothic pulpit of *c*.1500 in the Cathedral of St Stephen in Vienna. 'Master Pilgram' refers to Anton Pilgram, believed to have been the original sculptor of the pulpit. The bricks were of course to protect these precious works of art.

23 Abbreviation of *Nationalpolitische Erziehungsanstalt*, National Political Educational Establishment, for fast-tracking the next generation of Party officials and army personnel.

24 Empress Zita of Austria, 1892–1989, wife of Karl (1887–1922),

the last Emperor of Austria, who was deposed in 1919. Empress Zita's sympathies had been with the Western Allies in the First World War.

25 Henry the Fowler, 876–936, German king by election in 919, father of Emperor Otto the Great. According to legend, Henry was occupied with a bird decoy when news of his election arrived, hence his nickname.

26 The species is *Elaphe longissima*.

27 Karl Renner, 1870–1950, socialist politician, first Chancellor of the Austrian republic after the abdication of Emperor Karl in 1919. On the liberation of Austria in 1945 he was elected president of the republic.

28 Alfred Rosenberg, 1893–1946, Nazi ideologist, tried at Nuremberg and hanged.

29 In many parts of Europe, fuel for motor vehicles was in such short supply at the end of the war that wood had to be burned to produce gas to power them.

30 *Goldfasan*, golden pheasant, also the term for a high-ranking Nazi in his uniform.

31 Alfred Jerger, 1889–1976, Austrian bass-baritone.

32 Anny (1902–68) and Hilde (1905–80) Konetzny, Austrian sopranos.

33 Hilde Gueden, 1917–88, Austrian soprano.

34 The Albertina art gallery (graphics, prints, watercolours).

35 Hitler's mountain retreat in Bavaria.

36 Giovanni Antonio Canaletto (real name Canal), 1697–1768, famous Venetian painter. Presumably the child's mother means that the picture is more likely by his nephew Bernardo Bellotto, who continued to work in his uncle's style.

37 Ferdinand Georg Waldmüller, 1793–1865.

38 Hermann Leopoldi, pseudonym of Hersch Kohn, Viennese Jewish songwriter and cabaret artist.

39 Franz Völker, 1899–1965, German tenor.

40 *The Decline of the West* (*Der Untergang des Abendlandes*), the title of a famous work by Oswald Spengler, a historical philosopher, published in 1918–22.

41 Sven Hedin, 1865–1952, Swedish explorer.

42 The Central European region of the Danube basin between the rivers Tisza and Mures.

43 The SS had their blood groups tattooed on their arms to facilitate rapid treatment if they were wounded. After the war then, ironically, both they and their victims, the survivors of concentration camps who carried their camp numbers on their arms, could be identified by the mere presence of a tattoo.

44 The Austrian flag at this time; under Nazi rule it had of course been abandoned in favour of the swastika banner.

45 The 'teaching language' was of course German, the mother tongue of Austrians. Post-war efforts to disclaim any connection with Nazi Germany led to such bizarre linguistic constructions.

46 Traditionally, red is associated in Austria with the Social Democratic party, black with the more conservative Austrian People's Party.

47 A march popular with the German army, much played at Nazi Party rallies, and said to be one of Hitler's favourites.

48 One of the denazification tribunals set up to adjudicate on the degree of guilt of former Nazi party members.

49 The songs are *Gretchen am Spinnrade* (Gretchen at the spinning wheel), the famous poem by Goethe from *Faust*, and *Fremd bin ich eingezogen* (A stranger came I here), by Wilhelm Müller, from *Die Winterreise*, both set to music by Schubert.

50 Although Hitler was born in Braunau, he went to school in Linz and regarded it as his home town.

51 Vereinigte Österreichische Eisen-und Stahlwerke (United Austrian Iron and Steel Works).

52 A member of the Nazi party in Austria after it was banned in the country in 1933.

53 Wilhelm Furtwängler, 1886–1954, whose possible association with the Nazi regime (a matter of controversy, since he helped many Jewish musicians to escape) darkened the last decade of his life.

54 Bruno Walter, 1876–1962, who settled in the USA in 1939. After the war he paid many return visits to Europe.

55 Richard Strauss, 1864–1949, composer of *Der Rosenkavalier*, in which the boy's mother is to sing, and many other operas.

56 Herbert von Karajan, 1908–89, director of the Salzburg Festival from 1956 until his death.

57 *Jedermann* (Everyman), a version by Hugo von Hofmannsthal

of the old medieval morality play known in several European languages, including English, had its première at the Salzburg Festival of 1920, and has been closely associated with the Festival.

58   The three main parts in *Der Rosenkavalier* are all for women's voices: the Marschallin, Octavian (a trouser role) and Sophie. In Act 3 Octavian, disguised as the chambermaid Mariandel, eggs on the amorous Baron Ochs, who is courting Sophie, with whom Octavian himself has fallen in love.

59   Marianne, Sophie von Faninal's duenna, appears with her charge in Act 2. The narrator's mother had once sung the much larger part of Sophie.

60   A quotation from the libretto of the opera. 'Die Zeit, die ist ein sonderbar Ding,' sings the Marschallin as she realizes that she is growing older, and her lover Octavian will leave her for a younger woman.

61   The League of German Maidens, the girls' equivalent of the Hitlerjugend for boys.

62   Hahnenschwanzler, pre-war Fascist Austrian militia, so called from the feathers they wore in their hats.

63   A wine-growing region of Lower Austria.

64   Untranslatable term for a certain kind of Viennese youth from the late 1940s, when they had incurred the enmity of neo-fascist organizations. Schlurfs, mainly working-class in origin, cultivated a certain style of elegance and a louche way of life. In some ways they were not unlike the post-war British teddy boys, but with additional political baggage in their past history.

65   In Austria and Bavaria, a traditional companion of St Nicholas at Christmas time, causing much knockabout fun.

66   Klement Gottwald, 1896–1953, Czech Communist politician.

67   Either Wolfgang or Wieland Wagner, grandsons of the composer Richard Wagner. Wieland died in 1966; his brother continued running the Bayreuth theatre.

68   Otto Klemperer, 1885–1973, the famous conductor. He emigrated to the USA in 1933, and despite ill health continued conducting into old age.

69   Karl Gruber, 1895–1969, first post-war Foreign Minister of Austria.

70 Archbishop Marcus Sitticus, who had Schloss Hellbrunn built for himself and his mistress in the early 17th century.

71 The colour always associated with the Nazis.

72 Frederick the Fair, c.1286–1330, duke of Austria.

73 Benito Mussolini, 1883–1945, Fascist dictator of Italy.

74 Also known as the Brownshirts, the body of men recruited originally to support and protect Nazi speakers as the Party rose to power. In later years often at odds in its own power struggle with the SS.

75 A civil defence militia.

76 Ignaz Seipel, a Roman Catholic priest who was Chancellor of Austria in 1922–4 and 1926–9.

77 Engelbert Dollfuss, Chancellor of Austria 1932–34. Although an Austro-Fascist who suspended democracy in favour of dictatorial government, he was also in opposition to the Nazis, who assassinated him.

78 *Ein Kampf um Rom*, a once very popular historical novel about the Romans and the Ostrogoths by the late 19th-century writer Felix Dahn.

79 Marcus Aurelius, born AD 121, Emperor of Rome AD 161–80.

80 According to the Roman historian Cassius Dio, when the Romans were campaigning in what is now Austria against German tribes including the Quadi, the prayers of Christian soldiers in the Roman army brought heavy rain to disperse the enemy.

81 Noble family of Austrian dukes; the line died out in the mid-13th century.

82 The Tivoli Gardens, the famous amusement park in Copenhagen.

83 Matthias Grünewald, c.1460–1528, the 16th-century German painter.

84 The öre is a Swedish unit of currency.

85 The building of the Volkswagen, the People's Car, was a favourite project of Hitler's. Its first factory was at Fallersleben, in the Wolfsburg urban district. In fact the 'Wolf's Lair', the most famous of Hitler's various headquarters outside Berlin, was near Rastenburg in East Prussia.

86 *Die Heilige und ihr Narr*, a popular novel by Agnes Günther published in 1918.

87 Zarah Leander, the famous Swedish-born actress and singer, popular during the Nazi period in Germany. 'Davon geht die Welt nicht unter' was the title of her biggest hit.

88 The heroine of Mozart's *The Magic Flute*.

89 Bertel Thorvaldsen, *c*.1770–1844, Danish sculptor.

90 The tower of the church of St Michael, the emblem of the city of Hamburg.

91 Ludwig Erhard, 1897–1977, economist and politician, second Chancellor of the post-war Federal Republic of Germany.

92 Søren Kierkegaard, *Repetition, An Essay in Experimental Psychology*, 1843.

93 Green is the ecclesiastical colour for those times of the year which are not marked by any particular Church festival.

94 Milchreis Trautmannsdorf is the name of an Austrian milk pudding.

95 A reference to the *Blut und Boden* (blood and the soil) school of literature favoured by the Nazi regime.

96 Max Mell, 1882–1971, Austrian writer.

97 Karl Heinrich Waggerl, 1897–1973, Austrian writer.

98 Conductor at the time of this famous ensemble, founded in 1920.

99 Not the original Austrian national anthem with music by Haydn, the tune of which features in his Emperor Quartet, but an immediate post-war effort, with words written by Paula von Preradovic, mother of the Education Minister Felix Hurdes. The music of the new anthem, sometimes claimed to be by Mozart, is more likely taken from the works of his contemporary Johann Holzer. The quotations in the text are from Paula von Preradovic's words.

100 The German translation of a play by the Spanish dramatist Calderón. An English translation exists under the name of *The Phantom Lady*.

101 Orson Welles, star of *The Third Man*.

102 Graham Greene, who worked on the screenplay of *The Third Man*.

103 Willy Forst, 1903–80, actor and director.

104 The references are to the word *braun* in as much as it was connected with Hitler: Braunau, his birthplace in Austria; Braunschweig in Germany; the Brownshirts or SA (*Sturmabteilung*); his mistress Eva Braun.

105 The colours of the German flag.

106 Wolfsburg, the original home of the Volkswagen car; the Wolfsschanze or Wolf's Lair, Hitler's HQ at Rastenburg; the Werewolves underground army recruited for guerrilla warfare at the end of the war.

107 Quotation from Johann Nepomuk Nestroy, 1801–62, Austrian dramatist.

108 Ibid.

109 Leopold Figl, Chancellor of Austria from 1945 to 1953.

110 The boys are attempting a phonetic reproduction of the English term 'body-building'.

111 Hilde Krahl, 1917–99, Austrian actress born in Croatia; married to the director Wolfgang Liebeneiner.

112 Curd Jürgens, 1915–82, German-born actor who became an Austrian citizen, and had a successful career in English-language films, where he was known as Curt Jurgens.

113 Werner Krauss, 1884–1959, well-known German actor of the first half of the 20th century. His portrayal of Jewish characters in anti-Semitic Nazi films meant that his career was in difficulties after the war.

114 Paul Hörbiger, Austrian actor who had a small part in *The Third Man*.

115 Judith Holzmeister, Austrian actress born 1920, daughter of the architect Clemens Holzmeister, designer of a number of buildings for the Turkish government in Ankara.

116 Prince Eugen of Savoy, 1663–1736, the famous military commander who defended Austria from the invading Turks.

117 The famous amusement park in Vienna.

118 Helmut Qualtinger, Austrian actor, writer and cabaret artist.

119 A quotation from the dramatic fragment *Woyzeck* by Georg Büchner, 1813–37. It was later set as an opera by Alban Berg.

120 Wilhelm Busch, 1832–1908, author of comic tales in verse, illustrated by his own line drawings.

121 The radio has evidently reached Act II of Verdi's *La Traviata*.

122 Two cheerful pieces of light Viennese music: the Schönfeld March by Carl Michael Ziehrer, 1843–1922, and the Radetzky March by Johann Strauss the elder, 1804–49.